Peter Ganas,

the

guide to dating in America

> "Full of great ideas and great resources. A true treasure for singles."
>
> ~
>
> Gregory J.P. Godek, author of
> *1001 Ways To Be Romantic*

the IT'S just LUNCH!® guide to dating in America

by **Andrea McGinty, Nancy Kirsch and Alana Beyer**

& the dating experts at It's Just Lunch

FROM THE EXPERTS AT IT'S JUST LUNCH
RESPONSIBLE FOR OVER **2,000,000** FUN FIRST DATES

10 Finger Press
Wellington, FL

The It's Just Lunch Guide to Dating in America.

Copyright © 2005 by IJL Advertising, LLC. Manufactured in the United States of America. All rights reserved. No part of this book may be reproduced in any form or by any electronic or mechanical means including information storage and retrieval systems without permission in writing from the publisher, except by a reviewer, who may quote brief passages in a review.

Published by 10 Finger Press, 8435 Belize Place, Wellington, FL 33414. Distributed to the book trade by Midpoint Trade Books.

For more information about It's Just Lunch, go to www.itsjustlunch.com

All dating statistics used in this book are based on surveys conducted by It's Just Lunch.

Series edited by The Authors Team
www.AuthorsTeam.com

Cover and interior design by Pneuma Books, LLC
Visit www.pneumabooks.com for more information

ISBN 1-933174-48-X
LCCN 2004097711

09 08 07 06 05   5 4 3 2

The It's Just Lunch Dating Series
includes guides to dating
in these locations:

America	Northern Virginia
Albany and Saratoga	Omaha
Albuquerque	Orange County
Atlanta	Orlando
Austin	Philadelphia
Baltimore	Phoenix
Birmingham and Huntsville	Pittsburgh
	Portland
Central Pennsylvania	Raleigh-Durham
Charlotte	Sacramento
Chicago	San Antonio
Cincinnati	San Diego County
Cleveland	San Francisco
Dallas	Seattle
Denver	Silicon Valley
East Bay	Singapore
Honolulu	South Florida
Houston	Southeastern Michigan
Jacksonville	St. Louis
Kansas City	Tampa
Las Vegas	Toronto
Los Angeles	Twin Cities
Milwaukee	Washington, D.C.
Naples, Ft. Myers and Sarasota	West Texas
	Western New York
New York City	Wilmington
Northern New Jersey	

The It's Just Lunch Story

When founder Andrea McGinty's engagement was suddenly called off, she began the tedious search for a way to meet "normal," well-educated professionals. The ideal date, she decided, was a lunch date. In 1991, McGinty launched the company's first office in Chicago. The premise was simple: a dating service based on a personalized screening and a painless meeting with her to determine whether she had the type of people the client would like to meet.

It's Just Lunch caught on quickly! The company has over 70 offices worldwide, with new locations added nearly every month. These offices cater to an upscale audience of over 30,000 clients. Most clients have college degrees and many have a graduate degree.

The total results are astonishing: over two million fun first dates and thousands of marriages.

Their secret to success? Founder McGinty's certainty that when you explore enough avenues to meet people, "there's absolutely somebody for everyone."

www.itsjustlunch.com

Acknowledgements

This book is dedicated to a few very special people in my life... My father who taught me much about business and was so supportive of *It's Just Lunch*, especially in the early days. To my mother, who I know would be so proud of me. To my husband, Daniel, whose enthusiasm for this book never wavered. (And, whose idea it was!!)

This book is dedicated to all those singles searching for that one special person... I hope this book will give you some fresh perspectives on dating and just a tiny reminder to keep dating light, keep your attitude up and very open — because I truly believe there is a lid for every pot!!

I am so appreciative to Mahesh Grossman who guided our book and never, ever lost his excitement! (or mind!!) Special thanks to Michele Gough for her wit, humor and help putting our words to paper.

— Andrea McGinty

Contents

PART 1: THE TOPICAL GUIDE TO DATING IN AMERICA

Chapter 1 — Change Your Outlook and Your Luck Will Change 1
Ten Best Places to Boost Your Ego 9
Ten Places to Sweeten You Up 11

Chapter 2 — Where to Begin 15
Ten Best Singles Bars 23
Ten Best Nightclubs 25

Chapter 3 — Places to Go, People to See 29
Ten Best Places to Take Classes 34
Ten Best Coffee Shops, Book Stores & Juice Bars 36
Ten Best Sports Leagues 38
Ten Best Health Clubs & Gyms 40
Ten Best Bars for Wine, Martinis or Tapas 42
Ten Best Sports Bars or Pubs 44
Ten Best Restaurants 46
Ten Best After-Hours Spots 48
Ten Best Happy Hours 49

Chapter 4 — The "It's Just Lunchbox" of Flirting Tips and Tools 52
Ten Best Annual Events for Flirting Opportunities 67
Ten Best Hotspots 70
Ten Best Places to Flirt with Rhythm
   (Live Music Venues) 72
Ten Best Neighborhoods For Singles 74
Ten Best Places to Flirt 78

Chapter 5 — It's a Date! 82
Ten Best Places To Relax before a Date 89
Ten Best Places To Put You in a Dating Mood 90

Chapter 6 — The First Date 93
Ten Best Places for a Lunch or Brunch First Date 106
Ten Best Places for After-Work
   Drinks & Conversation 108
Ten Best Places for a First Dinner Date 110

Chapter 7 — Beyond the First Date 113
Ten Best Places for a Second Dinner Date 121
Ten Best Cheap Dates 123
Ten Best Creative Dates 125
Ten Best Places for Coffee & Dessert 126
Ten Best Places for a Laugh 128
Ten Great Dates 130

Chapter 8 — Going Steady 134
Ten Best Places for Valentine's Day Dates 146
Ten Best Special-Occasion Restaurants 148
Ten Best Places to Find Gifts They'll Love 150

PART 2: THE GEOGRAPHICAL GUIDE TO DATING IN AMERICA

Albany 155
Albuquerque 158
Atlanta 162
Austin 166
Baltimore 170
Birmingham and Huntsville 174
Boise 178
Boston 182
Charlotte 186
Chicago 190
Cincinnati 194
Cleveland 198
Columbus 202
Dallas 206
Denver 210
Des Moines 214
Detroit 218
East Bay 222
Greenville / Spartanburg 226
Harrisburg and Central Pennsylvania 230
Hartford / New Haven 234
Honolulu 238
Indianapolis 242
Houston 246
Jackson 250
Jacksonville 254
Kansas City 258
Las Vegas 262

Little Rock	266
Los Angeles	270
Louisville	274
Maine	278
Memphis	282
Milwaukee	286
Montana	290
Naples, Ft. Myers and Sarasota	294
Nashville	298
New Hampshire	302
New Orleans	306
New York City	310
Northern New Jersey	314
Northern Virginia	318
Oklahoma City	322
Omaha	326
Orange County	330
Orlando	334
Philadelphia	338
Phoenix	342
Pittsburgh	346
Portland	350
Providence	354
Raleigh	358
Sacramento	362
Salt Lake City	366
San Antonio	370
San Diego	374
San Francisco	378
Seattle	381
Silicon Valley	385
South Florida	389
St. Louis	393
Tampa	397
Twin Cities	401
Washington, D.C.	404
Western New York	408
Wilmington	412
Vermont	416
West Texas	420

Appendix — What's Your Dating I.Q.? 424

How to Reach the Nearest It's Just Lunch Office ...430

PART ONE

the
IT'S *just* LUNCH!®
Topical guide to dating in America

Chapter 1

Change Your Outlook and Your Luck Will Change

Here you are, about to start your great dating adventure. You've been dreaming about meeting someone special for a while now, but the idea of actually getting out there and doing it is a little scary.

You spend time and energy on your career, your workouts and your finances, and now you're ready for romance. You've tried the traditional ways to meet new people — blind dates set up by friends, the Internet, the bar scene. But none of that has worked out. The next step is to go out into the world and meet new people, but where and how? You're busy and don't have a lot of time for trial and error.

That's where we come in.

There is no better place to find good advice about dating than from people who have gone through it before — in our case, more than 50,000 times a month. *It's Just Lunch* is responsible for millions of fun first dates, so we know a thing or two about successful dating.

How to Use This Book

In each chapter, we'll demystify some aspect of the dating process, as well as provide tips and suggestions to boost your prospects. At the end of each chapter, we'll point you in the right direction with a current list of the best places to date or find dates in America.

Welcome to the Wonderful World of Dating

Perhaps you've picked up this book because you recently went through a divorce or a breakup, or maybe you've been single for some time and just haven't met the right person yet. Whatever brings you here, let us first say, congratulations on being single. Yes, we mean it! Being single is an exciting time in your life. It's a chance to learn more about yourself, to understand what you want for the future, and to discover the qualities you'd really like in a partner. And you're in for a treat — there are a whopping 110 million singles in the United States to choose from.

Of course, not everybody has a positive outlook on singledom. In fact, some people are downright negative, especially about dating. If you think like this, you might want to take a look at how you could be sabotaging your chances. Are you the type who loses hope if a date turns out not to be what you expected? Do you judge every date as a marriage prospect? Do you try so hard to impress that you end up scaring the other person away? If this sounds like you, chances are you take dating way too seriously.

It's hardly unusual. These days we're inundated with reality shows and movies that depict two incredibly beautiful people meeting for the first time, barely getting to know each other, quickly falling in love and then deciding to spend the rest of their lives together. With expectations like that, it's no surprise that we're all wondering, "Where's mine?"

In addition, chances are you've been hurt or suffered some pain or loss along the way. The idea of facing that ordeal again is enough to make you want to stay in bed with a good book and a pint of Ben and Jerry's Chubby Hubby ice cream.

If you're reading this book, you probably *do* want to date. If you're not feeling enthusiastic yet, you might need a little attitude adjustment to get you mentally prepared for your dating journey. Having a positive outlook as well as knowing the pitfalls and how to overcome them will make all the difference.

Start by putting all those bad relationships and dates from hell behind you. That's all in the past, and you can't do anything about them. Think about the *future* and make a promise to give yourself the time to enjoy the dating process — and try not to take it too seriously.

Here's the scoop: Dating can and should be lots of fun. Keep this in mind and you'll have a much better time than you think.

Successful Dating Guidelines

The key to successful dating is to focus on enjoyment and friendship. Date with the intention of making a new friend rather than expecting to meet your life partner. You'll have more fun and way less "performance" anxiety.

Six Ways to Maximize Your Fun
1. Approach dating as not just looking for an important relationship, but as enjoying life.
2. View dating as a chance to increase your circle of friends.
3. Find innovative and unusual places to meet people. Join a club, volunteer or take up a sport.
4. Take one positive aspect away from each date. For example, "I liked his values, her sense of style or his humor." Pick a quality or characteristic that you would like in your future mate. This benefits you, even if you aren't attracted to that person.
5. Become the person you'd like to date. Use your experiences as an opportunity for personal growth.
6. Embrace your singledom. You have the freedom to do anything you want, meet everyone you want and learn everything you can about yourself.

The point is to keep dating light and casual, especially early on. On a first date, go out to lunch, drinks or brunch and split the check. This keeps the expectations and pressure lower. If you decide to see each other again, you know your date is interested in you.

It's that simple.

As you get to know each new person, you'll have an opportunity to "try each other out" and see if the relationship might work. Pay attention to what you're discovering. As you progress on your dating journey, you'll be exposed to new types of people and new ideas. Even if a date doesn't develop into a full-blown relationship, you're still growing and learning as a human being, which makes life interesting and exciting.

If dating still sounds daunting to you, keep reading. You'll find many suggestions throughout this book that will make it easier than you imagine.

Breaking "The Rules"
The first and only rule we have here at *It's Just Lunch* is to throw out all your old ideas and rules about dating!

Dating is not about playing games, using clever tactics or making sure you come out on top. There are no winners and losers as far as we're concerned.

While other guides might instruct you to hold out, be mysterious and develop a game plan to trap your mate, we don't believe in that. Those games don't work in the long run and they're exhausting. If you present a fake exterior and try to be someone you're not, you deny yourself the opportunity to be liked for who you really are. And that's what real love is all about, folks — just be yourself from beginning to end!

DON'T:
- Play games
- Play hard to get
- Pretend you're not interested
- Wait three days to return his or her call

In other words, don't utilize any other ploy that seems like game playing.

Dating Karma

It's true — what you put out is what you get back! Whether you believe in the whole principle of karma or not, the idea behind it makes sense. If you are constantly thinking you're too fat, too skinny, too old, too poor, too stupid or too anything to attract a love match, chances are you probably won't.

If you believe there are only jerks, gold diggers or messed up freaks out there, these are the people you will meet. If you think dating is a complete waste of time, then it sure as heck will be! Negative thoughts produce negative results. It becomes a self-fulfilling prophecy.

If this sounds like you, then make a promise to yourself to stop it RIGHT NOW! When you catch yourself in a negative thought, give yourself a little pep talk. Say, "stop," and turn the thought around to something more positive such as, "I'm hot, smart and one helluva catch." You get the idea.

Would *You* Date You?

Think about it. Would you? This is a very important point. Unless you become the type of person who you're looking for, you won't attract the type of person you seek.

Have you ever known men or women who aren't necessarily the most handsome or pretty individuals, but they never lack dates? What makes them so attractive? You guessed it: self-confidence, and it's contagious. It also screams sex appeal. These folks are glowing with a bright, friendly, fun attitude, and they have a genuine interest in others. They're happy with who they are and appreciate what they have to offer. This positive energy attracts an abundance of people who want to meet them.

Self-confidence produces the most amazing results. Here's why:
- It's sexy!
- It allows you to relax and have fun.
- It means you take rejection lightly and not personally.
- It makes it clear that you are not desperate.
- It means you're content with yourself, your looks and your life — which only makes you more attractive.

In order to gain self-confidence, you must first learn how to love yourself. It's important that you recognize and appreciate what's great about you — and accept what's not so great. If you don't love and accept who you are, how do you expect someone else to?

DO the Following for Yourself
Try these six boosters to improve your self-confidence and sex appeal.

- Stop measuring yourself against others, especially celebrities or fashion models. Recognize that you are a hot ticket with a unique set of qualities and attributes. If you believe you are special, you will attract a partner who appreciates what you have to offer. Tell yourself, "I'm great just the way I am" or "I'm exciting" or "I'm loveable." You are! This kind of pep talk helps imprint positive messages into your brain and eventually will change your outlook.

    Remember, the very characteristic or behavior that turns one person off may turn another person on. Don't waste your time with people who don't recognize what you have to offer. Learn to love yourself for everything you are and everything you're not. When you like who you are, people will naturally be drawn to you.

- Surround yourself with people who treat you with the love and respect that you deserve. If you have people in your life who are overly critical or negative, weed them out.

- If you're not happy with the way you look, treat

yourself to a new look. Join a gym and get in shape. You'll feel like a million bucks. Dress and act your best at all times, because you never know when you might run into your dream date. When you look good, you feel good too.

- Step outside your own boundaries. Join Toastmasters, take a dance class or a stand-up comedy class, go horseback riding or parachuting. Push through your fears, and you'll find yourself alive with confidence.

- Finally, date more. As you handle all the different situations you come across, it will reinforce positive feelings about yourself and boost your confidence in your dating ability.

At the end of the day, everybody could use a little improvement. But nobody's perfect and no one ever will be, so you have to balance your desire to be all that you can be with your willingness to accept who you are.

Know What You Want: If You Build Them, They Will Come!

When you're looking for that special someone, you need to figure out who this person is going to be. Knowing what you want and who you're looking for really helps you find the right person.

We once attended a seminar on relationships where attendees were asked to design their perfect mates as specifically as possible. The goal was to create a wish list of all the qualities and characteristics we felt were important. It was a great exercise — a lot of the attendees realized that they didn't know what they wanted, although they had very specific ideas of what they *didn't* want. A few months later, the participants reunited to complete the final part of the seminar, which analyzed our results. We were blown away by how many participants had met people who matched most of the criteria on their list. It was as if putting it down on paper reinforced the belief in their mind's eye. Or perhaps by defining what they wanted, they became more conscious of those qualities when they saw them in a potential partner. Either way, this exercise worked for a large number of people.

Visualizing your ideal partner and the relationship you want is a great motivator. Athletes have long understood this process of imagery and will visualize a goal before acting on it. You can do the same with your love life. Give it a shot now! You have nothing to lose.

Close your eyes and picture your ideal partner. Engage all your senses. How does this person smell? What does he or she look like? Listen to this person's voice. How does it sound? When you kiss, how do you feel? Where are you? What are you doing? Are your friends and family around? How does he or she interact with them? Try this a few times until the picture becomes clear, then take out a piece of paper and make a list of the most important characteristics of this partner.

List about 20 qualities that mean something to you. What values and attributes does this person have?

Look over your list and separate your "deal breakers" from your "ideals." "Deal breakers" are the absolute non-negotiable traits, like finding a partner who wants children or is of the same religion (if those traits are important to you). "Ideals" are more about the attributes or traits you'd prefer, like "ambitious" or "good sense of humor."

By prioritizing which qualities are important and which are ideal, you'll discover what you're absolutely unwilling to accept and where you've got some flexibility.

Be Flexible

Don't be overly specific when you think about your ideal partner — such as wanting "tall blondes" or "no bald guys."

Celebrate individuality and be open to new possibilities. You could end up ruling out the woman or man of your dreams simply because they have the wrong hair color or are a few hairs short. Remember, it's a wish list, and nobody's perfect. Over the coming months, it will change and grow as you discover what's really important to you in a relationship. Remain flexible and open with your "ideals."

Fools Rush In

One of the biggest dating mistakes we see at *It's Just Lunch* is when people are in too much of a rush to settle down. Disaster! They hook up with the first compatible person who comes along, instead of dating several people and then making a powerful choice as to what's best for them.

Give yourself time to choose. The dating experience teaches you a great deal about what's really important to you in a partner and what you have to offer. By observing yourself, you will gain new insight into how you react to different situations, and which problems you bring into each relationship. It's only when you are inside the dynamic of a relationship that you can truly discover these things — otherwise it's all "in your head."

Now Get Out There!

Over the years we've met with hundreds of thousands of active daters and heard the inside scoop on just about every dating scenario one could possibly imagine. All of this has provided us at *It's Just Lunch* with the most up-to-date, insightful information on successful approaches to dating, which we're happy to share in this book. But the truth is that all the knowledge in the world won't make the slightest difference in your life, unless you physically get out there and date.

Since you've picked up this book, you're heading in the right direction and taking a proactive approach to meeting new men or women. Now you need to get off the couch, turn off another episode of *The Bachelor* or *Bachelorette*, and get out there and star in your own reality show. Consider these points:

1. Dating is a numbers game. The more potential mates you meet, the more likely it is that you will find "the one." If you're hoping that fate will drop him or her off at your door, think again, unless you have a penchant for UPS drivers.

2. Joining a dating agency like *It's Just Lunch* is not an act of desperation. It's the smartest way to meet the type of people you're interested in. It means you are the driver in your own life, not a bystander who leaves things up to chance.

3. You can get over your ex. Let's face it. If you're still hankering after your last love, then your heart isn't going to be open to meeting someone new. You are emotionally unavailable. Write a note to yourself that reads "single and unavailable" and stick it on your computer. Laugh at yourself. It helps. You'll get there eventually, just give it time. In the meantime, enjoy being single.

4. Dating doesn't have to take a great deal of time. If you're an *It's Just Lunch* member, we set up your dates so you only need an hour for lunch or for drinks after work.

Okay, no more excuses. You can sit back and wait forever or get out there and have some fun!

The Lists

Ten Places to Boost Your Ego

Baltimore
Trapeze School New York / Baltimore
Inner Harbor at Rash Field
(410) 459-6839 • http://baltimore.trapezeschool.com

Fly through the air with the greatest of ease. You'll never be the same! Lessons for this new event are drawing major attention.

Birmingham
Barber Motorsports Park
6040 Barber Motorsports Pkwy.
(205) 298-9040 • www.barbermotorsports.com

Home of the Porsche Driving Experience School, the park also features a collection of antique motorcycles in the Barber Vintage Motor Sports Museum.

Las Vegas
Second City Training Center (Flamingo Hotel)
3555 Las Vegas Boulevard S.
(702) 697-2653 • www.secondcity.com
Other Locations: Detroit, Chicago, Los Angeles

Closet comedians or busy professionals can try a three-hour Improv Workshop or a class on being a more effective presenter.

San Diego County
Language World
3741 India St., San Diego
(619) 692-3181 • www.language-world.com

Butcher a new language with other singles. Language World teaches conversational courses in Spanish, Italian and French in a small, intimate setting.

Tucson
Canyon Ranch
8600 E. Rockcliff Rd.
(800) 742-6494 • www.canyonranch.com
Other locations: Las Vegas, Kissimmee, FL and Lenox, MA
Let this high desert spa pamper your body, mind and spirit. Their goal is to help you "find greater joy in living." We believe this "best spa in America" succeeds.

Seattle
Boys and Girls Club of King County
603 Stewart #300
(206) 461-3890
Call for other locations. • www.positiveplace.org
This club's mission is to inspire and enable young people. Nothing boosts your ego faster than a grateful little smile from a child.

Charlotte
Belly-Dancing with Yasmine
(704) 752-8323 • www.magic-hips.com
Learn to perform a captivating dance while you tone your stomach. There are many styles of belly-dancing lessons offered.

Orange County
Corky Carroll's Surf School
624 20th St., Huntington Beach
(714) 960-8187 • www.surfschool.net
The key to boosting your ego may lie in the waves. The quintessential Orange County pastime, surfing is the ideal challenge to build grit, guts and even attract a few girls or guys.

East Bay
Introduction to Medieval Swordsmanship at
Union City Leisure Services
34009 Alvarado-Niles Rd., Union City, CA
(510) 675-5494
www.ci.union-city.ca.us/leisure/lifestyle.html
Try authentic European martial arts using fencing gear to let the inner "Lord of the Rings" out in you.

Denver
Krav Maga Israeli Contact Combat, Inc.
10 Grand Ave., 2nd Fl., Englewood
(201) 894-1996 • www.contactcombat.com

Listed as the most modern self-defense you can learn, Krav Maga has long captured the attention of busy Hollywood professionals looking for that superior burn.

BONUS LISTINGS

Why not boost your ego wherever you are? These next two listings are available all over America.

Toastmasters International
www.toastmasters.org

Get comfortable speaking in front of a group and one-on-one conversations will be a breeze. A Toastmasters Club is the best place to practice public speaking. And who doesn't feel good after applause?

The International Coach Federation
1444 I St. N.W. Suite 700, Washington, D.C.
(888) 423-3131 • www.coachfederation.org

Professional life coaches help people discover how to revamp and enrich their careers and personal lives. To learn more or to find a coach, visit their website.

Thirteen Places to Sweeten You Up

Wilmington
Woodside Farm
1310 Little Baltimore Rd., Hockessin
(302) 239-9847

Want ice cream right from the source? Yes, it's a farm, and yes, the cows are right there. Woodside makes the best ice cream you'll ever taste.

Chicago
Margie's Candies
1960 N. Western Ave.
(773) 384-1035 • www.margiescandies.com

Drop by this Chicago landmark in Mayor Daley's old neighborhood for old-fashioned hot-fudge sundaes or hand-dipped chocolates. The Beatles did after their concert in Comiskey Park.

Central Pennsylvania
Edwards-Freeman
441 E. Hector St., Conshohocken
(877) 448-NUTS • www.edwardsfreeman.com

Edwards-Freeman is an old-school candy store. They have everything from candies and nuts to seeds. Try popular candy from yesteryear like Dots, lemon slices and black licorice.

San Francisco
Kona Shores Extreme Ice Cream and Surf Company
1206 Masonic
(415) 861-3172 • www.konashores.com

San Francisco's only surf and ice cream shop, featuring Lapperts Hawaiian ice cream and coffee.

Seattle
Cupcake Royale
1101 34th Avenue
(206) 709-4497 • www.cupcakeroyale.com

The ballerina cupcake will definitely put a smile on your face. These cupcakes are baked fresh every day and lovingly hand-frosted with real, rich butter-cream frosting.

Charlotte
Original Pie Safe
10915 Monroe Rd., Suite F
(704) 708-4833 • www.originalpiesafe.com

With a large variety of yummy pies, they even feature a wonderful chicken pot pie.

Cleveland
Max's Deli
19337 Detroit Rd.
(440) 356-2226

Try one of their special cheesecake concoctions. They're big enough for two.

Dylan's Candy Bar
1011 Third Ave., Manhattan
(646) 735-0078 • www.dylanscandybar.com

Not just paradise for kids, this sweet destination is a hotspot for any Upper East Sider — the kind of place that makes it easy to start chatting with the person standing next to you.

Central Pennsylvania
Hershey Chocolate World
Kit Kat "Gimme A Break" Café, Hershey
(800) Hershey • www.hersheyschocolateworld.com

This could be the sweetest place on earth. Make sure you take the free tour to see the Hershey's Kisses Chocolate manufacturing line. Try the café for personalized desserts.

Northern New Jersey
Schnackenberg's Luncheonette
1110 Washington St., Hoboken
(201) 659-9836

It's a cute little luncheonette offering sandwiches and burgers, but it's the candy and confectionery aspects that make Schnackenberg's a Hoboken landmark.

Baltimore
Baltimore Cupcake Company
1433 E. Fort Ave.
(410) 783-7227 • www.baltimorecupcakecompany.com

Voted by locals as the best bakery in South Baltimore, it's housed in a Pepto-pink building. They offer decadent cupcakes, gifts and trinkets in pink take-away boxes.

BONUS LISTINGS

Los Angeles
Maison Richard Patisserie
310 S. Robertson Blvd.
(310) 275-5707 • www.maisonrichard.com

This landmark Patisserie is located in the trendy Robertson Boulevard shopping district. It's a great spot for a light lunch and espresso in between rounds of shopping.

Portland
Papa Haydn East
5829 S.E. Milwaukee Ave.
(503) 232-9440 • www.papahaydn1.citysearch.com

This Portland mainstay is an absolute dessert standout. Coat your fork with a mouthful of their Black Velvet cake and you'll think you've died and gone to heaven.

Change Your Outlook and Your Luck Will Change

Atlanta
Dante's Down the Hatch
3380 Peachtree Rd.
(404) 266-1600 • www.dantesdownthehatch.com

Wander down the plank into an authentic wharf scene — complete with a full-scale sailing ship — and enjoy Atlanta's best chocolate fondue and cheesecake.

Chapter 2

Where to Begin

With your new positive outlook on dating, a rough idea of what you'd like in a partner, and confidence beaming all over your face, you're ready to take matters into your own hands and venture out to find Mr. or Ms. Right.

So where do you start looking?

Here's what we tell all of our clients: *Try everything out and see which option works best for you.* Each method has its pros and cons, and we'll take a look at those a little later in this chapter. But for the most part, it's vital to just get out there and start exploring your options.

With that in mind, here are four ways you can improve your dating odds no matter where you go:

1. Be proactive

    Most people know exactly what they want out of their careers and have a clearly defined set of goals. But when it comes to finding a partner, it's often left to chance. You'd never be that random with your job! If you really want to find that special someone, make dating as important as your career.

    The first step is to tell everyone you know that you're available. Tell your friends, your co-workers, your hairdresser and the neighbors. Heck, tell the cable guy. Get the word out. Don't make a big deal of it, just casually let them know you're on the lookout for eligible dates, so if they happen to know someone who you might hit it off with... you get the idea!

    If you keep it a secret, chances are you'll be home alone most weekends, so don't be shy, and drop the occasional hint. How else is the world supposed to know?

2. Be open

    The best advice we can give you (aside from joining *It's Just Lunch*, of course) is to be open to meeting someone everywhere you go. There are lots of opportunities throughout your regular day to meet your future partner. You just need to have your radar turned on. Think about it. You could meet her over your morning latte; on the train heading to work; while standing in line for a chicken salad, cruising through the produce aisle, at the dry cleaners or the gym.

Interesting people are all around us, but we're all so consumed with our busy lives that we rarely take the time to look up. So start today! Notice your surroundings and the people who cohabit them. Here's what will make the biggest difference and allow serendipity to do its thing: being aware, keeping a friendly smile on your face and not being afraid to say hello once in a while.

3. Widen your scope
Don't limit your options by thinking someone is not right for you, is beneath or above you, or isn't your usual type. That high-powered corporate attorney who helped negotiate your company's last acquisition might be longing to go out with someone who is creative and free spirited — you!

Don't get turned off because of occupation, income, height, number of children, fitness level, hair color, hobbies, musical tastes, shyness, boldness or whatever. Right now you're just looking for dates — and like job opportunities or taxis — when one appears, a whole slew of others seem to follow. Try not to focus on the ultimate goal, but think more about putting your dating skills into practice and having some fun.

4. Create a ripple effect
Do you know why it's smart to talk to anyone, anywhere, even if that person doesn't seem to be your type? Well, if you throw a pebble into the dating pool, it can have a significant ripple effect that is sure to benefit you.

A 30-year-old female friend of ours recently met a 60-year-old woman at an art exhibition. Even though the older woman was twice her age, the two found they had many things in common, especially their taste in art. The woman later introduced our friend to her nephew and they've been out several times since.

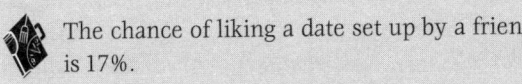
The chance of liking a date set up by a friend is 17%.

Having a genuine interest in getting to know new people and keeping an open mind while you're networking might end up being more valuable than you think. You just never know who that person might introduce you to in the future. Similarly, if you meet someone you like, but you don't feel a love connection, why not offer to set him or her up with a friend?

Never turn down a party invitation or an opportunity to expand your network of friends and potential dates. Seek like-minded people who can introduce you to colleagues of a similar quality. Expanding your network will ensure a life rich with opportunity and happy times.

Looking for Love in All the Right Places
Dating is a numbers game, but the odds of finding the right person increase if you look in the *right* places.

You Gotta Have Friends
Your friends are your number-one resource for finding a mate. Use them. However, don't rely solely on them.

Co-Workers
Just like your friends, co-workers are a great resource for finding possible dates. There are downsides, however. If you and your date end up falling out, or one of you breaks the other's heart, your co-worker could find himself or herself in an awkward position. The best solution is to try to keep the friendship, dating and work issues separate.

Expand Your Possibilities
A circle is exactly that — a circle! And often we get stuck inside our own. There's nothing wrong with that — after all, it's great to have people in your life who you know you can depend on. It's great to have a routine. But that circle can shrink.

While getting fixed up by friends and co-workers is a traditional approach to finding your soul mate, stepping outside of your comfort zone and trying some new dating avenues expands your possibilities and increases your confidence ten-fold.

In *The Artists Way*, creativity coach Julia Cameron states that she often sees synchronicity in the lives of her clients. When they develop a strong commitment to bringing their dreams to life, events around them start to fall into alignment with that vision. Little coincidences take place and lead them toward their true path. For example, a writer meets a producer at a party the day after he finishes his screenplay, or a personal trainer finds a studio for lease the day after she decides to go solo and start her own business.

This happens in love too. It has a lot to do with your *intention*. The moment you become open and accessible to meeting new people, miraculously, potential dates begin to materialize all over the place, often when you least expect it. Your circle expands.

This happens regularly to our clients, the moment they take action and join *It's Just Lunch*. One client, Lisa, went on three dates through our service. Each time we sent her to the same restaurant because it was close to her office and she really loved the atmosphere and food.

Although she enjoyed all three dates, there wasn't a strong love connection and she was happy to continue meeting a few more guys. At the end of her third date, after the man left and she was waiting for the valet to bring her car, Lisa started chatting with the restaurant manager, Brad. Each time Lisa had visited the restaurant previously, Brad, who found her attractive, had his eye on her. Because *It's Just Lunch* coordinators call and make lunch reservations, we become very familiar with many restaurant staffers, who usually take special care of our clients. Obviously, Brad knew Lisa was open to dating. When he saw his opportunity to ask her out for lunch, she was extremely flattered and agreed to go.

Of course, you know how this is going to end, right? Lisa and Brad fell in love and recently were married. Lisa says that just getting out there and being open to dating caused Brad to show up in her life. After all, if she hadn't been on an *It's Just Lunch* date, she never would have met her husband.

Every time you get out of the house and meet someone new, it sets off a domino effect that generates new opportunities.

Let's take a look at some non-traditional methods of dating:

Internet Dating

It doesn't matter if you're having a bad hair day, if you live in the boonies, or if there's three feet of snow outside your window — finding a date now is possible in a 24/7, instant-gratification moment through a slew of online dating services and chat rooms.

This approach to finding a date can be thoroughly enjoyable as long as you don't set your expectations too high. Let's face it, you can't really tell what people are like until you meet them in person — no matter how recent they say their photo is.

The Pros and Cons of Cyberdating

The Pros: It's immediate and convenient. It's cheap! You get to know basic information about your dates before you meet them in person. You have access to thousands of people and can narrow your search by criteria.

The Cons: The biggest con is also one of the most appealing parts of online dating. You can be anybody you want to be and so can he or she. Studies mentioned in *The Wall Street Journal* state that, "30% of online dating site visitors are married and countless others misrepresent themselves." Not exactly what you signed up for, huh? You'll find more than your fair share of untruths online, so don't believe everything you read or see.

More cons: Many Internet dating junkies are not interested in real relationships. Navigating through websites and wading through hundreds of profiles can be very time consuming. Also, safety is a big concern. Without a screening process, you haven't the faintest idea who you might be meeting for coffee.

Yes, it's a shot in the dark, so be prepared for some disappointments. On the upside, your odds are about the same as meeting your ideal mate in a bar, and you don't even have to put on a clean shirt. The best part of cyberdating is that you get to practice your flirting skills. You also get first-hand experience with your cyberdate's ability to string together sentences. By putting yourself out there, you gain more courage to try other ways to meet someone.

Here are a few basics to keep you safe and informed when meeting new folks via the Internet.

Dos and Don'ts of Online Dating
1. DO be honest. You're going to have to meet in person one day (or at least you hope to), so tell the truth early rather than having to face an awkward conversation later.
2. DON'T reveal too much about yourself until you become better acquainted.
3. DON'T use your last name or give out your personal information until you've known the person for a while.
4. DO dial *67 before dialing their phone number. It will block your phone number and name from appearing on a recipient's Caller ID unit. You also can use your cell phone so your address can't be tracked.
5. DO get a separate email account that does not give away your real name — some email providers allow you to create multiple addresses or names for free.
6. DO post an up-to-date photo, and ask if their photo is recent. Many aren't.
7. DON'T spend too much time emailing before talking on the phone or meeting in person. Nothing can replace face-to-face chemistry. Better to find out if you have any before you get too involved.
8. DON'T jump too quickly into sexy talk; it may send the wrong message.
9. DO meet in a public place.
10. DO make every word count. Keep your descriptions light hearted, to the point, and add a little teaser.
11. DO expect a flood of emails. Longtime users will jump at the opportunity to meet someone new.
12. DON'T be ambiguous. Be clear about what you want, your goals and desires.

Speed Dating

This is definitely not for the shy types, or those who take a little time to warm up. Speed dating is like horseracing: The bell rings and you're off! The pressure is on to be the best that you can be in six minutes or fewer. Still, if you want the opportunity to meet a dozen singles in one night, you can do just that.

First, you register online for an event in your city. Most

are held at local clubs and restaurants. Once there, you get a nametag and a worksheet. You then chat with about a dozen other singles in less than two hours via a series of six-minute "speed dates." At the end of the six minutes, a bell rings and you move on to your next date.

You keep track of who you'd like to get to know better, and they do the same on their worksheets. At evening's end, you turn in your worksheet, and if there's a match, the organization sends an email to both with the other's contact info so you can arrange your "first" date. After that it's up to you. Phew!

Dating Services

These services run the gamut, with some offering events, singles' nights and seminars while others provide introductions, video dating, computer dating and matchmaking services. Some focus on fixing up singles who are interested in sports. Others cater to specific religious groups. There are even some for millionaires.

When choosing a service, there are a few things to consider to ensure you don't get ripped off or unwittingly sign up with a fly-by-night service. Stick with busy, reputable services, and be sure to ask the following questions:

- How many years have they been around?
- What is their success rate?
- How many clients do they have?
- What are the demographics?
- Do both men and women pay?
- Are people available for questions you might have?
- How responsive are they?
- How many dates are you entitled to, and over what period of time?
- Do they tell you the price over the phone or do they make you come in to find out?

We can tell you all about the workings of one very successful dating service: *It's Just Lunch*.

Yeah, yeah, so we're a little biased on this one and who can blame us with a success rate of thousands of marriages? We've definitely got something to brag about.

Here's why we're so successful: Everyone has to eat. So why not consider a matchmaker who schedules lunch dates for you? Instead of popping out for a sandwich, you can use your time wisely and have a very productive and entertaining lunch.

Joining *It's Just Lunch* is not as expensive as some of the other professional matchmaking services, whose rates can run as high as $5,000 or more.

What makes us unique is that *It's Just Lunch* does all of the work for you — and we even make the lunch reservation! All of the people you meet will be busy professionals who want to meet singles outside of their office, client list or usual circle of friends. Our roster includes doctors, architects, journalists, engineers, lawyers, TV producers, management consultants, writers, teachers, business owners, advertising execs — and that's just for starters. The best part is that they all have the same objective as you: finding someone special in town.

This is how it works. First, you schedule a confidential interview with us. This no-pressure interview enables us to carefully discern what it is you look for in a potential partner. We talk about what has worked for you in the past (and what hasn't) and what your interests are. We'll know by the end of the hour if we have what you are looking for. If so, the fun begins!

After your date has been hand-selected by us, we will give you a call and tell you all about the person we've chosen. We don't give out last names, phone numbers or places of employment. Once the two of you give us your schedules, we choose a convenient restaurant and set up a lunch date. Sometimes it's a weekend brunch, sometimes a drink after work but never, ever dinner. It's a first date that's short and sweet, which you'll enjoy at one of the many fun, hip eateries on our preferred restaurant list.

Taking this light-hearted approach helps reduce nerves and anxiety so you can relax and enjoy the time together. What more could you ask for? (And no, we don't pick up the tab.)

After the date, we encourage you to call in and provide feedback so we can learn more about what you like and dislike. This helps us fine-tune the matching process.

If you do meet that special someone and decide to date exclusively, you can put the service "on hold" for up to a year. If your current beau fails to measure up, then you simply pick up the phone and we reactivate your membership right away.

Singles Events

When most people think of dating, they think of singles events and singles bars. To find some in your city, check the local paper or try an online search. You can find events in all types of venues from museums and theaters to bars and clubs. The best approach is to go as a non-member and check out the event before committing to a year's membership.

Social clubs are hotspots for active singles, and they offer a good opportunity to meet people with similar interests. It's much easier to strike up a conversation when you have something to talk about. You pay a lower-rate membership fee to participate in fun activities like kayaking, dining clubs, hiking and theater visits — to name a few. Check online to see if a group is available in your city.

The Lists

Ten Best Singles Bars

Albany
Pearl Restaurant & Lounge
One Steuben Pl.
(518) 433-0011

Mahogany woodwork, vaulted ceilings and parquet floors don this upscale restaurant and bar. They've got a great selection of designer martinis.

Albuquerque
OPM
211 Gold Ave. SW
(505) 243-0955 • www.opm.com

OPM is an upscale nightclub open Tuesday through Saturday with two levels: intimate seating upstairs and dancing downstairs.

Las Vegas
Rum Jungle (Mandalay Bay)
3950 S. Las Vegas Blvd.
(702) 636-7404

You'll find a young crowd comprised of locals and tourists, a large bar, tons of fun, outstanding rum drinks, and walls of water.

Sacramento
KBar
1200 K St.
(916) 669-5762 • www.cafebernardo.com/kbar

This is a hip and trendy place with good dance music and a very plush New York vibe.

Austin
Speakeasy
412D Congress Ave.
(512) 476-8017 • http://speakeasyaustin.com

With a rooftop terrace, happy hour specials, live music and a swanky atmosphere, this is one of the best singles bars around.

Chicago
Matilda
3101 N. Sheffield
(773) 883-4400 • www.matilda-babyatlas.com

This trendy Lakeview pub boasts a wicked martini menu and its lower level lounge, baby Atlas, is open Thursdays through Saturdays.

Southeastern Michigan
Ernie's Kings Mill
16655 19 Mile Rd., Clinton Township
(586) 286-8435 • www.erniesclub.com

Live acts five nights a week and great cover bands keep singles dancing the night away. In the summer, relish one of the 200 varieties of martinis on the deck or patio.

New York City
The Cabanas
The Maritime Hotel
363 16th St. at 9th Ave.
(212) 242-4300 • www.themaritimehotel.com

This rooftop bar in Chelsea has emerged as one of the hottest places to see and be seen in Manhattan.

San Diego County
Beach Bar at the W Hotel
421 W. "B" St., San Diego
(619) 231-8220 • www.starwood.com/whotels

Don't miss the rooftop Beach Bar, featuring a heated sand

floor and fire pit. Ladies, be aware it's hard to walk around the sand looking cute if you're wearing 4-inch heels!

Seattle
Viceroy
2332 2nd Ave.
(206) 956-VICE

A very sexy mix of hipsters and Belltown yuppies. The décor is urban and chic, so put on your lipgloss and wear the Manolos!

BONUS LISTING

Cleveland
The Treehouse
820 College Ave.
(216) 696-2505

The life-size faux tree growing from the bar continues to draw young singles into the Tremont area, but it's the corner bar atmosphere that keeps them coming back.

Ten Best Nightclubs

Tampa
Bahasa Lounge
2408 W. Kennedy Blvd.
(813) 251-3329 • www.bahasalounge.com

It's where the beautiful people come to pretend they're dancing in Bali, accompanied by reggae, hip-hop or live bands.

Miami
Mansion
1235 Washington Ave., Miami Beach
(305) 532-1525 • www.mansionmiami.com

This is *the* happening spot on South Beach. Great DJs from all over the world spin here and celebrities consistently host the hottest functions. Call for the week's current line-up.

San Antonio
Bonham Exchange
411 Bonham St.
(210) 271-3811 • www.bonhamexchange.net

This is one of San Antonio's oldest dance clubs. The five bars and three dance floors at the Bonham Exchange cater to any crowd.

Albuquerque
Sauce
401 Central Ave. NW
(505) 242-5839

This nightclub has it all — one side for intimate conversations and snuggling; the other for dancing and partying.

Las Vegas
Rain Las Vegas (The Palms)
4321 W. Flamingo Rd.
(702) 940-7246

"Rain in the Desert" has VIP skyboxes, cabanas and water booths that you can reserve — plus go-go dancers and a light show that looks like fire, fog and rain around the dance floor.

Austin
The Foundation
307 W. 5th St.
(512) 472-4256

One of Austin's newest additions to the Warehouse district, Foundation is best known for its roominess and high-end metropolitan style. The upstairs bar is a well-kept secret.

Chicago
Crobar
1543 N. Kingsbury
(312) 266-1900 • www.crobar.com

Funk, soul and R&B keep things hot in this hipster club. The staff and DJs are fantastic!

Detroit
Envy
234 W. Larned
(313) 962-3689

For an upscale experience that won't blow your budget, this hip club features a meld of DJ spins and live music — and it's never too loud for conversation.

Dallas
Obar
1602-B Main St.
(214) 747-OBAR • www.obar.com

This downtown subterranean bar is a perfect example why a book shouldn't be judged by its cover. Walk inside this nondescript locale and it's an intimate and swanky nightclub.

Milwaukee
Have A Nice Day Café
1103 Old World Third St.
(414) 270-9650 • www.cafemilwaukee.com

Only the most popular music from the '70s, '80s, and '90s with a great dance floor from Saturday Night Fever.

BONUS LISTINGS

Northern Virginia
eCITIE
8300 Tyce Rd., McLean
(703) 760 9000 • www.eciticafe.com

An upscale venue with a chic New York-style design, eCITIE is a great place for those who live by the saying "Work hard, play hard."

Pittsburgh
Matrix
7 E. Station Sq.
(412) 261-2220 • www.pghnightlife.com/matrix_home.php

Four distinctively themed rooms provide house beats, hip-hop, Latin-dance and Miami-style trance music.

San Francisco
Suite one8one
181 Eddy St.
(415) 345-9900 • www.suite181.com

Dress well, and drink and dance the night away with other fabulous people. Think incredible lounge with couches and a back patio for smokers, which is hard to find in this city.

Charlotte
Breakfast Club
225 N. Caldwell St.
(704) 374-1982 • www.that80sclub.com

Dance the night away to your favorite beats from the '80s. The multi-level club features '80s-inspired specialty drinks, memorabilia and unique events every night.

New York City
Marqui
289 Tenth Ave., Manhattan
(646) 473-0202

Experience the hot new A-list only club in Chelsea. Buy a

table or wait for hours behind the velvet rope. Obviously, this is the place to be if you want to be seen.

Central Pennsylvania
Eclipse
236 N. Second St., Harrisburg
(717) 221-0530

This is big-city nightlife in downtown Harrisburg. The first level has an art-deco lounge with couches and a bar. The second level features a dance floor with sexy cages.

Sarasota
Fandango International Café and Jazz Bar
1266 Old Stickney Point Rd.
(941) 346-1711 • www.fandango-cafe.com

Heat it up on the dance floor and then cool it off in the upstairs VIP lounge or by catching a breeze outside in the open-air loft bars.

Phoenix
Mr. Lucky's
3660 N.W. Grand Ave.,
(602) 246-0686 • www.mrluckys.com

If "dancin' " translates into "boot scootin'," then Mr. Lucky's is the two-stepping honky tonk for you. Be sure to wear your tight jeans and Stetson hat.

Silicon Valley
Usual
400 S. 1st St., San Jose
(408) 535-0330

This unusual nightclub boasts a European atmosphere. Enjoy the café-style menu all day and night. They serve up everything from cappuccino to Guinness and martinis.

Indianapolis
The Vogue
6259 N. College Ave.
(317) 259-7029

Get up and dance at this Indy hotspot. Locals swear the Wednesday Night Retro Rewind is not to be missed. The live acts vary from local bands to major headliners.

Chapter 3
Places to Go, People to See

Whether you're heading out for a few martinis with friends, volunteering at the local dog shelter or taking a class in feng shui, you increase your chances of meeting Mr. or Ms. Right ten-fold simply by getting out of the house.

So you've gotten as far as the doorstep — now what? In this chapter we'll take a look at some of best venues to scope out potential dates and offer a few suggestions for making the most of them.

Beyond the Bar
If the bar scene just isn't cutting it for you, we offer a whole slew of fun and interesting activities where you could easily run into your soul mate.

Spend time in places you like, doing the types of things you really enjoy. Choose activities that will put you in a position to meet people who are like you or who at least have similar interests.

Coffee Shops/Juice Bars/Bookstores
Bookstores with coffee shops are great locales to make new friends. Try scoping out approachable people in sections of the bookstore that reflect your interests. With all those book titles, you've got thousands of potential conversation starters. If you spot a hottie, check out the book section he or she is browsing, and if you know something about the subject, speak up. If you don't, pick up a book and ask if they know anything about the author you're perusing. Once you've broken the ice, suggest a move over to the coffee area for some frothy conversation.

Classes and Workshops
Signing up for classes at the local junior college or university is really a win-win situation: you're doing something you enjoy, expanding your knowledge and meeting like-minded people.

If you want to improve your odds, why not join a class that usually is frequented by the opposite sex? Guys, try interior design (it can't hurt), personal development or gourmet cooking. Ladies, look into business, management, computer classes and golf.

If no one in the class catches your eye, don't lose hope. Once you start to cultivate new relationships, these folks will introduce you to their friends and family.

Dance classes are a terrific way to meet other singles and are a whole lot of fun. Country and swing dancing are very popular. How about learning to tango, salsa or meringue? You'll pick up some hot moves, get in shape and best of all, dancing comes complete with partners who often rotate among the class.

Sports Leagues

If you're a sports enthusiast, joining a league is one way to meet other athletic and sports-minded people in a non-threatening environment. Socializing after the game provides further opportunities to meet and mingle, but there are some downsides to the league approach. As with any other bunch that meets regularly, some people won't want to "date" within a group or a team because they are afraid of ruining the group's chemistry.

Golf, tennis, softball and polo are among the best sports to find successful eligible professionals.

Health and Sports Clubs

Fitness-conscious singles invest a lot of time working out by playing sports, visiting the gym or taking fitness classes.

Sports clubs (like a hiking club) and leagues are especially popular with men, so ladies, this is a great opportunity to meet athletic guys. Most of the people you meet at these places are fun. They are outdoorsy, adventurous, often well traveled, fit and outgoing people who love to meet others.

Keep in mind that most members want to meet people who are competent and enjoy the sport, so don't join these clubs unless you have a real interest. If you are a beginner, there are groups and classes for every level to help you master the sport.

Golf is extremely popular these days, and the driving range, clubhouse, pro shop and putting green are great places to come across potential dates. Ski or sailing clubs are popular on both coasts and around cities with large lakes. There are several large ski clubs around the United

States. Many are involved in racing and offer their own leagues and activities.

Finally, there's always the local gym. If you spot someone attractive while working out, ask for advice on toning up your glutes or which cardio machine yields the best results. Stay alert and don't close yourself off to everyone by clamping on headphones or immersing yourself in a magazine while riding the stationary bike.

Wine Tastings and Dinners

If you enjoy the finer things in life, a wine tasting or gourmet dinner event is a great networking opportunity. Most attendees are 40 or over. This typically is a white-collar, professional crowd.

Some groups organize trips to vineyards and others hold tastings in local restaurants. If you really are up for an adventure, you can sign up for a wine-tasting trip to Italy, where you're sure to find romance.

Call some local restaurants that are known for their wine lists and see what events they're planning.

You can also log on to www.localwineevents.com, which bills itself as the "largest wine and spirits calendar in the world."

Volunteer/Fundraisers/Political Campaigns

Did you know that there are volunteer groups just for singles? In many large cities, organizations like the Single Volunteers of New York City or the Leukemia Society of America offer opportunities that bring together unattached volunteers. This is a rewarding way for you to connect with new people who share similar values. You get to make a difference in the world while meeting folks who are also giving back to the community. Search online for "volunteer groups for singles" and enter your city to find local organizations.

If you support a certain political party, you can volunteer to help with campaign efforts. Many cities have a Young Democrats or Young Republicans group. Political fundraising balls or parties that raise money for charities are another great way to meet people and network. Once again, you will encounter people who share your views and you'll build a strong camaraderie as you work together on projects.

Bars and Nightlife

Regardless of how you feel about it, the bar and club scene is still a feasible place to meet other singles. We know several people with happy marriages who met in a bar or a club, but we've also heard quite a few horror stories too. Even though the quality of dates cannot be guaranteed here — and it's more likely you'll find a one-night stand than a lasting relationship — you will socialize with members of the opposite sex, and that alone improves your chances of meeting a new love.

Going out and being social opens up opportunities, so go have some fun — you never know when cupid will strike! As long as you keep your expectations in check and don't confuse that warm heady rush you get after a few martinis with true love, you won't be disappointed.

Though the odds of meeting your soul mate in a bar may not be great, there are some things you can do to improve your chances.

Take time to observe people and don't allow yourself to be drawn to the best-looking person in the room. Instead, sit back and watch how that person interacts with others. Are they friendly, polite, do they seem interested or drunk?

Be open and accessible. Smiling and talking to various people sends the signal that you're approachable.

Bars and clubs, above all, are excellent places to test your conversation and flirting skills, to meet different types of people and observe body language first hand. (See more on this in chapter 4, "The Language of Love.")

Your choice of watering hole is vast, depending on the type of company you'd like to keep. Different breeds of the human species gather at different locales, and frequenting one of those venues will increase your chances of meeting that type. We hate to put people into *types* that frequent certain *types* of bars, but it's true!

Let's look at some of the more common establishments.

The Wine/Martini Bar

If you prefer to focus on conversation and cocktails, then the wine or martini bar is your best bet.

- **Who you'll find there:** Suburban hipsters and professionals, usually well groomed and sophisticated.
- **The Scene:** Swanky and cultured.
- **Dress Code:** Smart/Casual.

The Sports Bar

Catch a game and a buzz as armchair quarterbacks and football maniacs scream instructions at an impressive number of TV screens per square foot.

- **Who you'll find there:** Slightly younger crowd, blue-collar or collegiate sports fans.
- **The Scene:** Lively, loud, lots of woo-hooing!
- **Dress Code:** Casual.

The Hotel Lounge

Settle into a comfy couch, catch up on *The Wall Street Journal*, and tap your feet to the beat of the pianist's background jazz tunes.

- **Who you'll find there:** A more refined crowd; business types on expense accounts.
- **The Scene:** Relaxed and very posh. This is where the wealthy come to sip cocktails in comfort.
- **Dress Code:** Dressy.

The Pub

If you can't get to Dublin, you can find a wee bit o' Ireland in an authentic style pub. If it's not Irish, it's English style, so expect fish and chips, shepherd's pie and plenty of good old-fashioned brews on the menu.

- **Who you'll find there:** Ex-pats from the U.K., Australia, South Africa and New Zealand as well as friendly local natives digging the energy and the accents.
- **Vibe:** A hospitable crowd partaking in the "eat, drink and be merry" customs you'd find in any neighborhood pub anywhere in the U.K. crossed with the casual familiarity of the American "local."
- **Dress Code:** Casual.

The Hotspot

Ultra cool interiors gleam with modern architectural angles, plush velvet couches, plasma TVs and hardwood floors. Writhing sirens dance on elevated boxes as deejays spin a mix of juicy hip-hop and Top 40.

- **Who you'll find there:** The A-list crowd. You may find yourself dancing next to well-connected nightlife connoisseurs and local and visiting NBA stars.
- **The Scene:** Stylish, sophisticated and sexy.
- **Dress Code:** Designer duds.

The Dance Club

Once past the velvet-rope crush of wriggling bodies clamoring to be deemed worthy, the dance club offers infectious beats and eye-candy treats for those who want to get their groove on.

- **Who you'll find there:** A mixed crowd of young professionals and fabulous hipsters.
- **The Scene:** A well-dressed crowd looking to dance, flirt and dance some more.
- **Dress Code:** Sexy

The Lists

Ten Best Places to Take Classes

San Antonio
Sam's Swing Factory
330 E. Grayson
(210) 223-2830

Located in Sam's Burger Joint, these dance classes offer you the opportunity to get swingin' on Monday nights at 7 P.M.

Dallas
Guy Mezger's FS Martial Arts
12740 Merit Dr.
(214) 954-0022 • www.landmarkclub.com

Located inside The Landmark Fitness Club in the heart of North Dallas, this is a great place to meet other singles, practice lethal moves and have a great time doing it.

San Francisco
Beadissimo
1061 Valencia St.
(415) 282-BEAD • www.beadissimo.com

A fun and creative way to spend some time: beads for bracelets, necklaces and earrings from around the world. Make something personal for someone special.

New York City
The 92nd St. "Y"
1395 Lexington Ave.
(212) 415-5500 • www.92Y.org

This "Y" is famous for great lectures, performances and

meeting singles, plus classes in photography, traveling solo, career workshops, artsy stuff, writing fiction and more.

Atlanta
Margaret Mitchell House
999 Peachtree St. NE
(404) 249-7012 • www.gwtw.org

This is where would-be authors indulge their passion for writing. Who wouldn't be inspired working in the house where *Gone With the Wind* was written?

Houston
Skydive Space Land
1611 Farm Road 521
(281) 595-3772 • www.skydivespaceland.com

Thirty miles south of Houston is a skydiving resort with a restaurant, where ordinary people do extraordinary things!

Honolulu
Hans Hedemann Surf School
2586 Kalakaua Ave.
(808) 924-7778 • www.hhsurf.com

Hans has 17 years of professional experience surfing Oahu's legendary North Shore. Impress by learning to surf.

Northern New Jersey
2 for Tango
Bergen Museum Gallery, Bergen Mall, Midland Park
Call for other locations.
(201) 444-2249 • www.2fortango.org

These tango encounters pair you with other eager dance partners. Together you'll discover the Argentine dance of love as taught by tango aficionados!

Miami
Bikram Yoga Miami
1330 Ocean Dr., Miami Beach
(305) 534-2727 • www.bikramyogamiami.com

Yoga is a great way to physically relax and feel spiritually cleansed. Wear something cool and comfortable and go in with an open mind. Don't forget a sense of adventure!

Las Vegas
Creative Cooking School
7385 West Sahara
(702) 562-3900 • www.creativecookingschool.com

Creative Cooking School offers a range of classes from specialty menus to grilling techniques to spectacular desserts.

Ten Best Coffee Shops, Book Stores, and Juice Bars

Tampa
Tampa Antiquarian Books & Collectibles
6306 N. Armenia Ave.
(813) 871-3919

Linger amid stacks of rare books and other odds and ends at this favorite haunt of the intellectual set.

Albany
Shades of Green
187 Lark St.
(518) 434-1830

Stop by this vegetarian restaurant and juice bar for a wide assortment of yummy shakes that are nutritious, too. Order the Moon Shake — it's incredible!

Austin
Bookpeople
603 N. Lamar
(800) 823-9757 • www.bookpeople.com

The largest bookstore in Texas, Bookpeople is a refuge for literary enthusiasts. Choose from an amazing selection of books and enjoy a good cup of coffee while you're there.

Chicago
24-Hour Starbucks
Piper's Alley, 210 W. North Ave.
Call or check the website for other locations.
(312) 867-0186 • www.starbucks.com

Regulars tell tales of sharing a 3 A.M. Doppio Macchiato with the ghost of John Belushi at the mega-Starbucks located on the first floor of the Second City building.

Denver
The Tattered Cover
1628 16th St.
(303) 322-1965 • www.tatteredcover.com

This expansive bookstore features a fourth story restaurant and bar, providing a dramatic view of the Rocky Mountains and weekly live music.

Pittsburgh
The Quiet Storm
5430 Penn Ave.
(412) 661-9355 • www.quietstormcoffee.com

One of the most fashionable coffeehouses in Pittsburgh, with free wireless Internet, live bands, art displays and shelves of donated publications.

New York City
The Hungarian Pastry Shop
1030 Amsterdam Ave.
(212) 866-4230 • www.geocities.com/hungarianpastryshop

A local intellectuals' hangout where you join in with Columbia grads and undergrads and discuss the meaning of life and whether or not to order another slice of pie.

Boise
Flying M Coffeehouse
500 W Idaho St.
(208) 345-4320

The Flying M is downtown Boise's premier coffeehouse, serving gourmet blends and luscious homemade desserts with eclectic art-infused flair.

Boston
Mike's Pastry
300 Hanover St.
(617) 742-3050 • www.mikespastry.com

Mike's is practically a Boston institution, serving up the most delectable homemade desserts in the city. Order a cappuccino and the signature homemade cannoli!

Columbus
Coffee Table
731 High St.,
(614) 297-1177

This location has outdoor tables where you can enjoy your

choice of many different delicious pastries and coffees. As a bonus, they offer free dog treats.

Ten Best Sports Leagues

Tampa
Tampa Bay Sea Kayakers
Sweetwater Kayaks, 10000 Gandy Blvd. N., St. Petersburg
Call for other locations.
(727) 570-4844 • www.clubkayak.com

Get wet and have a great time while navigating the rivers and coasts of 10 counties. Choose from 15 to 20 trips each month.

Albany
Afrim's Soccer Leagues
636 Albany Shaker Rd.
Other location: Schenectady
(518) 438-3131 • www.afrimsports.com

If soccer's your game, this is a great way to get to know some new people and have some fun. Many adult leagues are offered at convenient times. It's not just for kids!

San Francisco
Golden Gate Sport and Social Club
1628 Lombard St.
(415) 921-1161 • www.ggsportandsocialclub.com

The recreational adult sport and social club to meet people in San Francisco. They have something for everyone — from coed softball teams to nighttime bike-riding clubs.

Seattle
The Mountaineers
300 3rd Ave. W
(206) 284-6310 • www.mountaineers.org

The largest outdoor adventure club in the Northwest, where you can meet someone who shares your love of the great outdoors!

New York City
Bowlmor Lanes
110 University Pl.
(212) 255-8188 • www.bowlmor.com

Bowlmor is hands-down the city's hottest bowling spot.

Get there on Monday nights when they host "Night Strike," their long-running bowling club.

Orange County
Huntington Central Park Equestrian Center
18381 Goldenwest St., Huntington Beach
(714) 536-5486

A competitive sports league for those who want to get serious about their equestrian skills. It offers complete hunter and jumper facilities, a polo club and reining.

East Bay
Bay Billiards
40515 Albrae St., Fremont
(510) 252-1311

Let the experts teach you how to shoot pool. Come and learn a few tricks to impress your friends at this super billiards parlor.

Atlanta
Ruff 'n Sluff Bridge Club
1809 Roswell Rd. NE
(770) 973-7717 • www.mindspring.com/~ruffnsluff

Believe it or not, bridge is hip again! If your mom didn't teach you how to play, Ruff 'n Sluff Bridge Club gives private lessons and will help place you on a team.

Cleveland
The Cleveland Darter Club
11624 Madison Ave.
(216) 226-2582 • www.darter.org

No Rust Belt city is complete without its own darting league. This league offers coed teams and a chance to meet in local bars for competitive darting.

South Florida
Florida Atlantic University L.I.F.T. Program
& Rock Climbing Club
777 Glades Rd., Boca Raton
(561) 297-3617 • www.shs.fau.edu/ropes

Offering challenging programs designed to help stimulate and inspire, the club also meets monthly for group climbing sessions and fun. All levels are welcome.

Ten Best Health Clubs And Gyms

Chicago
East Bank Club
500 North Kingsbury St.
(312) 527-5800 • www.eastbankclub.com

This is Oprah's uber-gym of choice! It features an indoor track, eight indoor tennis courts, an indoor golf driving range, a dry cleaner, a full-service salon and spa, and a 60,000-square-foot sun deck.

Houston
The Houstonian
111 North Post Oak Ln.
(713) 680-2626 • www.houstonian.com/club/abo.htm

An elegant, classy and gracious club, boasting more than 125,000 square feet of workout area. Great for people watching.

Columbus
LifeTime Fitness
Easton Town Center
3900 Easton Station
(614) 428-6000 • www.lifetimefitness.com

This club features a variety of dance classes, an indoor rock climbing wall, diving lessons for all skill levels and water slides.

Dallas
GoodBody's
5301 W. Lovers Ln., Ste. 114
(214) 351-9931 • www.goodbodyswellness.com

This casual gym has two locations where Dallas' finest singles come to get fit as well as to mingle.

Seattle
Bellevue Place Club
800 Bellevue Way N.E., Seattle
(425) 688-3155

A full-service athletic club, Bellevue is 22,000 square feet of pure health that offers organized group hiking, rafting and biking trips.

New York
Chelsea Piers
23rd St. and the Hudson River
(212) 336-6000 • www.chelseapiers.com

This vast gym defines everything in fitness at a trendy location. Work out; take sailing, golf or rock-climbing lessons; hit a puck at their Sky Rink or hire a personal trainer!

South Florida
Athletic Club Boca Raton
1499 Yamato Rd., Boca Raton
(561) 241-5088 • www.wellbridge.com

This is the area's top athletic club and also a day spa that offers full-service amenities. Exercise, socialize and get pampered all under one roof.

Sacramento
The Capital Athletic Club
1515 8th St., Sacramento
(916) 442-3927 • www.capitalac.com

Primarily serving the downtown business community, this club offers everything from free shoe service and laundry services to free Pilates classes with membership.

Denver
Greenwood Village Athletic Club
5801 S. Quebec St., Greenwood Village
(303) 770-CLUB • www.greenwoodthleticclub.com

Their motto is: "Greenwood Athletic Club... It just might change your life." It's quite possible, after all. It is a national award-winning health club!

Twin Cities
The Sweatshop
167 Snelling Ave. N., St. Paul
(651) 646-8418 • www.sweatshopfitness.com

The tremendously caring staff will help you set your goals for rehab, weight loss, or general conditioning.

10 Best Bars for Wine, Martinis, and Tapas

Tampa
Tinatapas
615 Channelside Dr., Ste.120, Tampa
(813) 514-8462 • www.tinatapas.com

Tinatapa's three commandments — share, socialize, and sangria! — liven up this tapas lounge. Try the guava ribs and chocolate con churros.

Detroit
Blue Martini
201 Hamilton Row, Birmingham
Other location: Pickney
(248) 258-3005

Here's where the rich and famous clientele — and wannabes — dance and network while they sip high-end drinks and listen to live music.

Milwaukee
Centanni
219 N. Water St., Milwaukee, WI 53202
414.221.4200 • www.centannipaniobar.com

This is a phenomenal piano bar with a great wine and martini selection. Cintanni blends the classic 1940's nightclub with an intriguing fusion of Art Deco, Italian, and Contemporary design.

San Francisco
Nectar Wine Lounge
3330 Steiner St., San Francisco
(415) 345-1377 • www.nectarwinelounge.com

Cool, chic place to enjoy wine paired with imaginative appetizers. Nectar boasts a 600-bottle wine list and 40 wines by the glass. You'll find big groups of singles.

Seattle
Tango
1100 Pike St., Seattle
(206) 583-0382

The people, food, and décor at Tango lend themselves to a sophisticated evening where we recommend the fiery prawns in adobo.

Twin Cities
Martini Blu
615 2nd Ave. S., Minneapolis
(612) 752-9595 • www.martiniblu.com

This is both a full restaurant and a sushi bar. Try their award-winning Sexy Blu Martini. Sunday night is all-you-can-eat sushi. Wednesdays through Saturday nights there are live DJs.

Northern New Jersey
Tapas de Espana
7909 Bergenline Ave., North Bergen
(201) 453-1690

Entrees here are on the large side but the paella Valenciana tastes like the real thing — those who've had the authentic one in Spain say this Jersey version tastes exactly like it!

Baltimore
The Wine Market
921 E. Fort Ave., Baltimore
(410) 244-6166 • www.the-wine-market.com

There'll be plenty to talk about as you take in the historic intensity of a restored foundry — not to mention the seven hundred wines to choose from.

Atlanta
Noche
1000 Virginia Ave. N.E., Atlanta
(404) 815-9155
www.heretoserverestaurants.com

This eclectic Mexican bistro in the heart of the trendy Highlands attracts plenty of young singles during Happy Hour, with its quaint patio and inviting bar.

South Florida
The Rose Bar
1685 Collins Ave., Miami Beach
(305) 672-2000
www.delano-hotel.net411.com

Enjoy sushi while sipping on a delicious glass of wine. This is a simple yet elegant bar located within the Delano Hotel.

Ten Best Sports Bars Or Pubs

Sacramento
Sidelines Sports Bar and Nightclub
1023 Front St.
(916) 447-2311

Lots of televisions, so sports fans are sure to catch all the action. It's a great place on Sundays and during any sports playoff series. At night, the club action begins.

Wilmington
Scrimmages
4723 Concord Pike
(302) 478-8638

Not only can you watch the game here, but you might find yourself hanging out with players. A popular spot for the softball, soccer and volleyball crowd.

Chicago
McGee's
950 W. Webster Ave.
(773) 549-8200 • www.mcgeestavern.com

This place has a TV everywhere you look. If you love meeting people who can talk sports, by all means don't miss McGee's Tavern.

San Diego County
Seau's The Restaurant
1640 N. Camino Del Rio, #1376, San Diego
(619) 291-SEAUS • www.seau.com

Seau's is owned by former San Diego Chargers linebacker Junior Seau and features 60 televisions in addition to a huge projection screen for major sporting events.

Northern Virginia
Crystal City Sports Pub
529 S. 23rd St., Arlington
(703) 521-8215

This three-level sports bar has 60 television screens! There are also foosball tables, dartboards and pool tables.

Pittsburgh
Hi-Tops
200 Federal St., North Shore
(412) 231-3310 • http://hi-topsusa.com/pittsburgh.htm

Located directly across from PNC Park, Hi-Tops is Pittsburgh's hottest pre-game, post-game and game-time party bar.

San Francisco
Bayside Sports
1787 Union St.
(415) 673-1565 • www.baysidesportssf.com

41 TVs showing just about anything involving a ball. Great mixed atmosphere and great food too.

Kansas City
Fox & Hound
10428 Metcalf Ave., Overland Park
Other location: Independence
(913) 649-1700

A sports lover's dream with many big screen TVs and billiard tables. The nachos are almost as high as the Broadway Bridge.

Twin Cities
Damon's
950 Helena Ave. N., Oakdale
(651) 501-2330
Other locations: Inver Grove Heights, Blaine
www.damons.com

The Club House offers five large-screen TVs with speakers on each table. This joint really fills up on game nights for the Vikings, Timberwolves, Twins and Wild.

East Bay
Ricky's Sports Theatre and Grill
15028 Hesperian Blvd., San Leandro
(510) 352-0200 • www.rickys.com

Ricky's has pool tables, darts and video games, along with 72 TVs and satellite feeds to soothe the sports junky in you.

Ten Best Restaurants

Las Vegas
Aureole (Mandalay Bay)
3950 S. Las Vegas Blvd.
(877) 632-7401 • www.aureolelv.com

Charlie Palmer's award-winning restaurant offers modern décor, lots of seafood, and a multi-story wine tower where "angels" trapeze up and down for your chosen vintage.

Pittsburgh
Le Mont
1114 Grandview Ave., Mt. Washington
(412) 431-3100 • www.lemontpittsburgh.com

Incredible food with a fantastic view of our fair city atop Mt. Washington. Le Mont is a great date… one that makes a lasting first impression.

Charlotte
La Vecchia's
225 East 6th St.
(704) 370-6776 • www.lavecchias.com

Partake of exquisite seafood or aged beef. Known as the best seafood restaurant in Charlotte.

Naples
The Grill Room at the Ritz-Carlton Golf Resort
280 Vanderbilt Beach Rd.
(239) 598-6644 • www.ritzcarlton.com

This restaurant is the perfect place to have a memorable dining experience. Make sure to call ahead and reserve the romantic table in front of the fireplace.

East Bay
Chez Panisse
1517 Shattuck Ave., Berkeley
(510) 548-5525 • www.chezpanisse.com

Local, organic ingredients turned into French and Italian inspired masterpieces make this a truly memorable and delicious experience.

South Florida
YUCA
501 Lincoln Rd., Miami Beach
(305) 532-9822 • www.yuca.com

YUCA is an acronym for Young Urban Cuban Americans — and that's precisely the type of ethnic flavor this trendy upscale restaurant represents.

Boise
The Milky Way
205 N. 10th St., Ste. 110
(208) 319-0123 • www.restaurantmilkyway.com

This urban retreat serves fine dining sensations that are out of this world. Try the pan-seared beef tenderloin, but save room for the lemongrass cardamom crème brulee!

Columbus
The Ocean Club
4002 East Station
(614) 416-CLUB

The Ocean Club gets rave reviews for its seafood dishes. One of the top 10 restaurants in Columbus, The Ocean Club has a well-trained staff and offers exceptional service.

Des Moines
Chat Noir Café
644 18th St., Des Moines
(515) 244-1353

Chat Noir — the black cat — is a cozy hideaway, know for European-influenced cooking. Not to be missed is the house specialty: crepes.

Boston
Tapeo Restaurant and Tapas Bar
266 Newbury St., Boston
(617) 267-4799 • www.tapeorestaurant.com

Share several of their more than 40 tapas dishes, order up a bottle of wine or a pitcher of sangria, sit back, chat and enjoy an adventurous and romantic dining experience.

Ten Best After-Hours Spots

Albuquerque
Frontier Restaurant
2400 Central Ave. SE
(505) 266-0550 • www.frontierrestaurant.com

Known for their great green chili stew, breakfast burritos, homemade tortillas and Frontier sweet rolls, this late-night spot is open 24 hours, seven days a week.

Austin
Katz's Deli and Bar
618 W. 6th St.
(512) 472-2037 • www.katzsneverkloses.com

The slogan — Katz's Never Kloses — says it all! Katz's claim to fame is its New York deli-style cuisine "with a Texas attitude," morning, noon and night — all night.

Northern Virginia
Silver Diner
11951 Killingsworth Ave., Reston
Other locations: McLean, Arlington
(703) 742-0801 • www.silverdiner.com

This old-style diner serves delicious food and large portions. Definitely try the caramel French toast if you go there for breakfast.

Seattle
13 Coins Restaurant
125 Boren Ave. N
(206) 682-2513

This original upscale diner has been open 24/7 since 1967. We love the high-backed booths. Where else can you order Chicken Piccata at 4 A.M.?

St. Louis
O'Connell's Pub
4652 Shaw St.
(314) 773-6600 • www.saucemagazine.com/oconnells

The bar is open until 3 A.M. on weekends and you can't beat the burgers. A true St. Louis tradition since 1962, the bartenders and waitresses are nice, too.

East Bay
Pring's
15015 E. 14th St., San Leandro
(510) 351-3266

This is a quiet haven in which to kick back, talk and get to know each other better after a busy night out.

Northern New Jersey
Mastoris
144 Highway 130-Rte 206, Bordentown
(609) 298-4650 • www.mastoris.com

Another Jersey landmark, Mastoris is considered the ultimate "gut-buster" of all the great diners. It's a real standout for its high-quality comfort food.

Los Angeles
Berri's Pizza Café
8410 W. Third St.
(323) 852-0642

When you pull up at 3 A.M. and the valet is jam-packed, you know you're at Berri's. This late-night eatery has some of the best New York-style pizza in Los Angeles.

Atlanta
Majestic Diner
1031 Ponce De Leon Ave.
(404) 875-0276

This local landmark is a great place to enjoy breakfast and hot black coffee in the wee hours of the morning. Try the pork chop and eggs with a pecan waffle!

South Florida
Porterhouse
7050 W. Palmetto Rd., Boca Raton
(561) 391-6601

Eat, drink and dance to a live band that plays the latest and hippest music in town. Open till 5 A.M.

Ten Best Happy Hours

Wilmington
Kid Sheleen's
14th & Scott St.
(302) 658-4600 • www.kidshelleens.com

Always happening and loud. The bar attracts singles from

all walks of life, but particularly upscale professionals finding refuge after a long day.

Orlando
Dexter's
808 E. Washington St., Thornton Park
Other location: Winter Park
(407) 648-2777 • www.dexwine.com

Choose from more than 30 wines, champagnes, ports and sherries by the glass. A great place for happy hour as well as a place to view (and buy) the works of local artists.

Philadelphia
The Irish Pub
1123 Walnut St.
(215) 925-3311 • www.theirishpub.com

This place has happy hour down to a science. The Irish Pub has exceptional munchies at the free buffet with extraordinary drink specials.

San Francisco
Royal Exchange
301 Sacramento St.
(415) 956-1710 • www.royalexchange.com

Locals like to call it "The Royal Exchange of phone numbers." That being said, it's a prime spot for financial-district types in this very happening after-work English pub.

Twin Cities
The Imperial Room
417 1st Ave. N., Minneapolis
(612) 376-7676 • www.imperialroom.com

Happy hour is from 3:30 P.M. to 8 P.M. weekdays. Enjoy half-price martinis and appetizers, 2-for-1 drinks, and a great downtown crowd.

Raleigh
Green Room
1108 Broad St., Durham
(919) 286-2359

Sixty types of beer, good conversation and 10 of the finest pool tables you'll ever see make this a welcome respite from the workweek.

Birmingham
Lou's Pub
726 29th St., Birmingham
(205) 322-7005

Hey baby! Lou's Pub is a classic. It's a package store that is literally a bar, and the staff has been there forever. This is the happy-hour spot for the media.

Atlanta
Atkins Park Tavern
2840 Atlanta Rd. SE, Smyrna
(770) 435-1887 • www.atkinspark.com

Atlanta's oldest continuously licensed tavern is a neighborhood pub with plenty of beer on tap, good tunes in the jukebox and lots of singles.

Cleveland
Kevin's Martini Lounge (basement of Pickwick & Frolic)
2035 E. 4th St.
(216) 241-7425 • www.pickwickandfrolic.com

Finally, the place to wear your black leather pants! You'll look as cool as the rest of the crowd and contrast nicely with the oh-so-swanky red-and-white decor.

Houston
Sam's Boat
5720 Richmond Ave.
Call for other locations.
(713) 781-BOAT

At Sam's, it's hard to beat their prices — 25-cent shrimp and oysters. Add loud music and beer and you have the recipe for a great time!

Places to Go, People to See

Chapter 4

The "It's Just Lunchbox" of Flirting Tips and Tools

Now that you're armed and ready with a great dating attitude, the lowdown on your options and places to go, it's time to get out and meet some people.

In this chapter we'll tackle the whole process from getting noticed to closing the deal in four simple steps.

Step 1: The Preliminaries

Rules of Attraction

Strike a Pose
Pause in the doorway with your head held high and shoulders back, and hold it there for a few seconds. The idea is to let all potential dates get a good look at you at your best. Then proceed across the room with confidence.

Divide and Conquer
Ladies: break up the pack. Men will never approach you when you are surrounded by your posse of girlfriends. And men, no woman in her right mind will stride up to a bunch of guys and shoulder her way through to you — no matter how cute you are. If you want to attract the opposite sex, make room for them to approach.

Smile
It lights up your face and will make you appear more friendly and open. If your attitude projects "speak to me at your own risk," people will stay away. Nobody likes rejection, so whoever appears most welcoming and approachable will be approached the most.

Use a Prop
What better way to bolster a conversation! Props come in

an infinite variety of packages, so carry one, wear one or bring one along at all times. For example, dogs are people magnets and natural-born flirts. Skilled at reading body language, they will walk right up to someone they're interested in and say hello (well sort of, since sniffing is basically the same thing), and they never take rejection personally.

Women can't resist a man with a small child. For some reason, many ladies believe that men who love children or animals are genuine sensitive types. A great prop for women is to wear something with a team logo. This never fails to attract men who love sports.

Another great flirting prop is a book — especially when the subject has a controversial or intriguing title. Hey, why not sit somewhere where you can be noticed and flash the cover of *this* book. That should get you some attention.

Step 2: The Approach

You spot someone across the room, your eyes lock, you feel a little giddy and there's a rush of blood to the head. Time to let them know you're interested, and at this stage of the game the eyes have it.

Close Encounters of the Opposite Sex Kind

Eye See You

The most effective flirting tools you have are your eyes. If you catch the eye of someone attractive, and they look back, don't become self-conscious and turn away. Women like men who are not afraid and know what they want, and men like women who give them clear signals. So be brave.

Do the glance — linger — look away — then reconnect routine. After a few times, the other person will know you're interested and will hopefully return the eye contact.

Guys, when you catch her eye on the reconnect, stay there until she looks away. Hold her gaze without giving her an *America's Most Wanted* stare, which means it's held just long enough to say, "I see you and I like you." Anything longer could scare her off. Then throw her a confident smile.

If a woman smiles at you a few times, this is your invitation to move in her direction. If you're up for it, go ahead. She could, of course, move over toward you, so smile and welcome her approach. Keep the eye-to-eye contact going and start putting those conversation skills to work.

> ## Men Only
> **The Romantic Return**
> A friend of ours insists this trick always works: You spot a pretty woman across the room and you make eye contact for a while, but you're not completely convinced that she's interested in talking to Mr. Staring Guy. So you pay and leave without approaching her. Ten minutes later, you walk back in and stride right up to her and explain that "you just couldn't let this opportunity go by." Chances are you'll get her number. You see, leaving the scene and returning because you'll regret missing the chance takes you out of the lecherous category and puts you in the romantic fool category. It's so Hugh Grant, most women can't resist.

Instant Confidence

There they are, sitting at the end of the bar, looking great, looking out of your league. You approach, hoping you won't get blown off quickly. Stop right there! Try this quick psychological booster. Instead of thinking *what will they think of me?* turn it around to *will I like them?* Changing your thinking will adjust your body language and your conversation from timid to friendly and self-assured.

Feeling better? Okay, proceed to establishing contact.

You Had Them at Hello... Er — Maybe Not!

Walking up to a total stranger and starting a conversation can be terrifying, but if you don't learn to overcome your fear and wait for them to approach you first, you might end up waiting in the wings forever. Remember, they have the same fears and desires as you, so go ahead and take a few risks.

Yes, we know it's tough. Guys: She could totally ignore you and you'll have to quickly save face by pretending to speak with the person behind her. Or worse, ladies: He could laugh, then dismiss you with one of those looks of scorn, while all your friends gaze on. Oh, the humiliation!

Don't make it a big deal. If you don't get a favorable response, just say, "nice to meet you," and move on — no harm done. Not everyone is going to be intrigued, so don't try to force things or be too pushy — but know that most people are polite and the consequence of approaching someone is always worse in our minds than it is in real life.

Just be yourself, be friendly and smile. The confidence and warmth you exude when you approach someone will determine how successful you will be with your introduction. A sense of humor is always appreciated, but it's also important to be sincere.

Your goal is to generate good conversation, relate to people and get them interested — and to find out if you're interested in what they have to say. No matter how much you stumble or stammer in your initial approach, you will do 100% better than those who do nothing at all.

Avoid predictable opening lines like: "Where are you from?" OR "What do you do for a living?" OR "What do you do for fun?" Those questions are BORING!

Find questions that would engage *your* interest and go from there. There's no perfect opener, so trust your instincts and do what works best for you.

Observe first, so you can get some information to use as an opening line. For example, "Great party! Did you try those amazing apple martinis?" If they haven't, then offer to go with them and get one.

Or try a compliment: "I love your tie/jacket/ring." Then tell them why you like it, "It reminds me of..."

A great low-pressure conversation starter is to ask about someone else: "Do you know who that woman in the red dress is? She looks familiar."

In a class or a volunteer group, it's easier to find a subject to talk about. Steer the conversation toward something personal so you don't remain in neutral forever — like, "Great night! What inspired you to join (name of event or class)?" This way you move the conversation to a more emotional connection.

Confidence always gets the girl or boy, so if you don't let fear get in the way of romance, try this great icebreaker: "*It just occurred to me that a third person wasn't going to introduce us. Hi, my name is...*"

One last thought on opening lines — don't get too caught up in getting it right. When you get into a conversation with someone, unless you say something offensive right off the bat, you'll probably get to a few more sentences. Those are what will keep the conversation going.

All right! You've made contact. Now it's time to flirt.

Men Only
Rules of Attraction

Women know within the first few minutes of interacting with you whether or not you're a sexually confident man. It's all about your voice tone and body language. If you're not sure whether you project this "sexy beast" persona, chances are you don't. So, what's a guy to do? These four basic skills will instantly make you irresistible:

- **Lesson One:** Learn how to hold eye contact for longer than she does. Don't gawk, cold stare, or use darting eye glances. Just gently hold her gaze until she looks away. Avoiding eye contact reeks of emotional insecurity.

- **Lesson Two:** Women look first at your attire and second at how you hold yourself. Keep your body posture in a stance that says, "I'm the dominant male and I own this place." Suck in your stomach, hold your head up, chest out, shoulders back...and generally hold yourself like you're the most powerful person you've ever known. We know it seems a little awkward at first, but trust us, it'll work. Carry yourself like a manly man and women will have a positive subconscious, and then conscious, reaction to you.

- **Lesson Three:** Slow down. Confident people are not in a hurry. Fidgeting or nervous behavior shows insecurity and self-consciousness. Use slow, calculated gestures and movements. Walk slowly and with purpose, turn your head slowly, gesture slowly, even blink slowly. Emulate John Wayne or James Bond. This transmits a feeling of "I'm comfortable in my own skin," and makes a huge impact on women. Don't overdo it and become the slo-mo guy, but always project an attitude that you know what you're doing and where you're going.

continued on p. 39...

...continued from p. 38...
- **Lesson Four:** Lower your voice. A wobbly or high-pitched voice is a big turn-off for women since it relays low self-esteem. Moderately deep conveys confidence. Learn how to speak from the chest and stomach and not from the throat. Speak slower, articulate your words, pause more...it creates anticipation, which is sexy. If you talk too fast and too much when you get nervous, take a deep breath, let it out slowly, and relax. Stand up and hum a little before you leave a voicemail message—it will lower your pitch.

Step 3: The Flirt

It's Saturday night in a crowded bar. A man and woman are locked in conversation. She's laughing, batting her eyelashes and playing with her hair. He's standing with his head tilted slightly, leaning in toward her and occasionally touching her arm. They're performing a social ritual that's been around for more than 5,000 years — flirting.

Flirting is one of the great joys in life. It's an ego booster that makes you feel more attractive and desirable. Flirt with someone and they feel excited, flattered, appreciated and darn good about themselves. So indulge yourself whenever possible.

Two things are going on when you flirt. The first is the actual conversation, and the second is your body language. Flirting is an enticement and an invitation that lets the other person catch glimpses of your most attractive characteristics and behaviors. These days, it's a lost art, but it's great fun when done well.

Practice flirting with acquaintances or friends of the opposite sex (without telling them) and see what techniques get the best response.

For those who feel clueless about where to even start, we assure you that flirting is a learned behavior. It's not only possible to pick up the basics, but with a little practice, you can perfect the art. Let's start with the flirting conversation.

Can We Talk?

Flirting is considered a meta-conversation, which means

> # Women Only
> **Rules of Attraction**
>
> If you don't have the nerve to walk right up to a man and say hello, you could always bump into him... literally. That should get you noticed. Or ask for the time, a light, last week's notes, or where he got his jacket because you want to buy your brother one just like it. Even better: Ask for his advice. This makes him feel important and helpful — men love that. Ask him to explain something, give you directions or help you pick between two sweaters for your Dad. Get it? It doesn't matter what you say as long as it initiates a conversation.

it's three or four degrees of separation from what you're really saying. There's an underlying meaning to everything that's said. You might say directly, "That's really interesting," but the underlying meaning is, "I'm interested in you — perhaps sexually." There's a lot of unspoken communication going on: suggesting without stating, eye contact, body language, nods, smiles, encouragement and perhaps the start of something big.

Some men believe flirting is teasing encouragement and expect something at the end of it. If this is you, let us set you straight: *If a woman flirts with you,* or you flirt with her, it's simply an opportunity for an entertaining exchange of playful banter. *It doesn't mean you are guaranteed anything — not a dance, a drink, a date and especially not sex!*

Flirting is all about showing interest in the other person. So *ask questions and be attentive to the answers.*

Sometimes you can get caught up in the seductive aspect of flirting and find yourself stuck without a word to say. If this happens, there is a very powerful technique you can use called active listening. It's easy and will help you think of topics to discuss in any situation.

The most interesting people are usually the ones who are most interested in others. Suppose your date (or potential date) tells you about her day and she mentions that she bought plants for her garden. You can use that to move into a fun conversation.

Her garden might not mean anything to you, but it's obviously important to her. So you could say, "What's it like?" She'll jump at the chance to answer and actually think you're more interesting because you are interested in HER garden. And she'll become more interested in you!

A Few Conversation Dos

- Do be sincere. If her smile lights up the room, then tell her, but don't say something just for the sake of it. Insincere compliments are transparent.

- Do be yourself. Whatever's on your mind and in your heart will be the most natural thing you can talk about. Remember, they'll either like you or not. If they like you, great, if not... next! Why waste time trying to get someone's approval?

- Do be funny. Being light with a sense of humor helps people let their guard down, which could allow you more room to move in!

- Do say his or her name a few times; it'll make them feel special. But don't say it too much, or you'll sound like you just attended a cheesy sales seminar.

- Do keep it positive. Stick to your best attributes and the things you are most positive about. People become sexier as they talk excitedly and passionately about things that interest them.

- Do have fun with it. It's all about play!

A Few Conversation Don'ts

- Don't criticize personal choices, like wearing fur or who they voted for in the last election.

- Don't hog the conversation. It should flow back and forth like a tennis volley — you hit, he or she returns.

- Don't start talking about marriage or commitment on the first three dates.

- Don't use cheesy opening lines like, "Are you an Aquarius?"

Warning:
A Few Conversation Don'ts for Men

Avoid these danger zones!

- Don't corner her into revealing her age — it's never welcome.
- Don't use an authoritative or formal tone — save it for the office.
- Don't ask if she has kids right away. Single moms are sensitive about this and fear that you might have your "avoid the instant family" radar turned on.
- Don't compliment below the neck. No woman wants to know how you've checked out her nether regions.
- Don't go overboard with the bravado. Bragging about past conquests, thinking you know more about her anatomy/job/family than she does, or trying to impress her with your salary and net worth will leave you solo. Confidence is alluring — cockiness is not.
- Don't "over-friend." This means you're acting like all you want is to chat, because that's exactly what you'll end up with. Inject a little flirty banter into the conversation and don't hide your intentions.
- Don't "self reject." Deciding that someone is out of your league and failing to make a move will ensure you never get rejected or accepted. Why? Because you rejected yourself first!

The Language of Love

Want to know if that person you've been flirting with all night really likes you? Even if you're chatting about the weather, how people hold their bodies will tell you more than they want you to know.

Signals He Sends

- **The Grooming.** Adjusting or stroking his tie, fiddling with his collar or hand combing his hair.
- **The Loosening Off.** Partly unbuttoning his shirt or loosening his tie.
- **The Eyebrow Flash.** Raising his eyebrows and flashing them upward signals a strong interest.

> ### Rules of Attraction
> When couples are connecting deeply, they subconsciously mimic the other's body movements. If she leans forward, he'll likely do the same thing. If he touches his hair, she'll flip or stroke her own without even realizing it, and even blink rates and breathing will synchronize. It's fun to watch. Check out couples that are locked in seduction mode next time you're in a restaurant or bar setting.

- **The Arm Guide.** Walking you through a room with his arm around the small of your back or holding your elbow.
- **The Head Tilt.** Standing with his head cocked slightly to one side.
- **The Walk.** It becomes strong and determined — he knows where he's going.

Signals She Sends

- **The Smiles.** Lots of them. If she laughs at your jokes too, she really likes you.
- **The Eye Linger.** Holding your gaze signals a strong sexual interest.
- **The Lip Lick.** Licking or biting her lips or running her tongue across her front teeth draws your attention to her mouth and is intriguing.
- **The Touch and the Lean.** Leaning forward and touching your arm is her way of bestowing affection on you — she's inviting you into her personal space.
- **The Fondle.** Plays with her jewelry, especially with stroking and pulling motions.
- **The Kick and Thrust.** Crossing one leg over the other and pointing it toward you or kicking it out and up while thrusting her body forward.

Signals You Both Send

- Accidental touches
- Leaning forward
- Eye contact
- Smiles
- Open body position

Road-Tested Flirting Techniques

Being a skillful flirt is all about using the correct body language and the right amount of attitude. Here are 10 steps to help you perfect the art of flirting.

- **Make meaningful eye contact and smile.** Let your eyes linger on his or her eyes while you're talking, then smile immediately when you feel a connection.

- **Get interested in them and they'll get interested in you.** What is it that people like to talk about most? Themselves, of course. Ask questions about where they like to go, what they like to do, who interests them, and why they do what they do, and you'll be talking all night.

- **Deliver a compliment.** Flattery may not get you everywhere, but it does open doors. Keep it sincere.

- **Listen attentively.** Being a good listener is a potent aphrodisiac.

- **Tell it like it is.** Being vulnerable and honest is the slam-dunk, sexiest thing a man or woman can be. Getting "real" with someone is not only easier than the pretense most people create, it also saves you unnecessary angst in the long run. Just don't get too personal, too soon.

- **Be enthusiastic.** As a flirt, you want the person you're flirting with to feel good about you and to experience you as a fun, happy, great-to-be-with person. If you feel that you are, it shows. If you sit next to them thinking, *I'm having fun, this is great, I'm so glad to be here,* it really comes across to the other person.

- **Draw them in.** Lean forward, not because you want to show off your cleavage or your muscles, but to convey interest. Talk to them actively, showing that you like them. Then start talking more quietly and intimately. They'll need to get closer to hear you so draw them in with your voice. Guys, gauge her "personal zone" and then encroach on it just an inch. Leaning in too far can seem too forceful.

- **Touch him or her.** The sense of touch heightens during flirting and can actually send tingles through a person's body. Realize this power and watch for ways to use it. Once you've become comfortable, lightly brush shoulders, or touch their hand or arm if they say something funny. This can work wonders if the signals are there.

Step 4: The Proposition

You've spent the entire evening flirting with a total dream. You're on fire, loving life, feeling wanted and bursting to know if they share your feelings. She (or he) hasn't made any moves to leave and scope out other prospects. The best way to find out is by going on a date.

What's stopping you?

Oh... you have to ask first.

You may yet be rejected, but if you don't make a move, they might never know how you feel. What's worse, someone else might take the plunge first and you know you'll hate yourself if that happens.

It's a dilemma. So, what should you do? You can start by briefing yourself on the following tips for popping the question:

What to Say

First, relax. Try not to view it as a date, look at asking her out as an invitation instead. Better still — take the pressure off by not using the "D" word altogether. Don't ask for a date and don't call it a date. It starts to get significant when that word appears, so focus on the activity and position it in the same informal way you would ask a friend.

Keep the invitation light and casual. The whole reason *It's Just Lunch* is the success it is today, arranging more than 50,000 first dates each month, is because we do just that.

A lunch date is low pressure — it has a beginning and an end, and both occur within an hour or so. It's easy to say goodbye, there's no goodnight kiss, no obligation, and so the pressure is off.

If you're dating through *It's Just Lunch*, we do the first-date asking for you, so it's really easy. But if you want to ask for a second date or if you're going it alone from the start, there are a few things to keep in mind when asking someone out.

Here's What *Not* to Say

- Don't ask, "You want to go out sometime?" It's too

open-ended and can lead to an awkward follow-up conversation.

- Don't ask, "What are you doing Friday night?" It's too vague and it might leave your potential date wondering if you're just curious about what he or she is doing on Friday night, or if you want to do something together.

- Don't use a sexually suggestive line like, "I'd love to have breakfast with you. Should I call you or nudge you?" It might be funny if you read it in a book, but in the real world, it's liable to get you a speedy rejection. These types of lines don't show that you're genuinely interested in a person — they make you seem a little too slick.

What Works Best?

Before you ask, consider the following:

- **Be a friend first, not a potential date.** If you really want to get to know someone better, the key is to relax and allow your own personality to shine through. There really is no need to be a smart-ass, or make them laugh out loud. You just need to be good company, because the more comfortable you both feel, the easier it is to recognize any chemistry between you. In short, forget the pickup lines. Show an interest in them, and they will only be flattered.

- **Create an opportunity for your date.** Once you know more about what that person likes to do, you can offer something. After all, a date is an invitation. If they love art, ask them to the latest big museum exhibition; if they like sports, offer tickets to a basketball game. If they enjoy wine, ask them to a wine tasting.

- **Drop a hint.** Ask about a subject and drop a hint. Say something like, "What do you like to do on the weekends?" As she responds, look for something you like to do too. If she says she loves to hike, respond with, "We should go hiking together sometime," then move on in the conversation and ask about her favorite hiking spots.

The Business Card

Handing someone your card is a less threatening way of putting the ball in their court. If you find you're just too shy to go over and strike up a conversation, or perhaps you're in a noisy location, which makes it difficult to break the ice, then make sure you carry a few extra business cards around with you. Write a short note on the back. Say something like, "The noise makes it difficult to talk, but I'd really like to meet you. You can reach me at _____." Or if you're shy, say, "I think you're really attractive but I'm a little shy. If you'd like to talk sometime please call me on _____."

You've just dropped a big hint, so let it sink in for a while. Listen carefully to her response and gauge her enthusiasm. If she stays upbeat and positive, ask her if she would like to go hiking with you next weekend.

- **Keep it casual.** If you feel uncomfortable saying, "Would you like to go to dinner Friday night?" try something like this:

    "I was thinking about going for a ride along the boardwalk on Sunday. It's going to be a beautiful day. Would you like to go with me?" Pose the question as if you're already going and they can join you, if interested. This will make you feel less desperate and take the pressure off them if they say no.

- **Be specific when asking for the date.** "I'd like to take you for coffee this Thursday" is more powerful than asking if she'd like to "go out sometime."

    Of course, you could always invite the person on a group date, since that really takes the pressure off. Invite them bowling, to play volleyball, or to join a bunch of friends for a drink or to a party. As soon as you say, "A bunch of us are going to..." it takes the pressure off. "Us" is the operative word here.

    Read the situation. If you've hung out for a while and all the signs suggest your potential date shares your feelings, then either a) you won't be able to keep your hands off each other, or b) you'll be able to suggest meeting up for an evening out knowing that's what they want too! If that vibe isn't happening, at the very least you'll have made a new friend.

So remember, when you are asking someone out, *plan ahead* and *be specific*. Know what you are going to say AND what you want to suggest doing on the date.

Your prospective dates will be much more comfortable if they know exactly what you want to do.

Just try to relax and enjoy yourself. Worst case scenario — they'll say they can't go out. And that will bring you one step closer to someone who can. Someone who appreciates you and where the chemistry connection is reciprocated and the sparks really fly. Let's face it, getting to that special someone inevitably means dealing with a few duds along the way. It'll be worth it in the end.

Should She Ask?

Absolutely! It's no longer fashionable to leave it up to the man. Most men will be flattered, impressed, and relieved if you have the courage to ask them out. These days, men appreciate women who take the initiative and go after what they want in life. Guys find confident women extremely sexy. It may seem hard to initiate a request for a date if you're not used to it, but do it a few times and it'll become a piece of cake.

Getting a No or Saying No

Dating is a numbers game. You may have several misses before you get a hit. Don't take it personally or assume you did something wrong. View each rejection as bringing you one step closer to your ideal mate.

If you're the one who isn't interested, most of all, be kind. Say something nice about them and then end it with a, "no, thank you."

Try not to be overly sensitive to rejection or get overly emotionally invested with the other person too soon. Either makes a rebuff become equally, if not more, painful. Simply move on!

The Lists

Ten Best Annual Events for Flirting Opportunities

Birmingham
Doo Dah Day
Caldwell and Rhodes Parks • www.dodahday.org
The annual Doo Dah Day festival was established to celebrate man's best friend. Festivities kick off on Friday night with Doo Dah Day eve at Zydeco and some great bands. Saturday starts off with the parade and continues all day with live music, food and fun including the naming of the king and queen contest. You have never seen anything like it. Plus, it is a great way to strike up a conversation!

Austin
Austin Under 40
Palmer Events Center
Held once a year, usually in February, this event is a "must attend" for the under 40 crowd. This is where the "who's who" of Austin in business is, and individuals in the community are recognized for their business accomplishments. Live music, a big dance floor, a silent auction and yummy food catered from Austin's favorite restaurants make this an event no single will want to miss!!

Atlanta
Steeple Chase at Kingston Downs, Georgia
It's not just a horse race, it's an opportunity to wear your best hat, and your girliest dress! Think Julia Roberts in *Pretty Woman* in the scene with the "replacing of the divets." Held every April, people plan for this event months in advance and go in groups of hundreds. It's an all-day affair, so pace yourself.

Dallas
Annual Cattle Baron's Ball
(408) 879-1049 • www.cattlebarons.com
A sellout crowd of 1,000 partygoers kick up their heels and let down their hair at this premier fund-raising event, which benefits the American Cancer Society. Check the website each year as the venues change regularly.

Las Vegas
NASCAR Weekend at Las Vegas Motor Speedway
7000 Las Vegas Blvd N.
(702) 644-4444 • www.lvms.com

This event draws both locals and fans from around the world and if cars are your thing, then you don't want to miss it. If you can't make the NASCAR Weekend, there are other events at Las Vegas Motor Speedway where you can still enjoy the races and hopefully chat up that single race fan sitting next to you.

Honolulu
Merrie Monarch Festival Hula Competition
Edith Kanaka'ole Stadium, Hilo
(808) 935-9168 • www.merriemonarchfestival.org

This is actually on a different island (the Big Island), but it is a mind-blowing event that is well worth the travel time. The pride and skill of these dancers is awesome.

Houston
Baylor college of Medicine Charity Ball
Houston Muesum of Natural Science
(713) 798-4600 • www.bcm.edu/osa/charityball

This charity ball is organized entirely by the students to celebrate philanthropy with the theme "Around the World."

Detroit
The Port Huron to Mackinac Race
www.porthuronmackinac.com

This race is one of the most talked about annual sailing event s on the Great Lakes. Sailing and boating enthusiast from all over come to watch the race. Every year, hundreds of sailing yachts take on the waters of Lake Huron and race along two different courses to the Island. Yachts range in size from 26 feet to more than 80 feet. The Thursday night before the race is know as "Family Night" in Port Huron. People stroll the docks along the Black River to admire the boats and watch the sailors prepare for the race. Friday night is Boat Night where thousands of people, sailors and wanna-bes line the Black River to view the yachts. Expect to participate in balloon fights between the boats. Parties last until dawn. On Mackinac, people gather below Fort Mackinac to watch for the boats on Monday morning.

Raleigh
Brookhill Steeplechase
(919) 713-0033 • www.Brookhillsteeplechase.com

Held annually on the first Saturday in May on the beautiful Brookhill Farm in Clayton, North Carolina, some say this event rivals the Kentucky Derby!

Northern New Jersey
St. Ann's Italian Street Festival
(201) 659-1116

This annual celebration turns July in Hoboken into a veritable Italian village for a few days. Vendors ply you with great Italian specialties, music and games. It's a big draw for singles to hang with old friends and hook up with new ones.

BONUS LISTINGS

Orange County
Huntington Beach Surfing Series
1 Main St., Huntington Beach • www.hbsurfseries.com
(714) 536-5511

One of the world's top professional surfing competitions takes place annually in Huntington Beach. Expect free concerts, a food festival, games and plenty of beach bodies to land an OC mate.

Naples, Ft. Meyers and Sarasota
Bachelor Ball & Action to benefit United Cerebral Palsy — Sarasota — Manatee Counties
1090 S. Tamiami Trail, Sarasota
Micheal's on East, 1212 S. East Ave., Sarasota
(941) 957-3599 • www.ucpbachelors.org

Every year in June the single ladies of the Sarasota-Bradenton get a little wild as they gather funds to bid on the eligible males taking part in the Bachelor Ball & Auction to benefit United Cerebral Palsy.

Twin Cities
Basilica Block Party
88 17th Street (at Hennepin Ave) Minneapolis
(612) 317.3511 • www.basilicablockparty.org

This is one of the largest outdoor concerts offered in Minnesota. Enjoy a weekend of great music while you benefit the Basilica of St. Mary. This event is attended by nearly 30,000 people. They have two stages with nationally recognized adult contemporary rock groups. Ages range from the 20s to the 40s.

Washington, D.C.
Halloween High Heel Race
17th St (between P and S streets NW)

Drag queens from all over town peel out in their best finery for this pre-Halloween event. It's a sight to see, but get there early!

Wilmington
Point to Point!

This is Delaware's best party of the year! Everyone who is anyone is here. Tailgate and participate in the decoration contest, or just come on out to see the horses run. Yes, there are horses — though most people come here for the fine food and drink!

San Diego County
Del Mar Thoroughbred Races
2260 Jimmy Durante Boulevard, Del Mar
(858) 755-1141 • www.delmarracing.com

The Del Mar horseracing season runs from mid-July through mid-September. It is the place to be and be seen. Don't miss opening day, where tradition has race fans and socialites alike donning their finest, and sometimes rather bizarre hats. Other hotspots at the track include the members' only Turf Club and 4 O'Clock Fridays, featuring a 4 P.M. post time followed by free concerts.

Ten Best Hotspots

Cincinnati
Newport on the Levee
1 Levee Way, Newport on the Levee
(866) LEV-EEKY • www.NewportontheLevee.com

The Levee features ten eclectic restaurants, 21 specialty shops, a 20-screen stadium-seat cinema, a live comedy club, a live blues and jazz club and a live cabaret.

Las Vegas
Ghostbar (Palms)
4321 W. Flamingo Rd.
(702) 938-2666

This trendy bar has one the best views in Las Vegas, inside

and out. Beautiful people (even some celebs) flock to this A-list bar. Get there early because the lines get long.

San Francisco
Sams
27 Main St., Tiburon
(415) 435-4527 • www.samscafe.com

You won't find a better place on a Sunday afternoon than the waterfront deck of Sams in Tiburon. Take the ferry, drive or bike, but do not miss this spot to sit in the sun.

Seattle
The Henry Art Gallery Annual Gala
University of Washington Campus

Seattle Magazine calls this black-tie affair Seattle's Signature Event, with tickets ranging from $300-$3,500. Proceeds support the art in The Henry, Seattle's finest museum.

Orange County
Splashes
1555 S. Coast Hwy., Laguna Beach
(949) 497-4477 • www.surfandsand.com

Splashes is a prized restaurant and bar that manages to attract the area's hottest and most eligible singles for drinks, dinner and the most romantic view in Orange County.

Phoenix
J Bar at the James Hotel
7353 E. Indian School Rd., Scottsdale
(866) 505-2637 • www.jameshotel.com

This is the Valley's equivalent of Hollywood's Standard or Manhattan's W. The lounge, lined with paparazzi-style photographs of celebrities, attracts celebs and local hotshots.

Western New York
Niagara Fallsview Casino
6380 Fallsview Blvd., Niagara Falls
(888) 888-1089 • www.discoverniagara.com/fallsviewcasino

The Niagara Fallsview Casino is not just a room full of slot machines. This place is classy, upscale and brimming with Western New York and Southern Ontario's elite.

Atlanta
Four Seasons Hotel
75 14th St., NE, Atlanta
(404) 253-3800 • www.fourseasons.com

The lounge at the Four Seasons Hotel gives new meaning to "swank." Cloth napkins and homemade potato chips add that certain *je ne sais quoi*, don't you think?

Cleveland
The Flats
Along the east and west banks of the Cuyahoga River,

There is no doubt that the Flats area is an inescapable entertainment hub in Cleveland. The area turns into an adult playground at night!

South Florida
The Shore Club
1901 Collins Ave., Miami Beach
(305) 695-3100

Here's a very trendy spot. Have dinner at their Japanese restaurant, Nobu, then go up to the open-air Sky Bar for a nightcap where you can lie on mattresses and view the stars.

Ten Best Places to Flirt with Rhythm (Live Music Venues)

Cincinnati
The Blue Wisp
318 E. 8th St.
(513) 241-9477 • www.bluewispjazzclub.com

Jazz lovers are frequent fixtures at Blue Wisp, and for good reason — it's arguably the best place to hear great jazz any night of the week.

Chicago
Double Door
1572 N. Milwaukee Ave.
(773) 489-3160 • www.doubledoor.com

Double Door is the premiere spot for meeting Young Wicker park singles. There is usually a cover, but the music is always worth it. Great deals on drinks, too.

San Diego County
The Belly Up Tavern
143 S. Cedros Ave., Solana Beach
(858) 481-9022 • www.bellyup.com

Live music is synonymous with the Belly Up Tavern, home to diverse acts of live entertainment ranging from nationally known recording artists to local bands.

Dallas
Gypsy Tea Room
2548 Main St.
(214) 747-9663 • www.gypsytearoom.com

Probably the best music joint in all of Texas, this swanky and upscale establishment offers two live music venues in a friendly atmosphere with gorgeous décor.

Philadelphia
The Kimmel Center for the Performing Arts
260 S. Broad St.
(215) 790-5800 • www.kimmelcenter.org

The Kimmel Center is quite new and devastatingly beautiful. It has quickly established itself as the premier Philadelphia music and performing arts location.

Seattle
Dimitriou's Jazz Alley
2033 6th Ave.
(206) 442-9729 • www.jazzalley.com

This jazz club is celebrated all over the country. The mix of music includes blues, Latin and big band.

Northern New Jersey
Maxwells
1039 Washington St., Hoboken
(201) 653-1703 • www.maxwellsnj.com

Rock, funk, punk, whatever you want, Maxwell's has been shaking Washington Street for decades. It's the place to be for cool crowds and cool tunes.

Raleigh
Cat's Cradle
300 E. Main St., Carrboro
(919) 967-9053 • www.catscradle.com

Many music savvy club-goers and musicians turn out for

the acts that play here. It's an eclectic mix of music in an intimate setting.

Atlanta
The Tabernacle
152 Luckie St. NW
(404) 659-9022

This venue is a favorite with die-hard blues fans, and its rich character makes any show memorable. Sit and listen or hit the dance floor — there's a great view from every angle.

Cleveland
Grog Shop
1765 Coventry Rd., Cleveland Heights
(216) 321-5588 • www.grogshop.gs

The Grog Shop is *the* place in Cleveland to see the best new bands from all over the country. Visit its sister bar in the basement, the B Side, for lesser-known performers.

Ten Best Neighborhoods For Singles

Atlanta
Virginia Highlands
www.virginiahighland.com

Casual and laid back, shorts, khakis and flip flops are the hallmark of this fun, relaxed neighborhood. One of the few walking neighborhoods in Atlanta, the Highlands has some of the coolest bars and greatest boutiques. Not to be missed is Fontaine's Oyster Bar ($2 Bass Ale pints and $6 dozen oysters on Tuesdays) and Metropolitan Deluxe, the home-store-slash-novelty-store with an attitude and a sense of humor! This is a great neighborhood for happy hours seven days a week, and Wednesday through Sunday nights.

Austin
South Congress (SoCo)
www.firstthursday.info

SoCo is just south of downtown and has turned "upscale trendy" in the last several years. This part of town used to be mainly artist and musician types. You must check out The Continental Club for live music and Guero's for the best Interior Mexican food in town. Jo's Coffee (a walk-up neighborhood coffee bar) shows movies once a week and hosts local bands as well. Also try Zen, Amy's Ice Cream and D & L's Texas Music Café, where you can listen to live

Austin music and eat great food under one roof!

Don't miss Lucy in Disguise with Diamonds, Austin's best-known costume and vintage clothing outlet that has the best selection for any dress-up occasion.

The first Thursday of every month there's a party on South Congress. All the shops are open late; there is live music, free beer plus vendors galore, selling their crafts ranging from handmade furniture to jewelry and paintings.

Western New York
Chippewa Street
www.westchippewa.com

Chippewa is the place to be and be seen. From the upper crust-elite to the hip and trendy to the alternative crowd, there is a place for everyone in and around Chippewa. The nightlife in Chippewa is unparalleled in Western New York with the Theater District and a multitude of bars, restaurants and nightclubs all within a few blocks. Park your car and stroll between Soho, with a hip younger crowd, Luna for Latin Lovers (and dancers), and the patio bar at Crocodile, where you can take in all the action. Or settle in for a New Orleans-style dinner at Bacchus.

Detroit
Ann Arbor
www.helloannarbor.com

If you are looking for an impressive array of diverse nationalities, ethnicities and social strata, Ann Arbor is the place to be single. Commonly known as the "Athens of the West," this sophisticated town has it all. The hottest area for singles of any age is the downtown area around Main, Liberty and State streets. Who hangs out there? Students from the University of Michigan, hip and trendy 20- and 30-year-olds and upscale townies in their 40s and 50s. In this small area you can enjoy galleries, boutiques, bookstores and some of the finest restaurants and bars. Try the Earle, Chop House, Cavern Club, Bab's or Gratzi's.

Kansas City

Rivermarket is the up and coming area of the city. The additions of lofts and concert series have made the Rivermarket a hotspot for singles. Visit the farmers market on weekends for a good detoxing of your body.

Milwaukee
Historic Third Ward

Milwaukee's newest hot spot. The Milwaukee Ale House makes its own brew and serves a delicious bite to eat. The streets are lined with a variety of fun shops. Check out Hers or Lela for new fashions. Pick up an exotic plant at the Private Gardener. Wrap a gift with paper from Broadway Paper. Check out the high-end furniture at Rubin's Furniture. Grab a cup of java at the Nova Cena café and bakery.

Northern Virginia
Old Town, Alexandria

Walking around Old Town, you're sure to find people of every age, race, class, gender and marital status. During the day, Old Town has more families, youngsters and tourists combing the gift shops that line King Street and enjoying the various restaurants. At night, couples and singles of all ages crowd the streets and converse in bars and restaurants. Bars to check out in Old Town Alexandria are: Murphy's, Bullfeather's and King Street Blues. There are a number of wonderful restaurants on nearby King Street, such as The Warehouse Bar and Grill, The Wharf Restaurant and The Fishmarket.

Whatever you do, make sure to take a walk along the waterfront in Old Town. This is a beautiful scene, especially around sunset. If you have time, take a dinner cruise. Early evening is the best time to venture into Old Town. The busiest evenings are Thursday through Saturday.

Philadelphia
Manayunk

Great eclectic mix of urban professionals, artists, musicians and families with a smattering of granola crunchers in the mix. Try Grape Street Pub for a flashback to your college days (or college daze). Farmer's Market remains a delight as well as the numerous, but frequently changing trendy clothing boutiques. Franchise stores (albeit cool ones) are invading the formerly home-grown patois of small, character-infused stores. Insist on visiting Le Bus for brunch and Bourbon Blue for dinner and after-dinner partying. Weekends are often crowded, but then, that's sometimes part of the fun.

San Francisco
The Marina & Cow Hollow

Think hip, happening ex-sorority and ex-fraternity type pretty people. No, make that VERY pretty people. Mid 20s to mid 30s (heavy on the mid 20s range). These areas are situated within blocks of each other and there is no shortage of bars and restaurants lining the streets. Take a cab here and walk from bar to bar the rest of then night. For spotting, spying and perusing the singles scene in San Francisco, you will not want to miss one of the best bets in town, "The Triangle." This is the name given to an area of three bars that face each other in the suggested shape. City Tavern, Balboa Café and East-Side West cover the corners of Fillmore and Greenwich streets. Singles swarm the streets and migrate between all three. Singles flock to Ace Wasabi for the sushi supposedly, but it's more likely the scene that's the attraction. The place is always crowded with fun trendy singles experimenting with the latest in saki-mixed concoctions. Around the corner is Cozmos Corner Grill, a neighborhood restaurant and bar inundated with a lively, buzzing, good-looking crowd clinking drinks and exchanging phone numbers. The Marina & Cow Hollow bars and restaurants are a standard for singles on any night of the week. In particular, you will find an incredible crowd Thursday through Saturday nights.

Tampa
Bayshore Boulevard
www.thenade.com

Nearly five miles of Bayshore Boulevard overlook the sparkling bay on one side and manicured estate homes on the other, making this Tampa's best outdoor track for active singles. Runners, bikers and skaters populate the wide, uninterrupted sidewalk nearly 24 hours a day, though sunset is undoubtedly the prettiest and busiest time. Jog over to nearby Hyde Park for a rinse at the gym, then sit down to a well-deserved lunch at The Collonnade.

BONUS LISTINGS

Washington, D.C.

Adams Morgan/U Street: During the day, these adjacent neighborhoods are great places to go exploring, with U Street's plentiful thrift shops and 18th Street's coffee joints (Jolt n' Bolt, Tryst). At night, however, much of the boho feel dissolves and bar-hoppers of all kinds find something to suit them here, from lounges such as Saki or Chi-Cha to hotspots such as Asylum or Millie and Al's.

San Diego
Gaslamp Quarter/Downtown San Diego

Don't miss the new Petco Park, home of the San Diego Padres. Baseball in a state-of-the-art, brand new ballpark played under a sunny sky in downtown San Diego... who could ask for more? The main drag of the Gaslamp is 5th Avenue, but be sure to explore the nearby streets that are continuously housing new shops, restaurants, bars and clubs. The Gaslamp is hopping on Friday and Saturday nights with singles hitting the restaurants, bars and clubs. Take a convenient pedi-cab when your feet get tired of walking around the busy streets! They are readily available at night and around Padres game times.

Chicago
Gold Coast

They don't call it Gold for nothing... if it were any more upscale, the Gold Cost would break the scale. Typically you'll find gentlemen in very expensive clothes made to look inexpensive and ladies in expensive clothing made to look casually expensive. Learn the true meaning of posh at the Red Line (the Bar not the CTA, not that the CTA isn't classy) at 228 W Chicago Ave. and all the swanky bars, restaurants and shops on Michigan Avenue. Stop by the Pump Room at 1301 N State Parkway: old school classy and worth the trip just for the pictures. (Guys: Remember, as Phil Collins will tell you... jackets required). Each month, The Museum of Contemporary Art, located at 220 E Chicago Ave, hosts a slew of events likely to impress your friends. Information can be found at www.mcachicago.org. The Gold Coast is unparalleled Saturday through Sunday morning.

Ten Best Places to Flirt

Austin

Town Lake Hike and Bike Trail is Austin's fitness enthusiasts' best hangout. Go for a walk, run or bike ride and then mingle with others while you stretch at "The Rock" under the Mopac Bridge. Run Tex provides water and sometimes

Powerade! This is a great place to see how those you admire look in a pair of shorts!

Cincinnati
Hyde Park Kroger
3760 Paxton Avenue in Hyde Park
(513) 871-4142

Is the meat department sexy or the produce department ripe? All that can be confirmed is that tons of singles shop at the Kroger in Hyde Park and have been known to notice more than the price of cheese. The neighborhood is home to lots of yuppie types and Baby Boomers but others drive a distance to be seen milling around the deli. The checkout line is a place to ask your crush from the frozen food aisle if he/she lives alone (or something slightly more subtle) but don't wait until unloading the cart ensues. Be bold. It is acceptable, if only slightly crazy.

Dallas
Sense/Candle Room
3001 Henderson Ave.
(214) 370-4445 • www.consilientrestaurants.com

Entrance to Sense and its sister establishment Candle Room is by membership or referral only. While both places offer an exclusive alternative to the crowded bar scene, Sense is the more upscale of the two.

Denver
5280's Single in the City Party
Filmore Auditorium • www.5280.com

What better venue to flirt than at the annual Single in the City event? This annual event follows 5280's Feb/March issue highlighting Denver's most amazing singles. 21 of Denver's hottest singles are selected from nominations gathered over the previous year. At the event, these 21 plus 250 other Denver singles join together for one of the hottest parties in town. An event not to be missed!

Kansas City
Kansas City has one of the largest St. Patrick's Day celebrations in the country. Treat yourself and take a day off of work. Attend the parade downtown, eat corn beef and check out the Pitch for bar events.

Orlando
The Winter Park Farmer's Market

Bring your dog and grab a cup of coffee and browse among the fresh flowers and foods brought to you by local farmers.

Sacramento

The Exotic ZONE Ball is a huge Halloween event in Sacramento, sponsored by 100.5 the ZONE (today's music alternative). You will see it all and meet it all here! People really get into character. This is a great place to flirt, with a younger crowd in their 20s and 30s. You'll find live music, great bars and downright crazy people looking to meet someone! You will see some outrageous get-ups here.

Phoenix
The Platinum Club at Phoenix Suns games
America West Arena
(602) 379-7878
www.nba.com/suns/tickets/arena.html#club

Nothing like athletes, competition and VIP status to get people's juices flowing. This leather-upholstered aerie at the top of the arena has plenty of mingle room by the carving station.

Seattle

The heart of Seattle is the Pike Place Market. Due to the vast size of the market, most people plan to meet under the famous neon sign at the main arcade standing next to the bronze pig, Rachel. It's the perfect place to strike up a fun conversation while you wait for your friends to find you!

Twin Cities
Minneapolis Skyways

Flirty eye contact can be found in just about any busy skyway in downtown Minneapolis. Try the Pillsbury building or the IDS courtyard. Making eye contact is the key, so keep your head up, a smile on your face and look available.

BONUS LISTING

San Diego County
San Diego Padres' Petco Park
7th and K streets
(888) MY-PADRES • www.padres.com

Petco Park is quickly becoming San Diego's most treasured

sporting facility. Friday and Saturday night games, in particular, seem to bring out the singles crowds intent on some Gaslamp-area socializing afterward. The Padres Hall of Fame Bar & Grill located in the Western Metal Supply Co. Building and any of the park's VIP suites/clubs seem to be great flirting hotspots!

Chapter 5

It's a Date!

Alright! You've got a date. You mustered up the courage to suggest a get-together and got a "yes." Don't you feel good? Yes... No? Well, chances are you could be slightly delirious at this point. It's perfectly natural to be nervous about looking good or anticipating that first kiss. Then there's the possibility of finding true love; one thing could lead to another and before you know it — enough! Stay grounded but enthusiastic.

There are two things you need to decide right now: What to do on your date (if you did the asking), and what to wear.

Where to Go

Figuring out the best place to go on a first date can be a bit daunting. If you're an *It's Just Lunch* member we set up the first date for you. We pick the restaurant, we make the reservation and arrangements with your date, and all you need to do is show up. Easy stuff!

If you're arranging the date yourself, you may think that you should do something impressive or unique. But in our experience — and that would be more than two million first dates — simple and casual is always better when you're meeting someone for the first time. Choose a place where you feel comfortable and familiar, so you don't waste time trying to figure out the lay of the land or that 20-page Japanese menu. This way, you can relax and focus on your date.

The purpose of a first date is to get to know each other better, so it's important to find a venue that isn't too distracting or too loud — somewhere you can have a nice, cozy chat without trying to outrap the sound system.

Lunch or Coffee Date

If it's a blind date or you're not sure how you feel about the person, keep it low pressure and go for coffee, lunch, or brunch. If you meet for lunch, you can use the excuse of having to get back to work if the date is a flop. And if it's fun, you can arrange to meet again and do something more exciting.

After-Work Drinks

This is another low-commitment, low-cost date that will allow you the option of continuing with dinner if things go well. Or you can call it a night after one drink — say you've got dinner plans elsewhere or you need to get an early start in the morning. Word to the wise: Alcohol on an empty stomach can cloud your judgment, so stick to one or two drinks.

Drinks and Dinner

Going out for dinner is a popular option for a first date, but one we don't recommend, especially if you don't know the person at all. Dinner puts you on the spot. If the two of you don't really "click," you're forced to sit and face each other while making polite chitchat.

Dress to Impress

Once you've agreed on a time and place for your date, it's time to figure out what to wear.

Though clothes can never be a substitute for self-confidence or a positive attitude, they can go a long way in making a good impression and give you a head start on landing a second date.

What's most important about dressing for a first date is wearing something that you feel comfortable in, both physically and mentally. Just reach for your favorite confidence-boosting outfit that makes you feel like a million bucks.

Keep It Simple

Fashion-wise, what works best for a first date? Obviously, tastes vary, but you'll come out a winner if you remember that less is more. Keep your overall style simple and stay away from anything extreme.

For example, don't choose really tight pants or extra baggy ones — wear something more classic. Once you get to know the other person better, you can start injecting the pieces that better reflect your personality.

Leave Some Things to the Imagination

Stay away from clothes that are too tight or revealing — even if you have a killer body. Let your date wonder what you look like under that shirt or sweater.

There's nothing wrong with wearing something fitted that emphasizes your physique — after all, you worked hard for it — but make sure you don't resemble an overstuffed turkey. On the other hand, if you're less buff and/or a little heavy, wear something to camouflage any problem areas.

Get Some Advice

If you're still having difficulty knowing what looks best on you, ask someone with a good sense of style for help. This someone should give you *honest* feedback, since it's not going to help if he or she insists you look great in everything. Go through your wardrobe and put together six outfits that look good on you, each one right for a different type of event, and then make the final decision.

Pick out clothes that make you feel attractive and confident, that best represent your personality and style, that aren't too over the top or make you look like you're trying too hard. You want to appear secure and relaxed.

Men Only

If you want to put a little distance between you and the average Joe, who frankly, isn't looking so stylish these days, a few simple fashion rules ensure great style and keep you ahead of the game.

- **Keep your colors to a minimum and work mostly with neutrals.** We're talking black, gray, navy, white or beige. And if you wear a black sweater, make sure you have a black belt and black shoes. That way, if your pants are a different color, you'll have a total of two colors.

    Stylish shoes are a must on your first date because women believe shoes reveal a lot about your personality, and they also complete your overall look. Make sure they're clean and polished — women notice this stuff and scuffed shoes look unkempt.

- **Keep accessories to a minimum too.** A watch is the only piece of jewelry any man really needs, and women know that a timepiece, like shoes, says a lot about a man. This is the one item you should invest in. It's better to have one good watch than several mediocre ones. If you're limited to one watch, make sure it can move easily from casual to dressy.

    If you must add additional jewelry, limit it to a

ring or a simple chain around the neck. The whole point of keeping it low key is so your date doesn't spend the night focusing on your "bling," but has her attention turned toward you.

Polishing Your Image

Now that you've got your ensemble figured out, let's move on to the grooming. Even if you're as handsome as George Clooney or Tom Cruise, it's important to look and smell your best when you're trying to impress a woman for the first time. Follow these guidelines to make sure all your angles are covered:

1. **Wash hair:** Definitely shampoo on the day you expect to meet up with your date. If your hair isn't clean, she will definitely notice. This is one of the most important criteria she'll judge you on, so make sure your hair is clean.

2. **Polish your face:** Wash your face and shave. Always shave in the direction your hair grows. If you go against the grain it can cause razor burn. *You'll score extra points with a woman if you moisturize your skin before you shave* — moist skin looks better than a scaly face.

3. **Clean and trim nails:** Dirty, messy nails are the number one turnoff for women. Put yourself in her shoes. How excited would you be to have some guy's grubby fingers all over you?

4. **Check Nose and Ears:** Make sure you possess and regularly use those simple but ingenious devices, the Q-tip and the nose-hair trimmer.

5. **Apply deodorant and cologne:** Don't forget to rub on plenty of underarm deodorant before you head out on that date. Damp armpits are obviously very high on the list of turnoffs.

    Here's something you might not know: Spraying on the right cologne could put her in the mood for love. Researchers have found that Oriental blends of spicy notes like ambergris, cinnamon and vanilla with sultry, animal odors like musk — are the perfume world's aphrodisiacs with warm, intoxicating qualities. In studies, the scent of pumpkin pie (which contains the same sweet and spicy notes) caused more sexual arousal than any other scent. But when it comes to cologne, remember less is more, so don't overdo it — and the same applies to pumpkin pie.

6. **Freshen breath:** Fresh breath is a must-have in any dating situation, especially so when it's time to deliver your first kiss. Make sure you brush and floss regularly, and keep plenty of breath mints, spray or gum at hand.

Piece of cake right? Now have a splendid first date.

Women Only: She's Gotta Have It

The right clothing might not change your life, but it can change your mood for the better. And while we always say that confidence is the sexiest thing you can wear on a first date, there are specific items that look great on every woman and will go a long way in making you feel extra flirty.

For starters, every woman should wear more cashmere. It not only feels good on your skin, it holds the curves of a woman without being too obvious. A snug three-quarter-sleeve sweater is an item every woman should have in her closet.

Of course he'll want to touch it too — no one can resist the feel of cashmere, so be prepared.

Anything made from silk charmeuse or satin, such as a bias-cut skirt, fitted blouse, scoop or V-neck top or camisole will work wonders for your sex appeal. Silk or satin tops are perfectly paired with fitted jeans. Skirts should be worn with a finely knit sweater or silk jersey top.

And don't forget the high heels. Platforms and wedges don't count. Guys love gals in sky-high heels.

Style Secrets

When you put your outfit together, start with a piece that you love and build the rest of the look around that. Never wear one designer outfit from head to toe — instead, mix high with low to create your own signature style.

Accessories can seal the deal when it comes to stylish dressing, but don't overdo it. Keep jewelry to a minimum. If you're wearing a low-cut top, pair it with a simple necklace and one statement ring, or do the earrings-bracelet approach. But never mix all four pieces.

Evocation, not Provocation
Flaunting your assets may show that you have no inhibitions, but it also shows a lack of self-confidence — like you need to be reassured of your beauty and sex appeal. Discretion is now the better part of sex appeal. Shoot for evocative — it's what he doesn't see but can imagine that's really titillating. A hint of gold-dusted cleavage; a skirt that stops at the knee revealing smooth, shimmery legs; pants that fit like a second skin, not tighter than your first; and floaty or sensual fabrics. These all say sexy, not smutty.

Accentuate the Positive
Pick your best feature and show it off. Great legs? Choose an above-the-knee skirt. Nice curves? Try a form-fitting dress. Great cleavage? Small waist? A wrap top will accentuate both. Whether you're a few pounds overweight or a skinny stick, there's something about you that *is* great and the world needs to know about it. If you can't figure it out, ask a friend.

Hair and Makeup from a Man's Perspective
A lot of men we talk to prefer women who wear little to no makeup and have that natural, un-fussed look. We agree! Flushed, dewy skin; moist, juicy lips; tousled hair — it's all so straight-from-the-bedroom sexy. Little do they know this can take a heck of a lot more time to create than slapping on the eye shadow and mascara Tammy Faye style.

Some guys appreciate a touch of drama like a smoky eye or a scarlet lip on the right occasion. If you decide to crank up the pace, a black eye pencil transforms a nicely natural face into a stylishly sexy one. Or go with a stronger lip and apply a classic red lipstick, but keep the rest of your makeup natural and neutral. One bold statement on the face is enough.

We suggest you keep makeup to a minimum and focus on your lips and hair, fuller and glossier for both. Also, now is not the time to try a new look, unless you've tried it before and know it looks good. You want to feel confident, so stick with colors you normally wear.

Showing off the décolletage area is flattering on most women at any age. The skin is extremely pretty there, as it hasn't had as much sun exposure. Add extra gleam to your skin with a light dusting of reflective gold powder along the collarbones. To make lips look fuller (and more kissable), apply a dab of shimmery lipgloss to the center of your bottom lip. Simply irresistible!

Get Your Own Make-Over

From *Queer Eye for the Straight Guy* to *Extreme Makeover*, everybody's indulging in a little body change madness these days — and why not? It makes you look and feel like a million dollars.

Most upscale hair salons provide makeup services, and they even offer lessons for those who would like to try a new look but are unsure where to start.

Why not stop by the cosmetics counter at your favorite department store and get a free makeover? You'll have to purchase a few of the recommended products, but it's well worth it.

A word of warning: Some sales associates can be a little heavy handed with the colors, so make sure you tell them that you prefer natural shades and don't want to look overdone. The best places to get a minimal makeup look are Laura Mercier, Clinique and Bobbi Brown.

Hot Heads

Ever since Rapunzel let down her long locks, gorgeous hair has ranked high on most men's lists of fetching female attributes. Whether you opt for long or short, straight or wavy, up or down, sexy hair must have two qualities: It has to be touchable and it has to smell good. Devote time to your tresses before your date.

Sexy hair is hair that doesn't look *done*, where he can actually run his fingers through it. Stay away from the hairspray. Instead, opt for a glossing balm to tame the frizzies and give you a super-smooth texture — a little goes a long way and it'll restore your luster. He'll long to reach out and touch.

Although many men say they love long hair, short styles can be incredibly sexy because they expose the neck. If you have good cheekbones and a small face, short hair looks extremely feminine — think Halle Berry, Ashley Judd or Sharon Stone.

The Lists

Ten Best Places To Relax Before a Date

Sacramento
Haggin Oaks Driving Range
3645 Fulton Ave.
(916) 461-GOLF • www.hagginoaks.com

This 24-hour lighted driving range has 100 hitting stalls. Bring some clubs, choose a stall, and use the time to loosen up prior to the big date.

Seattle
Nordstrom Day Spa at the Flagship Store
500 Pine St.
(206) 628-1670

The massage rooms are literally larger than most apartments. After the Java Lulur and honey-yogurt wrap, you can head downstairs to purchase a killer outfit.

Twin Cities
Schmidty's
1608 West Lake St., Minneapolis
(612) 822-HEAD • www.schmidtfaced.com
Other locations: Marshall Fields Downtown Minneapolis •

The only salon exclusively for men, Schmidty's offers all services from haircuts and colors to massages and facials.

Atlanta
Key Lime Pie Salon
806 N Highland Ave. NE
(404) 873-6512 • www.keylimepie.net

Its professional, down-to-earth staff and full-service salon and spa menu make this cozy hideaway a favorite stop for Atlanta's beautiful people.

Cleveland
Belly Dancing Class, HFC Athletic Club
1375 E. 9th St., Cleveland
(216) 621-0770 • www.troupeshabaana.com

To loosen up and feel sexy, belly dancing is the ultimate. Classes accommodate all skill levels and ages.

South Florida
The Spa at Mandarin Oriental
500 Brickell Key Dr., Miami
(305) 913-8332 • www.mandarinoriental.com

This holistic and Ayurvedic spa uses only the best products and proven techniques.

Tampa
Gandy Bridge Catwalks/ Friendship TrailBridge
Gandy Boulevard
(813) 835-5252 • www.friendshiptrail.org

Go fishing from one of the original wooden catwalks or stroll out onto the old Gandy Bridge to decompress with the help of sea, sun and salt air.

Las Vegas
Canyon Ranch Spa (The Venetian)
3355 Las Vegas Blvd. S.
(702) 414-3600 • www.canyonranch.com

Here you'll find stark décor, a climbing wall, fitness room and spa treatments. Try the Canyon Stone Massage, an 80-minute treatment that is sure to relax you.

Denver
The Spa at the Broadmoor
One Lake Ave., Colorado Springs
(800)-634-7711 • www.broadmoor.com

An amazing experience! Choose from 13 different types of massages at this five-star resort. Then check out the new personal shower featuring 17 shower heads.

Houston
Family Golf Center
13400 Westheimer Rd.
(281) 531-1156

If you love golf, nothing's as relaxing as hitting a bucket of balls at the driving range.

Ten Best Places To Put You In a Dating Mood

Cincinnati
Knickers of Hyde Park
2726 Erie Ave., Hyde Park
(513) 533-9592

There's nothing more "intimate" than intimate apparel.

Treat yourself to a soft, sexy piece of lingerie before getting ready for your hot date!

Tampa
The Pink Palm
1532 S. Dale Mabry Hwy.
(813) 259-9780 • www.pinkpalmflorida.com

Got a beach date? Tease your hair tastefully and slip into one of Lilly Pulitzer's sorbet-hued palm-print halter dresses.

Wilmington
Melissa's Basquetique
1700 North Scott St.
(302) 655-5229

The right fragrance can make a big first impression. Visit this marvelous little perfumery in the heart of Little Italy.

Dallas
The Glass Slipper
3699 McKinney Ave., Ste. 301
(214) 526-2115

This fabulous little boutique offers fine apparel for the fashion-savvy woman. Trendy but unique pieces, most of them imported from Italy.

Philadelphia
American Male
37 S. 16th St.
(215) 496-0229 • www.americanmale.com

This salon caters to men who are uneasy about going to salons. They offer expert grooming, hand massages, scalp massages and trimming in a male oriented atmosphere.

San Francisco
Samovar Tea Lounge
498 Sanchez St.
(415) 626-4700 • www.samovartea.com

Sit on a raised platform, sip one of their many fine teas, and enjoy the comfort and peace that surrounds you before your date.

Seattle
Elephant Car Wash
2763 4th St. S
(206) 622-2882
Call for other locations.

Okay guys, get a bit nostalgic and have the car detailed inside and out under the giant spinning mammal — a detailed car is impressive!

New York City
Kiehl's
109 Third Ave.
(212) 677-3171 • www.kiehls.com

Once a pharmacy, this store opened in 1851 and has since made products with the finest ingredients. Pick up some "Crème de Corps" to make your skin extra soft.

Western New York
Lotions & Potions
5543 Main St., Williamsville
(716) 565-0610 • www.lotionspotions.net

Indulge yourself with custom-made fragrances from around the world. Have them mix one up for your date, too!

Atlanta
Strings n' Strands
4632 Weiuca Rd.
(404) 252-9662

Hey, why not? Knitting is all the rage these days. This yarn boutique has the latest trends and fashions. So take a class — or just pick up a one-of-a-kind scarf to wear on your date.

Chapter 6
The First Date

Congratulations, you're officially dating!

However, if a little voice inside your head is trying to talk you out of it, don't panic. A little nervousness is perfectly natural.

Yes, it's true that dating means taking risks. Heaven forbid, you might get dumped. But the good news is, *you'll live*. The happiest people are those willing to step outside their comfort zones and take a few risks, because the potential for rewards is so great.

As for rejection, don't take it personally. It's just part of the dating journey. It will lead to bigger and better things — and eventually a few laughs as well.

Here's the key: Learn how to distinguish between describing the date as a failure and seeing *yourself* as a failure. It's not the same thing. Not everyone will be a match. And how else are you going to find the person who's right for you?

Every date is a learning opportunity — a chance to observe yourself. So there's really nothing to be nervous about. Treat dating as an adventure. Take it lightly and it can be fun.

Most of all, you'll be really, *really* living life to the max. Now what's so bad about that?

Safety First

Okay, we know this subject is not romantic, but it's necessary! Before you set out on your first date, there are a couple of safety measures you need to take so you can rest assured that even if you end up lunching with a Ted Bundy type, you'll be around to talk about it later.

Guys, this applies to you too. Before you groan, laugh or throw this book away in total disgust, we have five words for you: Glenn Close in *Fatal Attraction*. Convinced?

If it's an *It's Just Lunch* date, then you can rest assured that we've done our absolute best to pair you up with someone of sound mind. But we're not Big Brother, so use your best judgment when meeting someone the first few times. Our dates are set up with safety and discretion in mind. We work with both of you directly to arrange a time and place for you to meet, and we never give out any of your personal information.

If you're going it alone and meeting someone you've never met before (blind date, Internet date, someone you met in a bar) versus someone you've known for a while or who has been recommended by a mutual friend, then do the following:

- Arrange to meet your date in a public place like a restaurant or bar.
- Don't let them change the location at the last minute.
- Give out your cell phone number rather than home phone.
- Let friends know the details of your date and when you expect to be home.
- Don't get in a car with him or her.
- Trust your instincts. If you find yourself in a situation that makes you feel uncomfortable, leave.
- Don't hesitate to leave if your new date shows signs of drunkenness, rage, hysteria, rudeness, disrespect, recklessness or any other embarrassing or dangerous behavior.

What to Expect

A first date is all about getting to know the other person a little better and walking away with a sense of whether or not you want to see them again. *Stop right there!* That's all there is to it.

Don't go on a first date with an agenda or a checklist of non-negotiables. There will be subsequent dates to find out if he's open to having kids, or her views on the last election or his sexual history.

Keep It in Perspective

Try to keep it light and fun. Don't lose sight of the fact that *it's just a date!*

Marriage should not be the goal (or the topic of conversation). You have no idea how it will turn out and have no control over that anyway. It will either work or it won't. So relax, laugh at yourself if you notice you're getting a little absurd (like thinking about picking out your china pattern together) or making the date too significant.

Pay attention to what you are learning about your date. No matter how excited, thrilled or turned on you might

79% of men on a first date take 15 minutes to determine whether or not they want to see a woman again.

be, it's important to listen. Otherwise, you can go through the whole date in a giddy daze and not remember anything later.

Enjoy Yourself

Focus on being pleasant and having fun. And don't forget to smile. It makes you more attractive. And who knows, you might have a good time. You might even meet the love of your life!

Women Only

What Men Look for in a First Date

As much as some of us would like to believe that men are above judging a woman based on her looks, it's simply not true. (Actually, women do it too.) Men are very visual beings, and sexual attraction ranks highest on their list. The good news is that our national surveys show that looks are not the only attribute men look for; qualities like intelligence and a sense of humor are equally important.

So what really attracts men? Most men are attracted to women who are intelligent, witty, passionate, confident and who are good conversationalists.

What Turns Men On?

Eye contact — men love flirty eyes and lots of smiles. They like it when you focus your attention on them and are genuinely interested in getting to know them better. Men also love women who appreciate humor.

What Turns Men Off?

Being drunk, negative conversation, complaints, self-pity and not laughing at their jokes.

Men Only

What Women Look for in a First Date

Self-confidence is extremely sexy to a woman. In fact, we'd go as far as to say that, more than a man's looks, job status or good manners, confidence is a winning trait that gets the girl. As old-fashioned as it might sound, women want

What Men Look for on a First Date

Through the years we've talked with thousands of men about what they look for in a first date. A 38-year-old CEO gave us this checklist, which pretty much sums it up.

- Does she complain about men?
- Is she open to trying new things?
- Do I like her clothes and sense of style?
- Can she speak intelligently about more than one thing (such as her job)?
- Is she emotionally available or is she still talking to her ex a lot? *(This is very important!)*
- Can she maintain eye contact? Is she nervous? Is there some energy between us or is it flat? (Nervous is better than flat.)
- Is she generous or is she confrontational? Can she hold her own opinion without making me wrong?
- Does she have a good sense of humor and a "fun" attitude? Does she get my sense of humor? Is she happy?
- Do we have chemistry? How does she respond when I put my hand on the side of her arm or in the small of her back? Is she open and not afraid to show that she likes me?
- Is she high maintenance? Does she talk about nicer places than the one you are taking her to in a way that makes you think she would have rather gone there? Does she pick the most expensive thing on the menu on the first date?

someone who's not going to run from a fight; a man who is confident in his ability to provide and protect. Women also like men who aren't afraid of emotional intimacy, who can talk openly and are willing to share their thoughts and feelings. Our research shows that the top three qualities women seek in a man are good communication skills, intelligence and a sense of humor.

What Turns Women On?

Chivalry is not dead. Good manners (holding the door open, pulling out the chair and helping with her coat) are still attractive to women. Lots of eye contact, attentiveness and being a good listener are other traits women appreciate.

What Women Look for on a First Date

Wondering what really scores high with women? Here's a checklist we gathered from a number of women that may give you some insight:

- Does he carry himself with confidence?
- Did he complain about every aspect of his life?
- Does he appear trustworthy, dependable and honest?
- Do we have good chemistry? Am I attracted to him?
- Do I like his sense of humor? Does he have one? Did we have fun together?
- Was he complimentary? Did he say something positive about the way I look?
- Did he only have eyes for me? Or was he interested in other women in the room?
- Is he a good communicator? Did he listen and appear to be interested in what I had to say?
- Is he well groomed with good hygiene? Clothes clean and pressed?
- Is he interesting? Did we engage easily in conversation or was it a struggle? Did he only talk about himself?
- Is he intelligent? Does he seem interested in life? Is he the type of man who makes things happen?
- Does he have good manners? Did he show me consideration and treat me with respect? Is he polite to others? Was he insulting about his exes?

What Turns Women Off?

Unsolicited sexual advances. Bragging about past conquests. Checking out other women. Constantly talking about yourself and not listening to her. Calling her "babe" on the first date. Bad hygiene. Bad attitude. Bad manners!

Conversation Starters

It always helps to have a couple of topics in mind or a few questions handy should your conversation ever fall into one of those awkward silences. If that happens, don't start squirming in your seat and getting all self-conscious and weird. It's perfectly normal to fall into the occasional lull.

64% of women will take an hour on a first date to determine if they would see a man again.

In fact, it's a great icebreaker if you just acknowledge it by saying something like, "Are we having one of those weird silent moments?" Seriously, your date will probably laugh and that will put you both at ease.

Need a little help with some clever conversation? Check out these great starters:

- Find out what they like to do in their free time.
- Talk about your travel experiences — trips you've been on or places you'd like to visit and why.
- Mention current events or news. Ask your dates what they think about a topic.
- Talk about where you grew up, your family, then ask about theirs.
- Ask about their favorite sports teams, movies, plays and books.
- Talk about something exciting in your life. A high school reunion, a promotion, a new home.
- Notice something positive about your date (nice hair, eyes, an expression or gesture) and compliment them on it.
- Ask a fun question like, "If you could change places with anyone in the world, living or dead, who would it be?"
- Mention something beautiful or touching you've seen or experienced in the past week. Even if it was just in a movie!
- Talk about the things you're most passionate about, from volunteering at a homeless shelter to your 1980s record collection.
- Ask about their dreams for the future. This will get them excited. (*But please don't turn this into a deal breaker.*)

Conversation Killers

Try not to say things just to please or impress and stay away from sensitive or taboo subjects such as religion or politics — at least on the first few dates.

Avoid talking about the following:

- Ex-anything. Leave your past relationships in the past for the first date.
- Other people you're dating.

> ## 5 Talkin' Tips
> 1. Keep up with current events so you can talk intelligently about major developments.
> 2. When you talk about yourself, keep it positive. Stick to your best attributes and the interests you're most passionate about.
> 3. Ask open-ended question's that evoke a response beyond yes or no.
> 4. Practice listening. You could do this with a friend. Have them read you a story from the paper and see how much you remember.
> 5. Try learning five jokes that are clean and not demeaning to anyone. This may take a while, but it's actually a useful "tool" in many situations.

- Personal topics like cosmetic surgery, medical history or "if only I could lose 10 lbs."
- Marriage, or your plans for a large family.
- Superficial things such as an interest in money or that sexy little Porsche you just bought.
- How much you pay (or get) in alimony.
- Controversial political topics: capital punishment, abortion, and your cousin's gay rights — these topics are better left for a later date.
- Name dropping, bragging or showing off in general.

Who Pays?

If you're on an *It's Just Lunch* first date, it's our policy that you split the check. It's just easier that way and takes away the whole "who pays" dilemma. On subsequent dates we suggest the following:

- Whoever does the asking should pay for the date. If he asks you out to dinner, he picks up the check. If she asks you to the symphony, she gets the tickets.
- If one person makes significantly more money than the other, then he or she could carry the majority of the weight, but the other person can contribute by paying for less expensive dates or making dinner on a romantic night in.
- No matter who pays, it's generally a nice gesture for the other person to offer to contribute (if you have been dating for a while).

Visitors surveyed on our website say that these are the four worst conversation killers: past relationships—49%, dieting or body image—21%, politics—15% and marriage—15%.

Most Common Dating Mistakes

Oh, c'mon. We've all made them. Confession is good for the soul. Take a look at "Most Common Dating Mistakes" on page 69 to see how your mistakes compare to our national singles survey. Then we'll look at them one at a time.

Judging Your Date

Picture this. You're sitting at the table waiting for your date to arrive. He or she comes in, walks up to the table and says, "Hi." Do you respond by saying, a) "Pardon, you must have the wrong person," then grab your coat and leave or, b) "Take a seat, I've been looking forward to meeting you?" Tell the truth! Many people make the mistake of immediately judging their dates negatively and don't even give them a chance.

If you catch yourself stacking up hurdles in front of your potential love matches, chances are none of them will make it to the finish line.

Unrealistic Expectations

This one happens a lot. We get so excited about the fantasy of our date that we start imagining all sorts of unrealistic ideals. By the time we get there we're expecting to have lunch with George Clooney or Angelina Jolie. No wonder it's a letdown!

Get rid of all your expectations on a first date. This is not the time to decide whether or not he or she meets your criteria for everlasting love. *It's just a date!*

Not Paying Attention

So by now we know that the most important part of a first date is to get to know the other person a little better, right? Well, you'd think so. But what often happens is that we spend too much time in our own head preoccupied with our own thoughts about what our date thinks about us.

If you're wondering whether or not you are doing the right thing, if you look good in that light, or if she can see your bald spot, you're going to miss out on the actual date.

> **5 Questions You Should Never Ask Your Date**
> 1. Do I look fat?
> 2. What did you look like with hair?
> 3. How many lovers have you had?
> 4. How much can a partner at your law firm expect to make?
> 5. What is your ex like?

If your mind isn't focused on your date, how can your date get a sense of who you really are? And how will you know anything about him or her when you've spent most of the date worrying about yourself?

It's impossible to know for sure if your date likes you or not (unless they tell you), so give it up!

Not Listening and Talking Too Much

These two usually go hand in hand. It's really important to be able to listen to the other person, and that doesn't just mean letting them speak, but also not trying to figure out what you're going to say while they're speaking. There's no way you can listen and think of a smart response at the same time.

Rambling on or talking "at" someone kills the experience of communication and alienates people. It's a big turnoff.

Your aim is to learn about your date; so ask questions, listen and let them do roughly 50 percent of the talking.

First Date Dos

When it's time to go on your first date, don't forget the basics:
- DO smile. Smile a lot. You'll feel better.
- DO have fun. Remember, *it's just a date!*
- DO try to see the real him or her, not the person you'd like them to be.
- DO be on your best behavior.
- DO remember your manners. Treat a first date like an interview. We're not saying to be stuffy or overly formal, just polite.
- DO be positive. A good attitude lets a date know you're fun to be around.
- DO dress appropriately.
- DO turn your cellular phone off.

> ## Most Common Dating Mistakes
> - 35% Judging your date…"don't judge a book by its cover."
> - 27% Having too high expectations for the date
> - 25% Spilling your "history" and being too honest
> - 13% Talking too much

- DO pull the chair out for a lady or open the car door. Chivalry is NOT dead.
- DO be honest, be yourself and don't play games.
- DO listen.

First Date Don'ts

A few basics that will help avoid first date disasters:

- DON'T be late. One of the quickest ways to sabotage a date is to show up late. Tardiness sends out a message that says, "You're not really important so I didn't make much of an effort to be on time." A great mantra for all aspects of life, including dating is…*if you're not exactly on time (or early), you're late.*
- DON'T talk about yourself all the time.
- DON'T refer to your past dates or talk about past relationships. That doesn't belong in the first date.
- DON'T order spaghetti — it's just not pretty.
- DON'T try too hard. If there's a lull in the conversation, just let it be.
- DON'T wear too much makeup, cologne or perfume.
- DON'T get drunk!
- DON'T prejudge. It takes time to really get to know someone.
- DON'T worry or fret about what they are thinking about you.
- DON'T say, "Oh, you're not at all what I was expecting."

How to Tell If They're Interested or Not

It's really quite simple. There will be lots of clues, primarily given through body language. Don't worry, you don't have to get up close and check to see if their pupils are dilated. It's much easier than that. The non-verbal signals are pretty much the same in both men and women. Here's a quick checklist to help you gauge the chemistry clues:

- Are they smiling at you often?
- Do they compliment you?
- Are they making lots of eye contact or looking around the room?
- Are they leaning toward you?
- Do they try to make body contact, perhaps by touching your arm or putting their arm behind your back to walk you forward?
- Do they seem attentive and interested in what you are saying? Are they nodding a lot?
- Do they make reference to doing something together in the future?

Clues That They're Not Interested
- They look around the room a lot and don't make eye contact. (Even worse, they're checking out other people.)
- They talk about how busy they are, hinting that they don't really have time to date you.
- They talk all the time on the cell phone and ignore you — unacceptable even for a doctor.

The End of the Date
So the date is coming to a close and that confident, funny, super-sexy self that cruised through lunch just flew out the window leaving behind the insecure you.

Now what?

You realize there is a smidgen of a chance that you could be rejected at this point. Or perhaps you're the one who is going to say, "no thanks." Either way, this is often the part of the date that most people dislike.

It's important to be straightforward, however you feel about the other person. This might be a great time to thank your date for a wonderful lunch and leave it at that. If this person isn't right for you, then it's better to deal with it now.

So be honest. Tell them whether you're interested in seeing them again or not. Most people appreciate it when you speak your mind, but make sure you don't just dump your feelings on them. Be responsible and kind.

Let Them Down Gracefully
The great thing about having a lunch date is that if you're not having a good time, returning to work gives you a great out without having to invent some lame excuse. If you really don't want to see the other person again, be honest, but

not brutally so. Nobody likes to be rejected, so tell them you enjoyed their company but must get back to work.

If you don't ask for another date, the person will assume you're not interested. Whether it's an *It's Just Lunch* date or you're going it alone, *please don't say*, "I'll call you" if you know you won't. There is nothing worse than waiting around for someone to call. It's better to say nothing than to lead someone on. You wouldn't want someone to do that to you, now would you?

Asking for Another Date

If you've had a good time and you really like them, what do you need to do to seal the deal? How exactly do you leave it? Do you linger in the parking lot, lips puckered, waiting for your date to plant one? Or do you sit in the car talking incessantly for an hour or more, too afraid to make the first move?

Hopefully, you'll do neither. If you had a good time, don't be afraid to say so. Be as enthusiastic as you feel. Say, "I had a great time and I'd love to do it again soon." Then hand them one of your business cards. That way the ball is in their court and they'll call if interested. If you exchange cards, you can rest assured that you both like each other enough to go on another date.

Most women usually expect to hear from a man the next day. And based on our surveys, virtually all men will call within 48 hours if they are interested in seeing their date again. We recommend calling the day after to say thank you or to indicate you'd like to go on another date.

To Kiss or Not to Kiss?

There's really no hard rule when it comes to kissing. We know some women who find it inappropriate to kiss on a first date, and then again we know others who think it's perfectly natural, depending on how the date went. If it's a lunch date, it's probably best to just give each other a hug goodbye. If you've been out for drinks or dinner, let your intuition guide you.

Before you even go in for anything physical, you must first establish that the person you desire wants to be touched. It's easy to tell; just watch their body language. If in doubt, stay away until you receive stronger signals. Just leave it at a hug or a peck on the cheek. Strong sexual advances too early can be a turnoff, even for guys. So trust your instincts.

Five Things to Say If You Want to See Them Again
1. "I had a great time. Would you like to get together again soon?"
2. "Would you be interested in dinner next time?"
3. "This was a great lunch! I'd like to get to know you better."
4. "I'm going hiking on Saturday and would love for you to join me."
5. "Now that the hard part is out of the way, are you interested in going out again?"

Five Things to Say When You're Not Interested
1. "The best of luck and fun in your future dates. Thanks again."
2. "I can see us becoming friends. I'd like to invite you to my next party."
3. "I had a good time, but I just don't think we have that much in common." (Very politely point out the differences between your lifestyles, interests, etc., which will show why you're not a good match.)
4. "I have a friend you might like, can I give him/her your number?"
5. "I feel that the chemistry just isn't quite right between us." (This implies it's a mutual thing.)

A Second Chance?

Well, how did it go? At this point you could be in one of three places. Either you're excited and really want to see them again, or you're convinced that this is not the right person for you. Or perhaps you're unsure about how you feel.

Before you press your built-in reject button, remember that you only need to determine whether or not you want to see them for a second date. So, stop right there!

While first impressions are important — and your time is precious — there is a point to giving someone a second chance. A lot of people suffer from first-date jitters. In fact, fear is the number one cause for first-date disasters and often leads to over-talking or out-of-character shyness.

We usually recommend two or three dates before you rule someone out completely, unless they happened to show up with facial tattoos and a pet snake. By the third date, you'll have gathered enough information to make a solid assessment.

At that point there are two areas you should look at.

The first is compatibility. Do you have things in common? Then, it's a good idea to check in with your own instincts. Ask yourself, "How do they make me feel inside? Are they genuine and trustworthy? Do they treat me with kindness and consideration?"

Trust your instincts, and you'll be surprised at how perceptive you really are.

An instinctive "gut" feeling can draw you to Mr. or Ms. Right even if they don't match all your criteria on paper. You probably have friends who are with partners who you never thought they'd be with. What brings people like that together? They trusted their "gut."

Basically, we all want the same things in a partner: honesty, trust, good communication, confidence, fun and understanding. If we can add chemistry to that, then bingo!

All that's left to work out is the timing. Is this person ready to commit, and does he or she want to share these qualities with you?

The Lists

Ten Best Places for a Lunch or Brunch First Date

San Antonio
The Magnolia Pancake Haus
13444 W. Avenue
(210) 496-0828 • www.magnoliapancakehaus.com

This is a local favorite, serving old-fashioned brunches and lunches. Their batter is made from scratch several times a day.

Chicago
Nookies
1747 Wells St.
Call for other locations.
(312) 337-2454

The lunches are quick and filling — try the apple and cheddar-cheese omelet — and if you have time for dessert, splitting one is a guilt-free way to enjoy Nookie on a first date.

Orlando
The Lake Eola Yacht Club
407 E. Central Blvd.
(407) 841-0033 • www.lakeeolayachtclub.com

This lakeside eatery borders Lake Eola with views of the downtown skyline. Feast on a tropical buffet or sandwiches and soups. Sit inside or outside on the breathtaking patio.

Silicon Valley
Fuki Sushi
4119 El Camino Real at Page Mills Road, Palo Alto
(650) 494-9383 • www.fukisushi.com

This is Palo Alto's oldest sushi bar, with an authentic Japanese feel and specialties you won't find anywhere else.

Baltimore
Alonso's
415 W. Cold Spring Ln.
(410) 235-3433 • www.alonsos.com

A mainstay since 1931, this place will leave you all warm inside, like you just ate one of Mom's home-cooked meals.

Los Angeles
Polo Lounge
9641 Sunset Blvd., Beverly Hills
(310) 276-2251 • www.beverlyhillshotel.com

The best brunch in the most romantic setting is found here inside the Beverly Hills Hotel. Be sure to make reservations for seating on the lush outdoor patio.

Portland
Southpark Seafood Grill and Wine Bar
901 SW Salmon St.
(503) 326-1300

Located in the heart of Portland's cultural district, their menu features the freshest Northwest seafood and produce in dishes inspired by the culinary traditions of the Mediterranean.

Cleveland
Heck's Café
2927 Bridge Ave.
(216) 861-5464

Come sit in the porch-like garden room and enjoy Cajun cooking. It's just like being in New Orleans!

South Florida
Bimini Boatyard Bar & Grill
1555 S.E. 17th St., Fort Lauderdale
(954) 525-7400

Sit out on the brick-laid patio and dine on one of their popular pasta dishes while chatting and watching the yachts sail in and out of the marina.

Denver
Cherry Creek Grille
184 Steele St., Cherry Creek
(303) 322-3524 • www.houstons.com

At this fantastic Cherry Creek mainstay, the food is outstanding with wood-fired rotisserie chicken, to-die-for cornbread and a friendly warm atmosphere.

Ten Best Places for After-Work Drinks & Conversation

Las Vegas
Sky Lounge (Polo Towers)
3745 S. Las Vegas Blvd.
(702) 261-1000

On the 19th floor of the Polo Towers is a touch of old Vegas. Cozy couches for two and a view of the Bellagio fountains make for an intimate, quiet place for an after-work cocktail.

Sacramento
Lucca
1615 J St.
(916) 669-5300 • www.luccarestaurant.com

Lucca is a popular midtown location to grab a cocktail after work in an upscale atmosphere.

St. Louis
Remy's Kitchen & Wine Bar
222 S. Bemiston Ave.
(314) 726-5757 • www.grihome.com

Always full of Clayton professionals after work, this is a great place for your first lunch date. For an added bonus, meet area business singles by taking part in the wine tasting.

Phoenix
Zen 32
3160 E. Camelback Rd.
(602) 954-8700

Sit on the patio or the inside lounge, sipping a sake martini, and noshing on half-price sushi.

Silicon Valley
Elixir
420 S. First St., San Jose
(408) 294-7800

Elixir has a lot going for it, with a romantic but neighborhood feel, a fun happy hour and exciting live music from local bands.

Los Angeles
Barefoot
8722 W. Third St., West Hollywood
(310) 276-6223 • www.barefootrestaurant.com

After a light bite and happy-hour specials or drinks and dinner, enjoy a short walk to a movie at The Beverly Center or the Beverly Connection.

Washington, D.C.
The Big Hunt
1345 Connecticut Ave. NW, Washington, D.C.
(202) 785-2333

The Big Hunt is big all right, with plenty of seating and a rooftop deck for the after-work crowds that fill this safari-themed bar for dirt-cheap happy-hour specials.

Atlanta
Toulouse
2293 Peachtree Rd. NE
(404) 351-9533 • www.toulouserestaurant.com

Featuring a quaint patio and one of the most impressive wine lists in Atlanta, this conveniently located restaurant is a popular after-work spot. Casual, yet divine!

Cleveland
The Garage Bar
1859 W. 25th St.
(216) 696-7772 • www.thegaragebar.net

This is where guys will feel comfortable enough to really

talk. The beer tap is a gasoline pump, there is a dirt bike above the door, and the music is rock 'n roll straight up.

South Florida
Max's Beach Place
17 S. Fort Lauderdale Beach Blvd., Fort Lauderdale
(954) 525-5022

Max's 3-for-1 drink special really brings in the crowd. It's a casual place that features American cuisine and ocean views.

Ten Best Places for a First Dinner Date

Cincinnati
La Petite France
3177 Glendale-Milford Rd., Evendale
(513) 733-8383 • www.lapetitefrance.biz

This very classy, yet quiet French restaurant is more country French than Paris, with all the right romantic charm. No visit would be complete without dessert.

Dallas
Samba Room
4514 Travis St.
(214) 522-4137 • www.crww.com/sambaroom

An evening at this Cuban bar and Latin café, amid palms trees, glowing lights and the intoxicating rhythm of Congo drums just might get you a little "hot ,hot, hot!"

Chicago
Kiki's Bistro
900 N. Franklin
(312) 335-5454

This romantic country French restaurant is a favorite with locals…and local chefs! The Crème Brulee c'est magnifique.

Philadelphia
Dolce
241 Chestnut St.
(215) 238-9983 • www.dolcerestaurant.com

Romance, romance and more romance. A Southern Italian themed restaurant that is intimate and private. It is also conveniently located in a romantic walking area.

San Francisco
Grand Cafe
501 Geary St.
(415) 292-0101

Opulent, romantic, located in the Hotel Monaco and close to the theater district — this surely is a place to impress your date.

Charlotte
Red Star Tavern
East Blvd.
(704) 333-3393
www.redstartavern.net/charlotte/homeCNC.html

Upscale version of comfort food with a large beer selection in an urban, "clubby" atmosphere around an open fireplace.

Twin Cities
Café Twenty Eight
2724 West 43rd St., Minneapolis
(612) 926-2800 • www.cafetwentyeight.com

Located in the historic Linden Hills neighborhood, the restaurant is in a converted firehouse with a cozy, intimate dining room but very limited seating.

Birmingham
Little Savannah
3811 Clairmont Ave.
(205) 591-1119
www.birminghammenus.com/littlesavannah

This is great restaurant featuring progressive southern cuisine in an historic southern neighborhood. The atmosphere is warm and inviting; you can't help but feel romantic!

Houston
House in the Heights
1642 Arlington, Houston Heights
(713) 880-2166 • www.houseintheheights.com

A 1904 Victorian house located in Houston Heights is the setting for a gourmet three-course meal. There is no printed menu because it changes daily.

South Florida

Capriccio's
2424 N. University Dr., Pembroke Pines
(954) 432-7001 • www.capriccios.net

Known for "the best tossed salad in town," dining at Capriccio's is a true Italian experience. It's one of the area's great original restaurants.

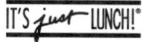

Chapter 7

Beyond the First Date

Well, you both enjoyed your first date experience so much that you've agreed to see each other again. Cool beans! While you might feel somewhat relieved that your dating prospects are finally looking brighter and the hope of finding someone you really like is imminent, just like the first time around, you're probably having similar anxieties about your second date. This time it could be worse because the stakes have been raised — you like this person and the fear of whether or not it will work out has caused that internal voice of doom to rear its ugly head again.

Try to stay in the NOW, the present moment. Don't let your mind get ahead of the actual events here. A second date is a second date is a second date. It's not happy coupledom, it's not the date on which you are guaranteed sex, and it's not the time to determine if he or she is "the one" — it's just an opportunity to spend a little more time with someone you like.

Trust us, you'll know exactly the right moment when the above should take place (if at all), but to relieve your anxiety, you can rest assured it's not on the second date. Remember to stay grounded, keep your expectations in check and your antenna high.

The Second Date

This could be the "make or break date" for you, depending upon how smoothly the evening flows. We usually recommend going on at least three dates before you decide not to see someone again. Sometimes it can take two or three meetings before the chemistry kicks in. On the other hand, if you have to give yourself a pep talk every time you go out to meet this person, you might want to consider calling it a day. Going with the flow too long isn't smart. One of you could get emotionally attached and that makes it harder to break it off later. Again, trust your instincts.

As you did before, choose a place where you feel comfortable and one that suits both of your tastes, otherwise you might be distracted and not able to focus your attention on your date.

Hopefully on this date you are both more relaxed and able to open up and reveal some juicy insight into the things that make you the unique and wonderful person that you are. Remember, your aim is to discover as much relevant information about him or her as possible. Take it easy and don't rush things. Remind yourself that perfect people do not exist in this world and everybody has strong and weak traits — you included.

Your goal is to gather some fundamental facts, discover more of his or her personality and notice your chemistry... oh, and have fun! To do that you should:

- Ask questions and listen carefully.
- Let them see the real you. Drop the façade, open up, disclose more detail and be vulnerable.
- Share yourself — express opinions, desires and interests.
- Know what you want — it's the only way you can determine if you are a match. If you are sure that you are not ready to be a step parent, find out if they have children from a previous marriage.
- Try to see them as they truly are, not as the people you want them to be. It's easy to get carried away with the excitement of meeting someone you really like and to place him or her on a pedestal, while losing sight of the real human being underneath it all.

Don't worry if all your questions aren't answered on this date. Give it time and let the information come out naturally. If you need a little help, check out the conversation starters in chapter six. You don't want to appear as if you're conducting a formal interview. At this stage you shouldn't be trying to determine if you've got a life match, so give yourself some room for romance.

What to Do on Date Number Two
You might feel like you have to do something lovely and amazing that will totally blow your date's mind, but it's really not necessary. At this stage you want to spend time alone, one-on-one, to see how you relate to one another and to notice if there's chemistry. You can move on to an adventurous activity or involve other people on your next and subsequent dates. That will give you a chance to see

how your main squeeze-to-be gets along with others (an important clue to their personality). But for now, keep it intimate.

Having dinner together is a great idea, especially if you didn't do it on your first rendezvous.

Check out the list at the end of this chapter for a variety of second date ideas. Any of the previous restaurants would be fine too. Whether you're looking for a laugh or good cheap eats; we've got you covered!

Say Goodnight, Gracie

At the end of the date, don't make false promises about what comes next if you know you're not interested in taking the relationship further. Be honest, tell them what you enjoyed about them and let them know you don't feel the chemistry.

Ladies need to know that if a guy doesn't ask to see you again it probably means that he's not interested. In this case, you probably won't hear from him again. *Guys need to know* that women are harder to read and often won't come right out and say if they're not interested. They don't want to hurt a man's feelings and are more likely to make excuses about not being available for another date. The best way to gauge a woman's feelings is to notice her body language (see chapter four). If she makes lots of eye contact, touches your arm and flips her hair then she's definitely keen. If she avoids you like the plague, you've got no chance, my friend.

If it ends, though, don't sweat it. Breathe a sigh of relief that you got out emotionally unscathed, and turn your attention to the 110 million other single men and women out there.

What to Do on Dates Number Three, Four, Five...

If you've made it this far, it probably means that the two of you are "in like," you enjoy being together and are eager to get to know each other better. Time to up the ante and try out a variety of fun activities that put you into all kinds of social situations. In short, you get to play at being partners by experiencing many different things together and seeing how well you fit and work as a team.

Spice up your dating game with some adventurous dates, play games and share activities, or try something simple and romantic like a moonlit walk. After a while, you might want to add in a few mundane activities to keep it real. Let's face it — long-term relationships include daily chores like shopping, taking the dog to the vet or fixing up the yard. Ask your date to hang out with you while you're at it or to help you out with these chores too.

If your long-term goal is to find a fulfilling relationship, you should pay attention at this stage and see how well you make decisions together or handle real-life situations such as dealing with crises or family obligations. Don't over-analyze every result, since that will kill the fun. Just be aware, observe and communicate your feelings. As each date progresses, you'll get a stronger sense of whether or not you are compatible.

Dating Dilemmas

When They Don't Call

If you've had what you thought was an incredible date and they don't call, it's normal to wonder what the heck went wrong. You start to think you imagined the chemistry, and that perhaps there's something wrong with you after all, or maybe blame is your thing and it must have been something you said or did. You're starting to obsess. Stop it! Don't go down that road. It's never pretty.

Who knows what happened? There are lots of reasons — he lost his job and slipped into depression, she's not over her last relationship, he's a non-committer (better you find out now), her self-esteem was too low, he fell down a well — hey, it's possible!

Whatever the reason, it may not have anything to do with you at all. So don't sweat it. Drop your date one follow-up email and if you don't receive a response, cut your emotional ties right away. Remember, there are six billion people on the planet, so even if there was no chemistry connection on his or her part, who cares? Give yourself a pat on the back for taking a chance. There are plenty more fish in the sea, so don't take it personally.

The Perfect Match

While there is no such thing as the perfect person, there *is* an ideal match out there for you, and actually, there are several. To find that special someone, you must first let go of your ideas about finding the perfect person.

Our fantasies are usually about Mr. or Ms. Perfect and often we eliminate Mr. or Ms. Right because they may not reveal all the perfect qualities. The older we get, the more we rationalize our way around things, and it can ultimately mean we never make any decisions. We get hung up on the "what ifs" and feel sure we know how it's going to turn out. The truth is you never know how something is going to turn out. At a certain point, if you determine that you really want to be in a lasting relationship, you will have to take a chance and work through the ups and downs.

Don't lose sight of the valuable lessons you learn while you're dating — you gain self-confidence, a stronger sense of self, a clear idea of what you can and can't compromise. More importantly, as an experienced dater, it becomes much easier for you to identify your soul mate when he or she finally shows up.

So keep the faith. Make sure your goals are clear from the get go, keep an open dialogue, have a no-bull policy, and you might find yourself in love before you know it.

Are We Exclusive?

Some people don't like to bring this subject up for fear of scaring off their new partner, but *until you actually have an agreement to stop seeing other people and focus solely on each other, you shouldn't assume that you are in an exclusive relationship*. The whole point of dating is to try out different people, and neither of you has to limit yourself to one person.

Don't rush into exclusivity until you know for sure that you want to focus solely on this person. If you were interviewing candidates for a partnership at your company, you wouldn't pick the first person who came along, would you? Well, you are the CEO of *your* life and the more potential partners you meet, the easier it will be for you to find your ideal candidate.

While you're interviewing, never stop learning about the opposite sex. Get interested in them. Imagine you're Barbara Walters or Larry King — and study and "interview" your subjects. The more you know about men or women, the better partner you will become. Talk to them, listen to them and most of all laugh with them.

When you decide to be exclusive with someone you've been dating, it's only fair and respectful to let your other dates know that you're no longer available. Don't just disappear out of their lives without so much as a "see ya." Tell them that someone you've been dating has become a serious relationship. Don't forget to mention how much you enjoyed dating them and what you liked about them. Try to leave them feeling good about the whole experience. You could even remain friends.

The Honeymoon Phase

Many relationships start off peachy keen. We've all been there: Every little mannerism is just adorable, every single statement they utter is worthy of a Nobel Prize, they're so understanding, so wonderful, so beautiful, and miraculously you seem to agree on everything. Welcome to the honeymoon phase.

Oh, it's a joyous time in those first three to six months; after all, there's never any bad news. Unfortunately, it can all come to a grinding halt. While you've spent the past several months eating off her plate and hand-feeding her dessert, you suddenly discover that you hate sauteed mushrooms and if you see one more lettuce cup you'll faint. Darn it, you're hungry!

Some relationships survive the end of the honeymoon period, other's fall by the wayside. But there's no need to feel bad if you can't make it past go and your engine loses steam. Believe it or not, that's how love works and this stage of romantic love is nothing more than Mother Nature's way of ensuring reproduction. Anthropologist Helen Fisher, author of *Why We Love*, claims that romantic love has a limited shelf life for a very good reason — we'd all die of sexual exhaustion if it didn't. She believes that romantic love wasn't built to last forever; it's there to fire our engines and get us all to work, making babies and building houses, and to keep us together during the early stages of child rearing. The intense attachment we feel toward each other ensures the survival of the species.

And to think, Hallmark has made a business off this!

So, how do we survive this period and keep the love alive? Well, according to Ms. Fisher, the answer is to do novel things together. Novelty, she says, drives up levels of dopamine — a brain chemical that is associated with arousal, motivation and goal-oriented behavior — the stuff love is made of.

So, there you have it: the answer to everlasting love.

Might we add one more piece of advice, just in case it turns out to be a false start? Pace yourself during this honeymoon stage. Don't drop your whole life because you're in lust. Don't spend every spare moment with your sweetheart and neglect your friends, family, career or self. Friends aren't there to fill in the gaps until that special someone comes along.

Remember, you're in the "getting to know you" stage. You might decide that this is not the right person for you and will have to return to your life. If you've blown off your friends and your work has suffered, don't expect to find things exactly the way you left them. Also, keeping your own life going while you are in the honeymoon phase takes the pressure off the other person "to be your everything."

You Can't Hurry Love: Is This Going Anywhere?

So, you've been out with your new sweetheart several times, but you're still unsure if the relationship is going anywhere and you find yourself wondering if this person could be "the one." How do you know she is right for you? Will he tell you he cares, will he show you he cares or will he only tell others he wants you in his life?

Timing is everything in a relationship. Some people take time to let things develop before making any serious commitments, while others jump right in and grab the bull by the horns. If you're not going at the same pace, there could be a clash. The truth of the matter is you're ready when you're ready and not a moment before. Try to let the relationship evolve at a natural pace without bulldozing ahead just because you're "primed" or imposing too many expectations on whether or not this can last forever.

Sometimes it can start off hot and heavy, but later you find out you're totally wrong for each other. Or you can start dating someone who may not be your usual type, but over time you fall for him anyway. Give it time to develop and you could be surprised.

You Have Passed Go: Sail Away with Your Sweetheart

Along the way there will be lots of positive signs if things are progressing nicely. These little gems have been culled from thousands of ex-clients who now are happily married:

- You can't stop thinking about each other when you're apart.
- He asks you what you would like, then does it.
- She can make you laugh and lift your spirits.
- He is caring and considerate, asks for and listens to your opinions and feelings.
- You communicate easily and can talk about a variety of things.

- You work together to solve problems.
- You accept each other's differences and can agree to disagree without resentment.
- She is an independent thinker and has her own thoughts and opinions, not just agreeing with yours.
- He is open and comfortable talking about himself.
- She is a well-adjusted, balanced person with a full, interesting life.
- You respect, admire and appreciate each other.

Warning Signs: Promptly Hit the Reject Button
- One of you makes all the effort to make plans.
- Her attention is inconsistent.
- She breaks dates often or cancels at the last minute.
- He doesn't call when he says he will, is frequently late or doesn't show up at all.
- He answers every cell phone call, regardless of where you are.
- He prefers spending time on the golf course with his buddies over taking you out.
- His eyes are wandering around the room checking out other women.
- She drinks more than three alcoholic beverages in an evening.
- He has controlling behavior, is angry or jealous and wants everything to go his way.
- She is neurotic about money and counts every penny, or is a compulsive spender and blows large sums of money frequently.
- He is dishonest or is reluctant to open up about past relationships.
- She is a loner and has no one in her life but you.

Wow, we've covered a lot in this chapter. Great ideas that will keep your dating journey fun and interesting, some of the dilemmas you might face along the way, the stages of hooking up and the signs to watch for on the road to a successful relationship.

You're fully armed with everything you need to do some honest evaluating of the whole experience and decide if you want to continue building this new relationship. The next step? Going steady.

The Lists

Ten Best Places for a Second Dinner Date

Albuquerque
The Melting Pot
2011 Mountain Rd. NW
(505) 843-6358 • www.meltingpot.com

This two-hour food sharing experience is best if the couple is pretty sure they like each other. There's something very romantic about dipping and swirling on a date.

Detroit
The Gandy Dancer
401 Depot St., Ann Arbor
(734) 769-0592 • www.muer.com

In the Michigan Central Depot train station, this quiet romantic spot has four separate dining rooms and is renowned for its fine seafood.

Philadelphia
Pasion
211 S. 15th St.
(215) 875-9895 • www.pasion.citysearch.com

Nuevo Latino is the theme of this restaurant that attracts a trendy crowd. It has an earthy, minimalist décor with draped ceilings and thumping salsa music.

San Francisco
North Beach Restaurant
1512 Stockton St.
(415) 392-1700 • www.northbeachrestaurant.com

Take a tour of their wine cellar and enjoy traditional Italian cooking and old-world service.

Naples, Ft. Meyers and Sarasota
Roy's
26831 South Bay Dr., Bonita Springs
(239) 498-7697 • www.roysrestaurant.com

This upscale, casual Hawaiian fusion is known for its Euro-Asian entrees such as the pot roast, rib eye and rack of lamb — but our favorite is the butter fish. Aloha!

Birmingham
Pauli's Chop House
109 Washington St., Huntsville
(256) 704-5555 • www.washingtonsq.com/paulis.htm

Consistently serving the best steaks and the freshest seafood, Pauli's is one of Huntsville's paramount locations for fine dining.

Portland
Portland City Grill
111 SW 5th Ave., 30th Fl.
(503) 450-0030 • www.portlandcitygrill.com

Here's where it all happens in downtown Portland. Elegant dining, swanky clientele and a separate, yet hoppin' bar scene punctuates this romantic, panoramic view destination.

South Florida
Bed
929 Washington Ave., Miami Beach
(305) 532-9070 • www.bedmiami.com

No, they don't offer chairs or tables at Bed; enjoy French cuisine and premium drinks atop a white mattress! It's a very chic feeling and a good way to cozy up on a date.

San Diego County
Old Venice Italian Restaurant
2910 Canon St.
(619) 222-5888

The quaint Old Venice restaurant is a fabulous place to go on any date, whether it's your second or your hundredth. Enjoy traditional pasta dishes, seafood, beef, chicken and veal.

Milwaukee
Coquette Café
316 N. Milwaukee St.
(414) 291-2655 • www.coquettecafe.com

Nestled in the Landmark Building in The Historic Third Ward, Coquette Café serves up authentic bistro fare in warm, casual surroundings.

Ten Best Cheap Dates

Sacramento
Jack's Urban Eats
1230 20th St.
Other location: Sacramento
(916) 444-0307

Cool, funky '70s interior and music to match. They have food to go, so you can take your order across the street for a picnic in the park.

Chicago
Movie in the Park Millennium Park
Millennium Park, Chicago • www.cityofchicago.org

Every Tuesday night in the new Millennium Park, one classic movie is shown after sundown. Pack some lawn chairs and a picnic. Admission is free.

Orlando
Aloma Cinema Grill
2155 Aloma Ave., Winter Park
(407) 678-8214 • www.orlandomovietimes.com

For only $2 you can watch blockbuster hits while you savor a cold beer, enjoy a sandwich or munch on pizza and a salad.

Seattle
The Center for Wooden Boats
1010 Valley St.
(206) 382-2628

This nonprofit center has a fleet of leisure-craft boats and sailboats that rent for around $5.

Kansas City
Boulevard Drive-In
1051 Merriam Ln.
(913) 262-0392 • www.boulevarddrivein.com

This isn't your parents' drive-in. The hundred-foot screen and state-of-the-art sound streaming from 600 speakers helps make you feel like you're right in the action.

New York City
Gray's Papaya
402 Avenue of the Americas
Call for other locations.
(212) 260-3532

Stop at this fun hotspot made famous in "Sex in the City." It's standing room only, no seats, but you and your date can share two hot dogs and a drink for under $3.

Orange County
Gypsy Den Grand Central Cafe
125 N. Broadway, Santa Ana
(714) 835-8840

Located in the trendy Santora Arts District of Santa Ana, Gypsy Den offers a cheap and cheerful dining experience with vegetable lasagna, quiches and tamale pies.

Twin Cities
Tailgating and a St. Paul Saints game
1771 Energy Park Dr., St. Paul
(651) 644-6659 • www.saintsbaseball.com

The parking lot is full of tailgaters with hibachi grills cooking up hot dogs, brats and burgers.

Charlotte
The Penguin
1921 Commonwealth Ave.
(704) 375-6959 • www.coldfury.com/Penguin

Ice cream parlor turned café and bar. A '50s soda shop serving beer and liquor. White-collar to body-art-painted diners come here. Try the fried pickles or banana pudding.

Cleveland
Arabica Coffee House
111300 Juniper Rd., Cleveland
(216) 791-0300 • www.arabica.com

Meet for a cup of coffee at Arabica and enjoy free music for the price of a cup of coffee. Wednesday is open-mic night. Call for dates and times of other performances.

Ten Best Creative Dates

Cincinnati
The Dude Ranch
3205 Waynesville Rd., Morrow
(513) 421-DUDE • www.TheDudeRanch.com

Is your date the adventurous type? How do horseback riding, paintball, ATV riding and cattle drives sound? Be sure to book ahead, as this place fills up fast.

Las Vegas
Helicopter Ride to Grand Canyon
6075 Las Vegas Blvd. S.
(702) 261-0007 • www.maverickhelicopter.com

Try the Wind Dancer tour, a trip that takes you from Vegas to the canyon floor for champagne and hors d'oeuvres, and ends with an aerial view of the Strip.

Sacramento
Jelly Belly Factory
One Jelly Belly Lane, Fairfield
(800) 9-JELLYBEAN • www.jellybelly.com

Learn the secrets of how they create the legendary Jelly Belly and taste the world of flavors at the jelly bean sampling bar.

Wilmington
Habitat for Humanity
1603 N. Jessup St.
302) 652-0334

Nonprofit organizations everywhere are in constant need of volunteers. Grab a hammer and paintbrush and go to work. You've never had a date like this!

Denver
Mataam Fez Moroccan Restaurant
2226 Pearl St., Colorado Springs
(303) 440-4167 • www.mataamfez.com

Enjoy belly dancing while being treated to Moroccan hospitality at its finest.

New York City
Horseback Riding In Central Park
The Claremont Riding Academy
(212) 724-5100

This is another great way to see Central Park. Rent a horse

at this venerable stable, trot around the park, and feel like you're at the Derby.

Orange County
Fairview Park
2501 Placentia Ave., Costa Mesa
(714) 754-5069 • www.cmfairviewpark.org

Adventurous types look to Fairview Park for action-packed dates that include gliding, horseback riding and trail jumping.

Phoenix
Drive-In Movie at Scottsdale 6 Drive-In
8101 E. McKellips Rd., Scottsdale
Other location: Glendale
(602) 949-9451 • www.drive-ins.com/theater/aztscot

The only armrest you have to share is the one in your car. Pop some popcorn and snuggle up. Maybe you will even watch the movie.

Washington, D.C.
International Spy Museum
800 "F" St. NW
(202) 393-7798 • www.spymuseum.org

Bring out your inner James or Jane Bond at the Spy Museum. Enjoy the world's largest collection of espionage artifacts and talk in funny Boris and Natasha accents for the rest of your date.

South Beach
Divers
850 Washington Ave., Miami Beach
(305) 531-6110 • www.southbeachdivers.com

Learn how to open-water dive. Start out slowly by practicing in a pool, then venture out to Key Largo and Miami Beach to really have some fun.

Ten Best Places for Coffee & Dessert

San Antonio
Nadler's Bakery & Deli
1621 Babcock Rd.
(210) 340-1021 • www.nadlers.com

Founded in 1963, Nadler's is a family owned bakery offering pastries, cakes, breads and anything else your sweet tooth desires.

Albuquerque
Theobroma Chocolatier
Central Ave. at 4th St.
Other location: Albuquerque Heights
(505) 247-0848 • www.theobromachocolatier.com

This is the place to go for luscious locally made chocolate, specialty desserts, chocolate-dipped strawberries and truffles, and more.

Las Vegas
Chocolate Swan (Mandalay Place)
3930 Las Vegas Blvd. S.
(702) 632-9366 • www.chocolateswan.com

Enjoy the upstairs location for a romantic dessert and coffee. You can sample many delicacies like homemade frozen custard or bite-sized cheesecakes.

Philadelphia
Pink Rose Pastry Shop
630 S. Fourth St.
(800) ROSE-383 • www.pinkrosepastry.com

A quaintly simple, English manor style bistro for coffee, tea and dessert. It is light and airy with a homey feel to it.

San Francisco
Cafe Cole
609 Cole
(415) 668-7771

Come for the coffee and pastries; stay for the warm neighborhood feeling.

Orange County
Haute Cakes Caffe & Bakery
1807 Westcliff Dr., Newport Beach
(949) 642-4114

Paintings from local artists, a freestanding flower store and a salon are but a few of the reasons to visit Haute Bakery, if not just for the delectable sweets themselves.

Northern New Jersey
CoCoLuxe Fine Pastries
161 Main St., Peapack
(908) 781-5554 • www.cocoluxepastry.com

Legendary chocolatier Joanne Gusweiler brings her pastries and chocolates to a brand-new shop in beautiful Jersey horse country. Live the manored life for an afternoon!

Atlanta
Café Intermezzo
4505 Ashford Dunwoody Rd. NE
Other location: Peachtree Rd. NE
(770) 396-1344

For the perfect end to an intimate evening, drop by for after-dinner conversation and dessert. Don't miss the cheesecake!

Cleveland
Truffles Pastry Shop
11122 Clifton Blvd.
(216) 961-7439

It doesn't get much trendier than Truffles on Clifton. Cookies, chocolate creations and enormous fruit tarts fill the display case.

South Florida
Segafredo Espresso
1040 Lincoln Rd., Miami Beach
(305) 673-0047

This awesome coffee venue offers outdoor seating with fantastic drinks, large couches and chairs and a very cool ambience with lounge music and great people watching.

Ten Best Places for a Laugh

San Antonio
Howl at the Moon
111 W. Crockett St.
(210) 212-4695 • www.howlatthemoon.com

This dueling piano bar will get you singing, dancing and laughing all night long, as the piano players get customers involved in the fun.

Providence
Stitches Komedy Kafe
2 Dudley St.
(401) 784-8243

Good comedy with gourmet eats like Brutus and Caesar salad and Groucho Sez Duck. Plus it does shows at Children's Hospital. That's something worth smiling about.

Austin
Capital City Comedy Club
8120 Research Blvd.
(512) 467-2333 • www.capcitycomedy.com

The comedians who show up at Capital City come pre-tested, with experience behind them from networks like HBO and Showtime. Be prepared to laugh out loud.

Chicago
The Elevated
Cherry Red Bar, 2833 N. Sheffield (back room)
(773) 477-3661

You never know who'll stop by this comedy showcase. Up-and-coming performers present comedy ranging from standard club comedy to the avant-garde.

San Diego County
Lips
2770 5th Ave., San Diego
(619) 295-7900 • www.lipsshow.biz

You never know which stars you'll see next during this bawdy female impersonator show. Don't miss Bitchy Bingo on Wednesdays and Gospel Brunch on Sundays.

St. Louis
Johnny Gitto's
6997 Chippewa St.
(314) 781-8111

For the diehard karaoke fanatic, this is where Billy Idol meets American Idol. Not for the timid; check your pride at the door and bring your best vocals and sense of humor.

Orange County
Irvine Improv
71 Fortune Dr., Suite 841, Irvine
(949) 854-5455 • www.symfonee.com/Improv/Irvine/home

Orange County's top comedy scene lures professionals and

TV personalities from their regular LA gigs to weekend performances and midweek comedy nights.

Washington, D.C.
Chaos
1603 17th St. NW
(202) 232-4141 • www.chaosdc.com

If you appreciate a good time intertwined with adventure, join the crowd and dance with well-dressed drag queens.

Atlanta
Improv in the Park
Lake lawn area, Piedmont Park
400 Park Dr. NE • www.piedmontpark.org

Free comedy shows are served up on Thursday evenings from late April through May. Large crowds come for hearty belly laughs from some of Atlanta's best comedians.

South Florida
Dolphins Plus
31 Corrine Pl., Key Largo
(866) 860-7946

Tickle noses while swimming with bottlenose dolphins in beautiful Key Largo. Be sure to make reservations.

Ten Great Dates

We mixed it up a bit in this category. We picked some dates that are one-of-a-kind experiences you can't get anywhere else. But we also chose some dates that you can go on in many cities in the U.S. This way, this list has something for everyone.

#10. Austin
Strike While You're Hot
Dart Bowl
5700 Grover Ave.
(512) 459-4181

Show off your bowling moves at Dart Bowl. Bowling is always fun, and it's nice to stir up a little healthy competition now and then. Once you build up an appetite, you can really score with Austin's best enchiladas (Austin Chronicle three years running) at the café. Tell Butch that *It's Just Lunch* sent you!

#9. Denver
How Much was That?
Stanley & Co. Auction Rooms, Ltd.
395 Corona St.
(303) 355-0506
From the speed talking to the final bang of the gavel, going to a high-end auction brings out the "Antiques Roadshow" in all of us. Educational, spellbinding, and always a fun thing to do, going to an auction can help spark mutual interests.

#8. Southeastern Michigan
Some Mighty Fine Wine
Wine Creation
31049 Dequindre Rd., Madison Heights
(248) 307-9463 • www.winecreations.com
Come taste the wonderful Chiantis, merlots and Rieslings produced by this winery. Then, design your own labels to create your own private-label wine.

#7. San Diego
Tide Pooling
Buster's Beach House
807 W. Harbor Dr.
(619) 233-4300 • www.bustersbeachhouse.com
Spend time in the Sunset Cliffs area exploring the tide pools. Everyone should feel relaxed walking by the great Pacific. It's so romantic, too. Afterwards, go to the Beach House in Seaport Village for some calamari and a Mai Tai; you'll feel like you took a mini-vacation.

#6. Milwaukee
Miller Time!
Miller Brewery Factory Tour
4251 W. State St.
(414) 931-BEER • www.millerbrewing.com
Free daily tours; see each step of the brewing process. The tours are offered every Monday through Saturday. Sample the brews at the end of the tour.

#5. Pittsburgh
8-Ball Corner Pocket
Breaker's
1413 Potomac Ave.
(412) 531-2250

Pittsburgh's history as a blue-collar town has several lasting traditions. The local pool hall is one of many you can use to your dating advantage. Raise the stakes by saying "Whoever loses makes dinner – winner's choice!" And, just like that, you've got your second date.

#4. Honolulu
Swim with the Dolphins
The Kahala Mandarin Oriental Hotel
5000 Kahala Ave.
(808) 739-8888 • www.mandarin-oriental.com

Take your date for a swim with six bottlenose dolphins in this twenty-six thousand-square foot natural lagoon. You will never view dolphins the same way after swimming up close with them.

#3. Northern New Jersey
Riding the Bulls
Cowtown Rodeo
780 Rte. 40, Pilesgrove
(856) 739-3200 • www.cowtownrodeo.com

Cowtown Rodeo is a professional circuit stop for hundreds of cowboys and cowgirls from across the nation. The longest-running Saturday night rodeo in the country, Cowtown is open May through September. It's a ride that makes for a really original date night!

#2. Atlanta
Saturday Night at the Drive-In
The Varsity
61 North Ave. N.W.
(404) 881-1706

Get your car detailed, pick up your date, and enjoy a blast from the past with curbside service at the world's largest drive-in. Wash those grilled chili dogs and onion rings down with a frosted orange and make sure that you bring along some peppermint breath mints to share. (And don't forget the popcorn!)

#1. Cleveland
A Roller Coaster For Two
Cedar Point
1 Cedar Point, Sandusky
(419) 627-2350 • www.cedarpoint.com
Snuggle up on one the 70 roller coasters at this amusement park, yet another unique dating gem available to the Cleveland area.

Chapter 8
Going Steady

You've made it past the three-month stage and you're still happily dating someone. Congratulations! You're moving out of the dating game and into relationship territory.

You no longer have to worry about attracting the opposite sex, going out to bars, getting set up by well-meaning friends, or any of those single life things. What a relief! But, being in a relationship does come with its own set of responsibilities and dilemmas. Working through them together will set the foundation on which to build something wonderful.

In this chapter we'll take a look at some of the fundamental issues and questions you might come across at this stage of the mating game. Things like coping with holidays and birthdays, saying "I love you" and ultimately, determining if he or she is "the one" or at least on the road to becoming that.

Holidating

Ah, 'tis the season of love, generosity, joy to the world and peace on earth... unless of course you're in the early throes of dating. Then it can just as easily feel like you are walking through a mine field of difficult choices with the pressure of family dinners, gift giving and all those parties to attend. You can be pushed right into happy coupledom way too soon or be accused of neglecting your new potential amour in favor of your friends and family.

Add to that the hassle of holiday shopping and the pressure to find the perfect gift — one that won't be deemed inadequate, or worse, be deemed as too much (which might make you come off as needy or desperate). It's no wonder the thought of hibernating suddenly seems very appealing.

So what is the right holiday protocol? After three months of dating, should you invite someone home to Wisconsin where your mother will inevitably express her desire for grandchildren while pulling on the wishbone?

Or will your date get the wrong idea and assume things are getting serious because you're introducing him or her to your folks? (Of course, if they're not invited, they might get offended and think you don't care. Oh, no! What are you going to do?)

In our experience, the top three issues that cause the biggest problems between couples during the holidays are gift giving, family dinners and party etiquette.

To keep you on track, we've put our heads together here at *It's Just Lunch* and come up with a few tips and ideas to help you navigate your way, peacefully, through the dating dilemmas of the holiday season. Our advice, of course, depends on how long you've been dating.

Thanksgiving/Christmas/Chanukah

Less Than Three Months
Spend it with your family and call him or her from home. It's too early to expect that you will spend these family-oriented holidays together. If you're in the same town, you can always invite your date over for dessert later.

Three to Six Months
If you've been dating for more than three months, bringing your partner to a friend's house for dinner is appropriate, but it's still a little early to bring them home to the folks if your parents live out of state. However, if you all live in the same city or reasonably close, it is probably okay. Feel it out.

Six Months Plus
If your new honey hasn't already met your family, now is the time. It can be a little nerve wracking and you might not have much of an appetite for your mom's turkey dinner, so be prepared. If you get invited to a family event, be on your best behavior and dress on the conservative side. Come bearing gifts and offer to do the dishes. Also, pay attention to how your significant other is around his or her family — you'll get a sneak peak of the real person coming out, so take notes!

New Year's Eve

Less than three months
New Year's Eve has taken over from Valentine's Day as the world's most high-pressured and overpriced date night. If you've been together *less than a month*, don't expect anything — continue with your previous plans. If you're doing something where you can bring a date, mention it lightly, but don't be offended if they already have other plans.

If the two of you have been dating for *more than a*

month, feel it out discreetly and make sure you have backup plans so you don't sit home alone sulking.

Three to Six Months
It's a date. Plan something fun and expect to bring in the New Year with a midnight kiss from your dream date.

Six Months Plus
This is your first New Year together and you're in the sweetest part of the Honeymoon period, so make it special and celebrate your coupledom.

Valentine's Day

Less than three months
Don't even bring it up if you've been dating for a month or less. *If you've been dating for more than a month*, bring it up casually, but don't expect anything.

Three to Six Months
If you've been together this long, it's reasonable to expect to exchange gifts and to enjoy a good dinner together. If one of you isn't up for that, it's likely you're in different places in your relationship.

Six Months Plus
This is a time for somewhat bigger romantic gestures — a special dinner together at a fancier restaurant than you usually go to and an exchange of gifts that are nicer.

Birthdays

Less Than Three Months
Under a month, just wish them a happy birthday and buy them a drink the next time you go out. *If you've been dating more than a month*, bring them a thoughtful (though not necessarily expensive) gift.

Three to Six Months
A nicer gift and/or flowers is reasonable, along with a nice dinner alone or with friends.

Six months plus
Invite a few of your honey's favorite friends and throw a surprise dinner party.

The Gift-Giving Guide

The hassle of fighting your way through all those pushy holiday shoppers is enough to give you a cardiac arrest without the added pressure of getting him or her that perfect gift that says it all.

The key is to plan ahead. It'll save you from rushing out in the last minute, spending extra money and compromising more than you planned.

The best way to figure out an appropriate and well-received gift is to be mindful of your mate's interests, dreams and desires. This will give you all the information you need to find that perfect gift.

It really is the thought that counts, and if you just put a little of it into your gift, it will make a colossal difference.

A husband we know always sends his wife flowers. What makes it so unique is that he hand selects the vase at Neiman's or Pottery Barn, matches it with the perfect card and gives everything to the florist to deliver with a beautiful arrangement. It's the hand selection of the vase and the personalized card (instead of the standard card the florist fills out) that makes it extra special. This is such a cool idea if you're a guy who wants to say thanks for a great date. (Girls, remember most guys do *not* want flowers.)

You don't have to wait for a special occasion to give something thoughtful. A woman we know, who met a man through a dating service, was blown away when he showed up for their second date with a small box of her favorite candy — chocolate dipped strawberries. How did he know? He remembered it was on her profile among her favorite things. Needless to say he won major points for being so thoughtful and going that extra mile to say she was special.

At the end of the day a gift will not make or break your relationship. Good communication will go further in creating a love affair than a piece of jewelry or a set of golf clubs.

What's Appropriate and When?

Less Than Three Months

For the guy or gal you've gone out with a dozen or so times, we suggest starting out with something thoughtful, rather than showy. Spending too much money on someone you just met will make you appear over invested and will make you look needy. They'll feel like they have to reciprocate and that could make them uncomfortable. Keep the gift simple and special.

Gifts for Him
- Melt his heart and bake him brownies.
- Buy him your favorite book and share something you love.
- If he's a sports fan, try a team logo sweatshirt or a golf shirt.

Steer clear of: Anything commitment driven like rings, watches, a mini-break in Hawaii... or anything too personal like nose-hair trimmers!

Gifts for Her
- Homemade CD of her favorite tunes.
- Godiva chocolates and/or flowers.
- Champagne flutes and a good bottle of champagne.

Steer clear of: Jewelry, lingerie or other sexy items and expensive gifts. (Oh, and nose-hair trimmers!)

Three to Six Months

At this point you're heading toward exclusivity, but most likely haven't committed to anything final or met the family yet. This is a pivotal point in the relationship and it's best to celebrate holidays and special occasions with a personal gift and a romantic dinner.

Gifts for Him
- Cook him a romantic dinner for two — wine, candles, soft music, a sexy outfit, the whole enchilada. This will show not only that you care, but that you can cook, too!
- The newest toy or gadget from the Sharper Image (www.sharperimage.com) or Hammacher Schlemmer (www.Hammacher.com). It need not be expensive or over the top.
- If you really like the guy but hate the way he dresses, a designer sweater goes a long way.

Stay clear of: Generic gifts like a wallet or pen. You want to let him know he's special.

Gifts for Her
- Romantic dinner for two at a little French bistro or surprise her with dinner at your place — the works (she'll love the gesture).

- Anything cashmere or pashmina.
- Tickets to the opera or ballet and have a courier deliver them to her office along with flowers. That way she can show off to her friends.

Steer clear of: Clothing. We all know that women love clothes, but don't even go there unless you know the following criteria:
- Her exact taste (unlikely)
- What's *in* for the season (pass). Better to stay well away, unless you happen to work for Gucci.
- Her exact size (too small she'll feel fat, too large she'll think you're saying she's fat, and remember it differs between brands).

Six months plus

Hallelujah! You're madly in love at this point. This is the time when you want your significant other to feel like the most special person in your life. Make your gifts personal, intimate and a true expression of your fabulous unity.

Gifts for Him
- Tickets for two to his favorite sporting event.
- Get him TiVo so he can create his own instant replays while watching the big game.
- A watch with a personal inscription from you

Steer clear of: Don't get him anything you think he *should* have, like a DustBuster or a particular tool, unless he's expressed specific interest in it.

Gifts for Her
- Arrange for a massage therapist to be at her home after a long day at work.
- Get her lingerie or other sexy items. (Warning! These should only be given for Valentine's Day or anniversaries, and are not right for holiday gifts or birthdays — otherwise they are considered gifts for *you*, not her!)
- Say it with diamonds and you've pretty much said everything your girlfriend needs to hear. A bracelet or pendant is appropriate.

When to Whisper Those Three Little Words

There comes a time in a relationship when one of you will

utter those three very important little words. It's a significant moment, often accompanied by fears of rejection, feeling silly, being misunderstood or worse still, pressure.

Don't ever feel pressured to say, "I love you" unless you really mean it. It's better to say that you sincerely care about your significant other than falsely claiming to love her. Lying will inevitably come back to bite you in the butt, so don't even go there.

By the same token, don't force your mate to say or feel it in return because you're afraid he or she doesn't. Saying "I love you" and being in integrity with that statement means you have no demands back. Love is a gift that is given freely and without expectation.

Partners often feel the urge to amplify their feelings by projecting their affection onto one another and in the heat of the moment will blurt things out. But if you're not sure of your feelings and your mate tells you they love you, you must respond honestly.

If you love them, tell them. If you're unsure say, "Thank you for being so open, that makes me feel wonderful." Or say, "That makes me very happy. I really care about you too." If you don't feel the same way be delicate when responding, as it could really hurt the other person.

Don't ever dump your feelings onto your partner by responding with, "don't say that," or, "I don't love you yet," or, "I'm not ready to hear that." It takes courage to be vulnerable, so handle with care and compassion.

Show How You Feel

It's possible to go a long time in a relationship without saying, "I love you." Often, actions speak louder than words and there are many other "little things" that indicate a person's level of affection for another.

Women respond to "little sentiments," those tidbits of information that might seem irrelevant to most men but become benchmarks in a woman's relationship — things like remembering the song that was playing on the radio when you first kissed or her favorite color or flower.

Men respond equally to small gestures. Leaving love notes under his pillow or packing a few power bars and a vitamin drink in his briefcase before he heads off for a long day at work can be extremely touching to a man.

You don't have to spend buckets of money to show your partner that he or she is precious to you. In the same respect, "talk is cheap," and you can throw about "I love yous" like plates at a Greek wedding, but in order for the words to really make an impact, they must be backed up with significant action.

It's important to observe all the non-verbal clues in a relationship too. Determining if someone is right for you lies as much in his or her actions and in what they don't do, as it does in what they say.

Telling your girlfriend that you want to spend more quality time with her and then spending weekends at the golf course just doesn't measure up. As time goes by, your endearments will lose their meaning and your trust will begin to deteriorate.

Pay attention to the special things that touch your girlfriend or boyfriend and make an effort to introduce these into your relationship on a regular basis. It takes effort and mindfulness to create a phenomenal affinity with another person. But it's worth it because ultimately you reap the rewards.

His Needs, Her Needs

Yes, by now we all know that men are from Mars and women are from Venus, but what we haven't quite figured out is how in the heck are we supposed to ever get it together? Here are a few guidelines to help you give each other what men and women need most in a relationship.

All the Dating Dos and Don'ts You'll Ever Need For Men

- DO agree to do things with her friends or family.
- DO listen attentively (lots of eye contact) and be interested in discovering her likes and dislikes.
- DO be affectionate and romantic. Send love notes and flowers, hold hands, give hugs and make loving phone calls.
- DO talk to your girlfriend. It's an important emotional need and you'll learn how to become more compatible through conversation.
- DO be honest and open. Build trust by sharing your thoughts, feelings, habits, likes, dislikes and daily activities.
- DON'T expect her to date you exclusively while you play around.
- DON'T expect sex.

Women Only:

Beware of the fix-and-change phenomena. There's a common pitfall that a lot of women fall into when deciding if their new beau is a Mr. Right candidate.

They focus too much on potential and whether or not a man is marriage material. That gets them into trouble because as soon as they find a man with potential they feel like they have to develop him and turn him into that perfect guy. Perhaps there are several really great things about him, but then there are those two or three little things, and if they could just change that then... get the picture? So they spend the next however many months or years trying to fix him and forget about having fun with him.

Ladies, you've got to give up trying to fix and change your guy. You don't do that to your friends. You accept that they have weaknesses and strengths as well as a whole slew of quirky behaviors. And you love them anyway.

Now, we're not being biased here. It's just that men usually don't do that to women, although there are some exceptions to the rule. (If you're one of them then take heed!) But, in our experience, if a man doesn't like something about a woman he'll either break up or accept her the way she is. He won't stick around for years trying to make her a better person.

A woman, on the other hand, will date a man and ask herself, "Is this who I want to spend the rest of my life with?" If the answer is, "yes, he could be," then she'll try to turn him into Mr. Perfect. If he's a bad communicator, she'll try to open him up and get him to share his feelings. If he's afraid of commitment, she'll try to become all he could ever want.

People don't change unless they want to. Unless he comes to you asking for support, don't take it upon yourself to show him a happier way. You might spend years wasting your time and never get what you really want anyway.

All the Dating Dos and Don'ts You'll Ever Need for Women

- DO let him go out with his friends.

- DO allow him to withdraw or go into his cave, once in a while, without insisting he talk about it.
- DO engage in recreational activities with him — watch football, play sports, go fishing.
- DO make an effort to look attractive and wear outfits that make you feel great.
- DO give him compliments and let him know he's appreciated.
- DON'T push him into commitment or saying he loves you.
- DON'T try to be who you think he wants you to be — be yourself.
- DON'T try to fix or change him.

Are We Ready for Commitment?

Are you and your partner both emotionally ready for a committed relationship at this time? If one of you is and one of you isn't, you are both wasting your time and energy.

Avoiding this conversation (or choosing to overlook the importance of it) is a major mistake. You could mislead someone into believing there is a future with you, or you might spend months or years fooling yourself with an unavailable partner.

In relationships, as in life, timing is everything. We all get to different stages of emotional growth at different times and there is no right or wrong time for commitment. It happens when you're ready. And for some, it may never come.

Relationship experts believe that we attract people who reflect some part of ourselves, so if you find that you frequently attract non-committal partners, you may have some subconscious motivation not to commit yourself.

One of the greatest benefits of joining a service like *It's Just Lunch* is that most people who register with us are looking for a committed relationship. It's an efficient way to weed out many time wasters, fence sitters and serial daters.

Is This "The One?"

Most people have an idea of what constitutes a desirable mate. We usually get fixated on superficial aspects like appearance, income or lifestyle and don't give enough thought to the quality of that relationship.

It's emotional intimacy, being able to share your truest, deepest, most vulnerable self with your significant other, which makes us feel loved. Skip judgments based on superficial aspects and focus on how you connect emotionally; how comfortable you are being yourself when you're around them, and how often you laugh and have fun together.

Really, that's all there is to it. If you can read the paragraph above and know in your heart that your partner meets all of these needs and makes you feel great about yourself, then he or she has all the qualities to become your ideal partner. The rest is up to the two of you.

A relationship is like any long-term investment: it requires a great deal of time, effort and devotion. Couples come and go, but real relationships are those that can survive whatever life throws at them. They go through it together and come out closer than before.

One final thing you should ask yourself before you decide that this is the person you want to spend the rest of your life with: Do you both share the same vision for the future?

Do you want the same things or are you at least committed to helping the other fulfill his or her dreams as well as your own? Do you both see yourselves together for many years to come? Can you imagine investing in a house, raising a family and eventually growing old together?

Recognizing Mr. or Ms. Right
Follow the steps that follow and you won't lose your head as you get to know your significant other better. Remain clear and confident and you'll make the right choices.

Before you choose to commit to someone, make sure you have no desperate need for attachment and that you are in a good place with your self-esteem. Be ready to walk away if things don't turn out as planned. Don't try to force a relationship to work or invest time trying to change someone. The whole purpose is to avoid ending up in divorce court. Why would you want to close a deal that has the wrong foundation or missing parts?

If you have seven or eight of the signs below in your relationship, then this could be it! Yeeeehaw!

Nine Signs for Recognizing Mr. or Ms. Right
- You listen to each other.
- You have a strong chemistry connection.
- He or she is a cheerleader for your hopes and dreams.

- You tell them what you want in a relationship and he or she steps up to the plate.
- Your partner is genuine, trustworthy and understanding.
- You can both compromise and work together to resolve disputes.
- You have a similar approach to life (values, morals, goals).
- Your partner shows you kindness, consideration and respect.
- You are focused on each other, not looking around for something better.

A relationship is a two-way street. Don't forget that you need to be all of these things back.

A Final Word

We hope this book has inspired you in some way to get out there and embark upon your dating adventure. We also hope it has helped you to replace any negativity you might have toward dating with faith and enthusiasm. At the risk of sounding like a Hallmark card, anything is possible if you believe. Take a few physical and emotional steps toward making it happen and you'll be amazed how the scales tip in your favor. It's all about attitude — your attitude.

If you're still reluctant to take control of your dating destiny, ask yourself this: If not now, when?

Seriously! This is your life happening, right now. Don't put off love until tomorrow, or it might never come.

Dating is the chance to try a few relationships, see how they fit and decide whether or not you want to make a long-term purchase.

Yes, there are emotions involved. Finding the love of your life means you'll have to take some risks and you could get hurt. But not dating doesn't mean you won't be exposed to emotional pain. Loneliness isn't much fun, either.

Remember, Mr. or Ms. Perfect only exist in the movies. Your goal is to find the perfect union, not the perfect person. The more you date, the more you develop your dating radar. You'll know quickly when a relationship has all the ingredients you're looking for.

Allow yourself to fail as many times as it takes before you prevail. If you find yourself single again, don't worry. There are endless options when it comes to being a proactive dater. Eventually you'll meet "the one." It takes time, so be patient.

You're armed and ready to go out into the world with hundreds of places to go, take or meet potential dates in your city. What more do you need?

Now get out there and have a blast!

The Lists

Ten Best Places for Valentine's Day Dates

Tampa
Six Tables
4267 Henderson Blvd.
(813) 207-0527 • www.sixtablestampa.com

This über-intimate setting is the perfect place to whisper into your lover's ear while anticipating your French-influenced six-course meal.

Greenville
33 Liberty Lane
33 Liberty Ln.
(864) 370-4888 • www.33liberty.com

Owned by a married pair of nationally known chefs, 33 Liberty presents food that is beyond belief! The culinary creativity and eclectic menus are exquisite.

San Diego County
Jake's Del Mar
1660 Coast Blvd., Del Mar
(858) 755-2002 • www.jakesdelmar.com

Jake's Del Mar sits right on the beach and offers magnificent oceanfront views through floor-to-ceiling windows. For that special night, be sure to ask for a window table.

Milwaukee
Celia
424 E. Wisconsin Ave.
(414) 273-8222 • www.knowingcelia.com

Located in the Pfister Hotel in downtown Milwaukee, this elegant establishment is a must for Valentine's Day or any other special occasion. The food is incredible.

Pittsburgh
Le Pommier
2104 East Carson St.
(412) 431-1901

This "country style" French restaurant brings old-world charm and romance to every meal, which is further enhanced by a superb wine list and the elegance of the staff.

Seattle
The Inn at Langley
4001 First St., Whidbey Island
(360) 221-3033

Take a quick ferry trip to this Feng-Shui inspired inn on Whidbey Island for truly romantic views and a cozy fire with a backdrop of the mountains and the sea.

Naples, Ft. Meyers and Sarasota
Carolina Catering
Naples
Other locations: Bonita Springs
(239) 285-6102

Instead of going out, stay in. Renowned chef Lisa Resch of Carolina Catering will prepare her Aphrodisiacs Dinner, complete with fabulous wines and champagnes.

Birmingham
Bistro de Soleil
300 Franklin St., Huntsville
(256) 539-7777

Ahhh...this small, quaint and romantic restaurant is the perfect place to proclaim your love.

Atlanta
Ray's on the River Seafood House
6700 Powers Ferry Rd.
(770) 955-1187 • www.raysontheriver.com

This romantic Marietta hotspot on the beautiful Chattahoochee River has been the setting for many engagement celebrations. (And critics consistently praise the seafood here.)

South Florida
The Breakers Palm Beach
One South Country Rd., Palm Beach
(561) 655-6611 • www.thebreakers.com

Built in 1896, The Breakers sits right on the ocean and is a great choice for a romantic dinner and drinks by the sea.

Ten Best Special-Occasion Restaurants

Cincinnati
Jag's Steak & Seafood
5980 West Chester Rd., West Chester
(513) 860-5353 • www.jags.com

Jag's is where Chicago turf meets Boston surf. Be assured that you will have a fine dining experience in one of their seven individually themed dining rooms.

Las Vegas
Renoir (Mirage)
3400 S. Las Vegas Blvd.
(702) 791-7223

This small, intimate restaurant is truly a work of art, in terms of the ambiance, artwork and menu. Dine among authentic Renoirs. This restaurant is pricey, but worth it.

Wilmington
Christiana Hilton
100 Continental Dr., Newark
(302) 454-1500

The only 5-diamond restaurant in Delaware. Try the Caesar salad made table-side! Lots of fun, with a great atmosphere.

Chicago
Tru
676 N. Saint Clair
(312) 202-0001 • www.trurestaurant.com

Enjoy progressive French cuisine in a whimsical setting. For a truly special occasion, book a private party with a custom menu created by Tru's chefs.

Denver
Opus Restaurant
2575 W. Main St., Littleton
(303) 703-6787

When making the best impression matters, try the subtle elegance of Opus, a fine dining experience without all the fuss.

Detroit
The Palm
5600 Crooks Rd., Troy
(248) 813-7256

For huge lobsters, this is the place. Feast on surf and turf and a bowl of lobster bisque while you see how many caricatures of local celebrities you can identify.

Philadelphia
Vetri
1312 Spruce St., Philadelphia
(215) 732-3478 • www.vetriristorante.com

A grand occasion destination housed in a Spruce Street town home. This place can do things with pasta that defy description. It is homey and elegant at the same time.

Naples, Ft. Meyers and Sarasota
The Ritz Carlton
280 Vanderbilt Beach Rd., Naples
(239) 598-3300 • www.ritzcarlton.com/resorts/naples

Since we're lucky enough to be within driving distance of the Gulf of Mexico, it's a perfect date location. Everyone feels relaxed walking by the Gulf, and it's so romantic.

Honolulu
Roy's Restaurant
6600 Halanianaole Hwy.
(808) 396-7697 • www.pixi.com/roys

Roy's features really good food and an extensive selection to ensure there's something for everyone.

Los Angeles
Patina
141 S. Grand Ave.
(213) 972-3331 • www.patinagroup.com

Downtown dining just got better with the addition of Patina, located in the Walt Disney Concert Hall. It's the perfect locale for a classical night of fine dining.

Ten Best Places to Find Gifts They'll Love

Cincinnati
One in a Million
222 Wooster Pike, Terrace Park
(513) 248-9080 • www.oneinamillionllc.com

Find one-of-a-kind jewelry, furs and gifts from local, national and international designers and artists.

Providence
Oop!
297 Thayer St.
(800) 281-4147 • www.oopstuff.com
Other Location: Providence Place Mall

Crafts, jewelry, furniture and toys by local and national artisans. Whether you need a 50-cent nose pencil sharpener or a hand-crafted $3,000 grandfather clock, it's here.

Las Vegas
Virgin Megastore (The Forum Shops at Caesars)
3500 Las Vegas Blvd. S.
(702) 696-7100 • www.virgin.com

This huge store has a fantastic collection of CDs, books, games, movies and more. A great place to find a thoughtful gift that won't break the bank.

Denver
Chocolate Foundry
2625 E. 3rd Ave.
(303) 388-7800 • www.chocolatefoundry.com

Sometimes the best way to impress is to give one of Chocolate Foundry's artful delicious creations.

Philadelphia
Caviar Assoulline
505 Vine St.
(800) 521-4491 • www.icaviar.com

Both a wholesaler and retailer of fine food and gift baskets with an emphasis on caviar, they can create according to budget or desire. Excellent service!

San Francisco
Luscious Wear
1410 Polk St.
(415) 440-0172 • www.lusciouswear.com

Silky, intimate clothing for him or her, with a friendly staff to help you find that perfect gift.

Seattle
Burnt Sugar
601 N. 35th St.
(206) 545-0699

From shabby chic to funky, you can easily spend $20-$500 on must-haves. We dare you to come home empty-handed!

Silicon Valley
Only the Best
15954 Los Gatos Blvd., Los Gatos
(408) 356-7362

Looking for that certain something? Try a unique stationery store with an extensive selection of cards, gifts and specialty items.

Los Angeles
Fred Segal
8100 Melrose Ave.
(323) 651-4129

Inside this cluster of trendy boutiques is where you'll find the most current "must have" urban clothing, shoes, sunglasses and beauty items.

Atlanta
Highland Gifts for Men
1002 Virginia Ave. NE
(404) 817-0470

If you're dating the man who has everything, this store is for you. Choose from unique shaving kits, bar ware, tools and cool gadgets he loves (but would never buy for himself).

PART TWO

the
IT'S *just* LUNCH!®

Geographical guide to dating in America

Albany

Best Restaurant for Lunch or Brunch First Date
Calaway Grill
661 Albany Shaker Rd., Colonie
(518) 869-9976 • www.albanywingate.com

This restaurant is a clever golf-themed venue, offering lots of grilled and otherwise healthy fare. Look for the "sand wedges" (sandwiches) and the "main course" selections.

Best Restaurant for First Dinner Date
Nicole's Bistro at Quackenbush
633 Broadway, Albany
(518) 465-1111 • www.nicolesbistro.com

This upscale bistro is great for a first date, as the building's history provides much for conversation. Later, see a show; it's also conveniently located near the Palace Theatre.

Best Cheap Date
Bombers Burrito Bar and a walk down Lark Street
258 Lark St., Albany
(518) 463-9636

Stroll down Lark Street then pick up a burrito at Bombers, where the goodies are fresh, plentiful, and tasty. It's a no-frills kind of place, but hefty tacos start at only two bucks.

Best Restaurant for a Second Dinner Date
One Caroline
One Caroline St., Saratoga Springs
(518) 587-2026 • www.onecaroline.com

One Caroline is an intimate little bistro with fabulous food and a great wine list. They also offer live music nightly.

Best Place for Coffee and Dessert
Peaches Cafe
1475 Western Ave., Albany
(518) 482-3677

Peaches Cafe is well-known for its vast selection of desserts and homemade ice cream. Their baked goods are prepared fresh daily.

Best Place for a Laugh

The Original Comedy Works
142 State St., Albany
(518) 689-0490 • www.thecomedyworks.com

The Original Comedy Works is sure to provide a side-splitting live entertainment experience.

Best Creative Date

Albany Aqua Duck Historic Tour
Broadway and Clinton Ave., Albany
(518) 462-3825 • www.albanyaquaducks.com

Take a unique, educational, and fun filled tour of Albany's historic area — by land and water.

Best Club

Luna Lounge
17 Maple Ave., Saratoga Springs
(518) 583-6955 • www.thelunalounge.com

The Luna is an upscale late-night lounge with a true NYC feel. Saturday nights a local radio station broadcasts live from this favorite hot spot; it's the late night place to be.

Best After Hours Place

Justin's
301 Lark St., Albany
www.justins-albany.com

Now, where else can you dine this well until the wee hours of the morning? Menus serving up Justin's signature new American cuisine are available until 4 A.M..

Best Special Occasion Restaurant

The Scrimshaw at the Desmond Hotel
660 Albany Shaker Rd, Albany
(518) 869-8100

Fresh fish and fine meats are elegantly served in this dressy hotel dining room. Don't miss the American Wine Festival in February!

Best Place To Buy a Gift

Wit's End
1762 Rt. 9, Clifton Park
(518) 371-9273 • www.witsendgiftique.com

Enjoy the cobblestone streets in front of this charming turn-of-the-century shop, which is adorned with beautiful antiques and whimsical, artful treasures.

Top Five Dates

#1. Snug Harbor Marina
92 Black Point Rd., Ticonderoga
(518) 585-2628 • www.snugharbormarinainc.com
Rent a boat and spend the day exploring the beautiful waters of Lake George. Pack a picnic lunch and get some rays.

#2. The Original Comedy Works
142 State St., Albany
(518) 689-0490 • www.thecomedyworks.com
A great date location for a good laugh, The Original Comedy Works is sure to provide a side-splitting live entertainment experience.\

#3. Slipping and Sliding
Snow Skiing
www.goski.com/resorts/rusany/newyork.htm
Enjoy a day of cool thrills at one of the many New York area ski resorts. Check the website for complete area listings.

#4. Thatcher State Park
One Hailes Cave Rd., Voorheesville
(518) 872-1237 • http://nysparks.state.ny.us
Spend the day hiking through beautiful Thatcher Park. Bring a blanket, some wine, and a picnic lunch to make it an extra special experience.

#5. Dine at Home by Candlelight
Making your date a home-cooked meal with all the trimmings (candles, flowers, and champagne) says you really care. Kick it up a notch with a gourmet dinner prepared by a fine cuisine chef right in your own kitchen. Just go to www.personalchefsearch.com to find a chef.

Albuquerque

Best Restaurant for Lunch or Brunch First Date
Java Joe's
906 S.W. Park Ave., Albuquerque
(505) 765-1514

Cozier than Starbucks and featuring live music on the weekends, Java Joe's also makes all of their breakfast goodies from scratch.

Best Restaurant for First Dinner Date
Ambrozia
108 N.W. Rio Grande Blvd., Albuquerque
(505) 242-6560

Located in historic Old Town, this quaint restaurant combines intimacy with a five-star menu.

Best Cheap Date
Rio Grande Zoo
903 S.W. 10th St., Albuquerque
(505) 764-6200 • www.cabq.gov/biopark/zoo/

Rhinos and camels and bears — oh my! A day at the zoo is always a fun way to reach the inner child within.

Best Restaurant for a Second Dinner Date
The Melting Pot
2011 N.W. Mountain Rd., Albuquerque
(505) 843-6358 • www.meltingpot.com

This is a two-hour food sharing experience and best if the couple is pretty sure they like each other. There's something very romantic about dipping and swirling on a date.

Best Place for Coffee and Dessert
Theobroma Chocolatier
Central Ave. at 4th St., Albuquerque
Other locations: Albuquerque Heights
(505) 247-0848 • www.theobromachocolatier.com

This is the place to go for luscious locally-made chocolate, specialty desserts, chocolate-dipped strawberries and truffles and more.

Best Place for a Laugh
Laff's Comedy Club
6001 N.E. San Mateo Blvd., Albuquerque
(505) 296-5653 • www.laffscomedy.com

Laff's features America's hottest comics, five nights a week!

Best Creative Date
Rainbow Ryders
11520 San Bernadino NE, Albuquerque
(505) 823-1111 • www.rainbowryders.com

Take a hot air balloon ride and enjoy the scenery over the beautiful Rio Grande River.

Best Club
Sauce
401 N.W. Central Ave., Albuquerque
(505) 242-5839

This nightclub has it all — one side for intimate conversations and snuggling, the other for dancing and partying.

Best After Hours Place
Frontier Restaurant
2400 S.E. Central Ave., Albuquerque
(505) 266-0550 • www.frontierrestaurant.com

Known for their great green chile stew, breakfast burritos, homemade tortillas and Frontier sweet rolls, this late-night spot is open twenty-four-hours, seven days a week.

Best Special Occasion Restaurant
Bien Shur
30 N.E. Rainbow Rd., Albuquerque
(505) 796-7788

Bien Shur serves up superb nouveau cuisine with a spectacular view of the Sandia Mountains.

Best Place To Buy a Gift
Hey Johnnie
3418 N.E. Central Ave., Albuquerque
(505) 256-9244

Located in Nob Hill, Hey Johnnie carries a plethora of goodies for the home or office — boxes, jewelry, furniture, candles, incense, pottery and much more.

Top Five Dates

#1. *Solve The Mystery*
The Mystery Café
(505) 237-1385

The Mystery Café is always a fun date for mystery-solving fanatics. It frequents various hotels, restaurants and night clubs. Call for location and date information.

#2. *Sittin' On Top of the World*
Sandia Peak Tramway
Tramway Blvd., Albuquerque
(505) 856-7325 • www.sandiapeak.com

Albuquerque's Sandia Peak features the world's longest tram ride. Climb the five thousand feet to the summit and watch the sunset from the terrace of the tram.

#3. *Rock n' Roll Under the Stars*
Journal Pavilion
1700 University Blvd. S. E., Albuquerque
(505) 452-5100 • www.journalpavilion.com

The Journal Pavilion brings the country's top rock n' roll and pop acts to Albuquerque every spring, summer, and fall. For a more intimate experience, buy lawn seats and spread out with a picnic under the stars.

#4. *Massage This*
Mark Pardo Salon/Spa
8001 Wyoming Blvd. N. E., Albuquerque
Call for other locations
(505) 298-2983 • www.markpardo.com

Escaping the busy urban life and spending a day being pampered is pure luxury, and it's even more memorable to share it with someone. Mark Pado Salon/Spa offers a couple's spa retreat sure to impress. The sweet indulgence will be well worth the splurge.

#5. *Dining In*
Albuquerque Catering Co.
6220 Edith Blvd. N. E., Suite G, Albuquerque
(505) 299-3999

They say a way to a man's heart is through his stomach; well, I've got news for you…it works with women too. Making your date a home-cooked meal with all the trimmings (candles, flowers, and champagne) says you really care. Kick it up a notch with a gourmet dinner prepared by Albuquerque Catering Company right in your own kitchen.

Atlanta

Best Restaurant for Lunch or Brunch First Date
Bajarito's
3877 Peachtree Rd., Atlanta
(404) 239-9727 • www.puravidatapas.com

The cheery staff serves fantastic Mexican-Southwestern burritos and tapas. A great location for a casual date.

Best Restaurant for First Dinner Date
Violette
2948 Clairmont Rd. N.E., Atlanta
(404) 633-3363 • www.violetterestaurant.com

Offering the kind of romantic charm that's sometimes hard to find these days, Violette is a great place to sit and enjoy French cooking at its romantic best.

Best Cheap Date
The Flying Biscuit Café
1655 McLendon Ave., Atlanta
Other locations: Piedmont Ave.
(404) 687-8888 • www.flyingbiscuit.com

A twist on the classic southern breakfast, this favorite serves everything from fried green tomatoes to orange-scented French toast. But come early, they don't take reservations!

Best Restaurant for a Second Dinner Date
Spice
793 Juniper St., Atlanta
(404) 875-4242 • www.spicerestaurant.com

This chic midtown hot spot is the place where the ultra-hip gather for wine tasting and fabulous cuisine. The modern décor is accented by an impressive art collection.

Best Place for Coffee and Dessert
Cool Beans Coffee Roasters
31 Mill St., Marietta Square, Marietta
(770) 422-9866 • www.coolbeanscoffeeroasters.com

This shop roasts its own coffee beans. The coffee is super-fresh, and the atmosphere is mellow — even a little bit beatnik. Sit and chat or enjoy a game of chess.

Best Place for a Laugh
Laughing Matters
173 Cleveland Ave. S.E., Atlanta
(404) 225-5000 • www.laughingmatters.com

Laughing Matters is the innovative place, offering award-winning improv shows, private murder mystery events and classes in communication skills.

Best Creative Date
Wired & Fired
994 Virginia Ave. N.E., Atlanta
(404) 885-1024 • www.wiredfired.com

This "pottery playhouse" has been heating up Atlanta since 1996. Get your hands dirty and create something memorable with your date.

Best Club
Compound
1008 Brady Avenue N.W., Atlanta
(404) 872-4621 • www.compoundatl.com

Known for its "net parties" (single networking parties), this vast club is set amidst some of the lushest landscaping in Atlanta.

Best After Hours Place
Majestic Diner
1031 Ponce De Leon Ave., Atlanta
(404) 875-0276

This local landmark is a great place to enjoy breakfast and hot black coffee in the wee hours of the morning. Try the pork chop and eggs with a pecan waffle!

Best Special Occasion Restaurant
Dante's Down the Hatch
3380 Peachtree Rd. N.E., Atlanta
(404) 266-1600 • www.dantesdownthehatch.com

Not your run of the mill fondue joint, this one's got live alligators! The low-lit rooms are designed like an abandoned ship. With live jazz nightly, Dante's is an absolute must!

Best Place To Buy a Gift
Blue Genes
3400 Around Lenox Dr. N.E., Atlanta
(404) 231-3400 • www.bluegenesatlanta.com

Blue Genes recently added a men's store to the already established women's boutique. Choose urban designer clothing that will place you at the forefront of fashion.

Top Five Dates

#1. Helicopter Tour of Atlanta
Humes McCoy Aviation
570 Piedmont Ave., N.E., Hanger 54156, Atlanta
(877) 723-5898 • www.humesmccoyaviation.net

Tour the city with Atlanta's biggest and most reputable aviation company. You can create your own flight path so why not begin near your neighborhood and end up at your favorite restaurant?

#2. Saturday Night at the Drive-In
The Varsity
61 North Ave. N.W., Atlanta
(404) 881-1706

Get your car detailed, pick up your date, and enjoy a blast from the past with curbside service at the world's largest drive-in. Wash those grilled chili dogs and onion rings down with a frosted orange and make sure that you bring along some peppermint breath mints to share. (And don't forget the popcorn!)

#3. Let Life Imitate Art
High Museum of Art
1280 Peachtree St., Atlanta, GA
(404) 733-4550 • www.high.org

Take your date out on Friday night to check out the exhibitions and collections at Atlanta's home to the works of the great European and American masters. Participate in an art-making workshop. Then talk about what you saw (or what you made) over dessert and drinks while you listen to live jazz in the Robinson Atrium.

#4. *Stone Mountain Park*
   Hwy. 78 E, Exit 8, Stone Mountain.
   (770) 498-5690

   Spend a day together in the country at Stone Mountain Park. Take a hike, explore the 1870's old town, ride the train, and take the sky lift to see the memorial stone carving of three Confederate heroes. And when you're tired and hungry, stop at Miss Katie's Sideboard Restaurant and enjoy a home-style Southern dinner.

#5. *Chateau Elan Inn and Winery*
   6060 Golf Club Dr., Braselton
   (800) 233-WINE

   Spend a day at the world-class resort and winery Chateau Elan. Start off with a complimentary tour and wine tasting. Then treat yourself and your date to a relaxing European-style facial. Top that off with dinner at one of the six restaurants featured at this upscale resort and vineyard.

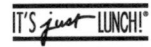

Austin

Best Restaurant for Lunch or Brunch First Date
Mother's Café & Garden
4215 Duval St., Austin
(888) 555-1212

Located in the fun and funky-turned-yuppie Hyde Park, Mother's has a relaxed atmosphere with a garden and indoor patio. Try the spinach lasagna, a signature dish.

Best Restaurant for First Dinner Date
Gumbos
710 Colorado St., Austin
(512) 480-8053

Feels like you're right in the heart of New Orleans' Bourbon Street! Delicious Cajun fare and the bread is to die for. Nice lighting and great service. Don't forget the gumbo!

Best Cheap Date
Republic Square Park, Austin
http://www.ci.austin.tx.us/events/city_calendar.cfm

Bring a blanket, a picnic and your date to the movies! Movies in the Park shows fun classics at no charge throughout the year. It's fun and free.

Best Restaurant for a Second Dinner Date
Clay Pit
1601 Guadalupe St., Austin
(512) 322-5131 • http://claypit.com/Home.asp

Enjoy Austin's best Indian food. The Clay Pit boasts an interesting wine cellar with over 100 different types of wine. Add to that a knowledgeable wait staff and great service.

Best Place for Coffee and Dessert
Mozart's
3825 Lake Austin Blvd., Austin
(512) 477-2900 • www.mozartscoffee.com

With its affluent clientele and lakeside decks, Mozart's is

both classy and romantic. Make sure to try the strawberry chocolate cheesecake.

Best Place for a Laugh
Capital City Comedy Club
8120 Research Blvd., Austin
(512) 467-2333 • www.capcitycomedy.com

The comedians who show up at Capital City come pre-tested, with experience behind them from networks like HBO and Showtime. Be prepared to laugh out loud.

Best Creative Date
Capital Cruises
8604 Lemen's Spice Trail, Austin
Hyatt Regency Boat Dock, 208 Barton Springs Rd., Austin
(512) 480-9264 • www.capitalcruises.com

Get out of the ordinary and take a dinner cruise! Here you will be served great food from the Hyatt (try the fajitas) and enjoy a guided tour of the city.

Best Club
Light Bar
408 Congress, Austin
(512) 473-8544 • www.lightbaraustin.com

Upscale, urban club with water walls, ultramodern chairs and stainless steel fixtures. A sleek, clubby atmosphere. Sip a designer martini at the trendy front bar.

Best After Hours Place
Katz's Deli and Bar
618 W. 6th St., Austin
(512) 472-2037 • www.katzsneverkloses.com

The slogan — Katz's Never Kloses — says it all! Katz's claim to fame is its New York deli-style cuisine "with a Texas attitude," morning, noon and night — all night.

Best Special Occasion Restaurant
Mirabelle Restaurant
8127 Mesa Dr., Austin
(512) 346-7900 • www.mirabellerestaurant.com

Mirabelle's warm, intimate interior creates the ideal atmosphere for romantic dinners. The restaurant also boasts two private dining rooms for special occasions.

Best Place To Buy a Gift
Tesoros Trading Co
209 Congress Ave., Austin
(512) 479-8377 • www.tesoros.com

Looking for exotic gifts? Search no further. This is the place. Among the finds are colorful hand-woven cloth from Guatemala, and glassware and tinwork from Mexico.

Top Five Dates

#1. Make a Day at Zilker Park
2100 Barton Springs Rd., Austin
(512) 974-3329 • http://www.ci.austin.tx.us/zilker
Rent a canoe, have a picnic, ride the train, fly a kite, stroll through the botanical gardens and take a dip in the springs if you dare. If you want something more substantial to eat after the day's events, try one of the many "Austiny" restaurants on Barton Springs road: the original Chuy's, Baby Acapulco's, Shady Grove and Romeo's, just to name a few.

#2. A Fredericksburg wine tour
www.spicewoodvineyards.com/home4.htm or
www.txwinetours.com
Texas' own little "Napa." Take off for a relaxing and beautiful scenic drive through the hill country, where you can sample wine from our own Texas vineyards. Afterwards, if you don't trust yourself behind the wheel, seek out one of the many Bed and Breakfasts that the hill country has to offer.

#3. Let your inner child out — Fiesta Texas
17000 IH 10 West, San Antonio
(210) 697-5050
www.sixflags.com/parks/fiestatexas/index.asp
Just a hop, skip and an hour jump from Austin, you can visit one of the state's largest wooden roller coasters and be a kid again at this water theme park. There are also some amazing laser light shows, as well as a variety of rides and musical performances. Don't forget to bring your swimsuit just in case you want to test the waters.

#4. *The Oasis*
   6550 Commanche Trail, Austin
   (512) 266-2442 • www.oasis-austin.com

   Best known for its scenic views and sunsets, The Oasis sits on Lake Travis and has over 20 decks for you to view the sun setting on the lake. You can always count on a great margarita at The Oasis. Come on Sundays during the spring and summer for live salsa music and dancing.

#5. *An evening on 6th Street: dinner, live music, dessert*
   Old Pecan Street Café
   310 E. 6th St., Austin
   (512) 478-2491

   Go to the heart of Downtown Austin for a complete date evening. Start out at the Historic Pecan Street Café for dinner. Catch live music at Stubbs BBQ (restaurant that doubles as a live music venue). Then journey down Austin's famous 6th Street to find the right bar for a nightcap and dessert. We recommend the Iron Cactus.

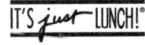

Baltimore

Best Restaurant for Lunch or Brunch First Date
Alonso's
415 W. Cold Spring Ln., Baltimore
(410) 235-3433 • www.alonsos.com

A mainstay since 1931, this place will leave you all warm inside, like you just ate one of Mom's home-cooked meals.

Best Restaurant for First Dinner Date
Ruth's Chris Steakhouse
600 Water St., Baltimore
Call for other locations
(410) 783-0033 • www.ruthschris.com

The very name of this establishment is an icon in Baltimore and the way they describe preparing their steak (not to mention the actual experience of eating it) is pure poetry.

Best Cheap Date
The Baltimore Zoo
One Druid Park Lake Dr., Baltimore
(410) 366-5466 • www.baltimorezoo.org

Is there anything sweeter than strolling hand-in-hand and giggling at a yawning hippopotamus? The Zoo is fun for both young and old.

Best Restaurant for a Second Dinner Date
Rusty Scupper
402 Key Hwy., Baltimore
(410) 727-3678 • www.selectrestaurants.com/rusty/

A harbor favorite, this location is perfect for a romantic sunset dinner and a short stroll to the Inner Harbor shops. Enjoy classic Baltimore seafood on a terrace by the water.

Best Place for Coffee and Dessert
Uncle Wiggly's Ice Cream and Coffee Cafe
6911 York Rd., Baltimore
(410) 377-3373

Open later than most, this place suits the urge when the timing needs to be just right.

Best Place for a Laugh
Burke's Café and Comedy Factory
36 Light St., Baltimore
(410) 752-4189

This place is just pure fun. A fixture at the harbor since 1934, it's noted for frosted goblets and huge onion rings. Comedy shows are on Friday and Saturday nights

Best Creative Date
Gardel's Argentinean Supper Club
29 S. Front Street, Baltimore
(410) 837-3737 • www.baltimoretanguero.com

Unbutton your shirt and feel the beat of the Latin drum as you mix fine dining with Tango passion. A "Tea Time tango" is offered on Sundays; it's a great way to get started.

Best Club
Baja Beach Club
55 Market Pl., Baltimore
(410) 752-7188

Any place that boasts of nightlife frenzies featuring "foam parties" and trays of dance- provoking shooters has got to be hot. This place is the stuff of legend.

Best After Hours Place
Nam King
2126 Maryland Ave., Baltimore
(410) 685-6237

If the night has been too good to end with a sloppy burger and diner coffee, then a hearty multiple course Korean meal may be the ticket

Best Special Occasion Restaurant
Aldo's Ristorante Italiano
306 S. High St., Baltimore
(410) 727-0700 • www.aldositaly.com

Here's an Italian restaurant that treats every night like it's a special occasion. Chef Aldo Vitale uses the best seasonal ingredients, all grown locally.

Best Place To Buy a Gift
Glauber's Home Chocolates
18 W. Ridgley Rd., Towson
Call for other locations
(410) 252-5080 • www.glaubers.com

Chocolate is always the pathway to the heart. You'll find lots to choose from here.

Top Five Dates

#1. *Toby's Dinner Theater*
3820 Falls Rd., Columbia
(410) 995-1969 • www.tobysdinnertheatre.com
Where else will your waitress serve your meal and moments later crash the stage to the opening chorus of "Miss Saigon?" There's nothing like the artist-audience bond at this fun dinner-date locale.

#2. *Bengies Drive-In Theatre*
3417 Eastern Blvd., Aberdeen
(410) 687-5627 • www.bengies.com
Who knows what the night may bring when you snuggle up in your Chrysler PT Cruiser around some greasy fries and "The Night of the Living Dead."

#3. *Boordy Vineyard Summer Concert Series*
12820 Long Green Pike, Hydes
(410) 592-5015 • www.boordy.com
Be it Big Band sounds or Cajun Zydeco, good music, a good wine buzz and a full moon will have you kissing on the dance floor by night's end.

#4. *Clipper City Dinner Sailing*
803 Light St., Baltimore
(410) 539-6277 • www.clippercity.com
With all the romance of a tall ship and ports unknown, this is just a great way to get away from it all and enjoy the moment. Try a romantic sunset sail or sign up for their Wind, Wine and Dine Wednesdays for a cruise featuring a special meal of gourmet hors d'oeuvres and wines from Boordy Vineyards.

#5. *Howl at the Moon*
   22 Market Pl., Baltimore
   (410) 783-5111

This dueling piano bar is side-splittingly funny and just downright fascinating to watch. After a night here, you'll appreciate talented musicianship in a whole new way.

Birmingham and Huntsville

Best Restaurant for Lunch or Brunch First Date
Sol Y Luna
2811 7th Ave. S., Birmingham
(205) 322-1186 • www.solyluna.net
For a first date brunch, the funky patio at Sol Y Luna is perfect: Enjoy authentic Mexican-style tapas featuring fresh seafood, as well as the best margaritas in Birmingham.

Best Restaurant for First Dinner Date
Little Savannah
3811 Clairmont Ave., Birmingham
(205) 591-1119
www.birminghammenus.com/littlesavannah
This is great restaurant featuring Progressive Southern cuisine in a historic Southern neighborhood. The atmosphere is warm and inviting; you cannot help but feel romantic!

Best Cheap Date
Jim Davenport's Pizza Palace
2837 Cahaba Rd., Mountain Brook
(205) 879-8603
Davenport's takes you back to a simpler time. Classic celebrity memorabilia, thin-crust pizza, plenty of beer and classic video games make this is a great place for a cheap date.

Best Restaurant for a Second Dinner Date
Pauli's Chop House
109 Washington St., Huntsville
(256) 704-5555 • www.washingtonsq.com/paulis.htm
Consistently serving the best steaks and the freshest seafood, Pauli's is one of the paramount locations for fine dining.

Best Place for Coffee and Dessert
O'Henry's
18th St. S., Homewood
(205) 870-1198
With its good coffee and fabulous deserts by Edgar's bak-

ery, this neighborhood coffee shop is a great place to meet friends or finish up a dinner date!

Best Place for a Laugh
The Hippodrum
2007 Highland Ave. S., Birmingham
(205) 933-6565

Looking for a laugh? Monday nights are karaoke nights at this hard-to-miss nightclub. Have a few drinks, grab the microphone, and enjoy yourself — or just laugh at the others.

Best Creative Date
Flying Monkey Arts Center
1230 Putnam Dr., Huntsville
(256) 489-7000 • www.flyingmonkeyarts.org

FMAC is a serious laboratory for the arts. It is an art gallery and performance facility for music, theater, dance, puppetry, etc. You could easily spend the day here!

Best Club
Club Red
2015 Highland Ave., Birmingham
(205) 933-1983 • www.theclubred.com

This upscale club is hip and trendy and caters to young professionals. Its awesome dance floor lighting and great DJ keep the crowds dancing well into the morning.

Best After Hours Place
Hogan's Irish Pub and Grill
507 Cahaba Park Cir., Birmingham
(205) 995-0533

A member of the Irish pubs of America, this beer and whiskey joint has late night munchies until 4 A.M..

Best Special Occasion Restaurant
Gorham Bluff
101 Gorham Dr., Gorham's Bluff, Pisgah
(256) 451-ARTS

Dinner is a four-course, chef's-choice, gourmet meal served on white tablecloths with flattering candlelight and fresh flowers. You are welcome to bring your own wine.

Best Place To Buy a Gift

Dorothy McDaniel
2824 18th Street, Homewood
(205) 871-0092

You will love giving and receiving flowers from this exquisite one of a kind floral shop! They also have a distinctive selection of vases, flowerpots and candles.

Top Five Dates

#1. See the Sea
The Dauphin Island Sea Lab
(251) 861-7500 • www.disl.org
This is Alabama's marine education and research center. The island's peaceful atmosphere and natural beauty are something to behold. It has tons of things to do, from an aquarium to interactive exhibits that will entrance you. Take a quiet walk on the beach. Bring a picnic, some wine, some cheese and let the day take you away!

#2. Art and Music Nights
Art and Wine Birmingham Gallery
2119 First Ave. N., Birmingham
(205) 252-5567 • www.synthesissouth.com/events.htm
Art and Wine pairs wine tastings with exhibitions of some of Alabama's fine artists. Then they mix in some of the best music found in the city. Nights such as Sultry Sushi, and Caviar and Friends bring great music and fine food together. Your date will love your sophistication!

#3. Step Back in Time
Burritt on the Mountain
3101 Burritt Dr., Huntsville
(256) 536-2882 • www.burrittmuseum.com
Take a break from the 21st Century and discover how much simpler and more fun the past was by visiting an authentic farm. They offer many different types of events to suit any taste, but a favorite is enjoying live music under the stars. Order a fancy picnic basket in advance. Enjoy the sunset and watch the stars come out while live jazz, gospel or even New Orleans Gris Gris plays. There's no better way to relax than this.

#4. It's Show Time
Alabama Theatre for the Performing Arts
1811 3rd Ave. N., Birmingham
(205) 252-2262 • www.alabamatheatre.com

Built in 1925 for Paramount Studios to showcase their movies, this restored movie theater is an amazing example of Spanish architecture. The Wurlitzer organ forms the central attraction, but the lovely terra cotta columns and lobby with gold-leafed ceiling and thousand-plus pound chandelier are stunning. It's an incredible visual spectacle.

#5. Fast Date
Barber Vintage Motorsports Museum
2721 5th Ave. S., Birmingham
(205) 252-8377

This is the best motorcycle and car museum in North America, period. If your date likes cars or bikes, there isn't a better place to spend the day. Come for the vintage Ferraris, Ducatis, and other fascinating vehicles. As an extra goody, there's a race track next door.

Boise

Best Restaurant for Lunch or Brunch First Date
Berryhill & Co.
2170 Broadway Ave., Boise
(208) 387-3553 • www.berryhillandco.com

Fresh local and organic ingredients form the foundation at this Boise hideaway. Go for the Sunday brunch — the fresh vegetable quiche with asiago cream sauce is a must try!

Best Restaurant for First Dinner Date
Asiago's Ristorante
3423 N. Cole Rd., Boise
(208) 323-1469 • www.asiagos.com

The authentic Italian cuisine and extensive wine list at this rustic-chic locale are just a few reasons why it's been voted the Best and Most Romantic Restaurant by Boise Weekly.

Best Cheap Date
Jessica's Mexican Restaurant
(208) 343-6403
6882 W. State St.

Offering something for everyone, even vegetarians, this restaurant's selection includes inexpensive enchiladas, fajitas, burritos, tacos and tamales.

Best Restaurant for a Second Dinner Date
The Milky Way
205 N. 10th St., Ste. 110, Boise
(208) 319-0123 • www.restaurantmilkyway.com

This urban retreat serves fine dining sensations that are out of this world. Try the pan-seared beef tenderloin, but save room for the lemongrass cardamom crème brulee!

Best Place for Coffee and Dessert
Flying M Coffeehouse
500 W. Idaho St., Boise
(208) 345-4320

The Flying M is downtown Boise's premier coffeehouse,

serving gourmet blends and luscious homemade desserts with eclectic art-infused flair.

Best Place for a Laugh
Boogie Woogie's
800 W. Idaho St. 2nd Fl., Boise
(208) 367-0040 • www.boogiewoogies.com

It's always a raucous sing-along comedy fest at this dueling piano bar, where the patrons mingle with the entertainers as much as they do each other.

Best creative date
Payette National Forest
(208) 634-0700
http://www.recreation.gov/detail.cfm?ID=(1025)

Take your sweetheart on a whitewater rafting adventure through a stretch of Idaho's 3,100 miles of coursing: everything from relaxing float trips to experts-only paddling.

Best Club
The Big Easy
416 S. 9th St., Boise
(208) 367-1212 • www.bigeasyconcerts.com

Turn it up a notch at this hot club, featuring live-action video displays and up to 1,000 hot-to-trot clubbers. Next door, Bourbon Street Saloon keeps the buzz alive.

Best After Hours Place
Old Chicago
730 West Idaho St, Boise
(208) 363-0037

Pizza, sandwiches, and a variety of draft beers highlight this familiar Boise locale. It's a great place to sit, talk and look around, especially if you're a sports fan.

Best Special Occasion Restaurant
Desert Sage
750 West Idaho St, Boise
(208) 333-8400

This simple yet elegant restaurant has a national reputation for its cuisine, and the atmosphere is great: With jazz in the background, the excellent staff makes it memorable!

Best Place To Buy a Gift
Ten Thousand Villages
1609 N. 13th St., Boise
(208) 333-0535

You'll find hundreds of gift ideas, with each item personally handcrafted. Pick up a journal from Indonesia, pottery from Peru, fine jewels from Nepal and much more.

Top Five Dates

#1. Steeeee-rike!
Lake Hazel Lanes
10489 Lake Hazel Rd., Boise
(208) 362-2695 • http://lakehazellanes.com

There's nothing like bowling to make for an easy-going, fun-filled date. Spice it up a bit with a Lake Hazel specialty Bloody Mary or strawberry margarita. Then sweeten the stakes by deciding that whoever wins makes the other dinner.

#2. Sniff, Swirl, Sip…Smooch
Ste. Chapelle Winery
19348 Lowell Rd., Caldwell
(208) 453-7830 • www.stechapelle.com

Ste. Chapelle is just a short, 20-minute drive from Boise, yet the open-air atmosphere makes it feel like it's worlds away. Taste the winery's award-winning varietals, tour the vineyards, enjoy live music, picnic lunches, and special events and festivals. It's a fun and leisurely way to spend time with your date.

#3. Art Walk
First Thursday of the Month
Downtown Boise
www.downtownboise.org

The first Thursday of every month, head downtown and check out local and national art exhibits, live music events and free drink and appetizer specials. Walk the galleries and observe in comfortable silence or strike up an intellectual conversation. Either way you're sure to have fun. Pick up an event brochure at any downtown merchant.

#4. Catch Some R & R
Serenity Retreat Therapeutic Spa
2405 Bogus Basin Rd., Boise
(208) 333-8827

Make it a date of rest and relaxation at Serenity Retreat. Order the couples' spa package, with dual one-hour signature massages and an hour in a private spa room — a romantic set-up with a hot tub and sauna, CD stereo, "gentle rain" showers and a cool-down area in which to relax. Dim the lights for a view of the evening stars.

#5. A Midsummer Night's Dream
Idaho Shakespeare Festival
5657 Warm Springs Ave., Boise
(208) 336-9221 • www.idahoshakespeare.org

The stage is set: Nestled within Idaho state park greenery and wildlife is a fantastical world of Shakespearean poetry — and you're invited. Purchase a pair of open-seating tickets, bring a blanket or a couple of low-backed chairs and grab a to-go feast and a bottle of wine from the gourmet Shakespeare Café next door. Ah, romance is in the air.

Boston

Best Restaurant for Lunch or Brunch First Date
Croma Boston
269 Newbury St., Boston
(617) 247-3200 • www.cromaboston.com
This trendy European pizzeria delights with Mediterranean fare and a staggering wine list. Ask for a table out on the garden patio or inside by the fire for an intimate first date.

Best Restaurant for First Dinner Date
Excelsior
272 Boylston St., Boston
(617) 426-7878 • www.excelsiorrestaurant.com
An A-list crowd flocks to this romantic dinner destination overlooking the Boston Public Garden. Try the ginger lobster or splurge with specialized food and wine-paired menu.

Best Cheap Date
Anchovie's
433 Columbus Ave., Boston
(617) 266-5088
The combination of great Italian food (pasta, sandwiches, lasagna, etc.) and low prices makes this a perfect inexpensive date. The food is so good she won't know it's cheap!

Best Restaurant for a Second Dinner Date
Tapeo Restaurant and Tapas Bar
266 Newbury St., Boston
(617) 267-4799 • www.tapeorestaurant.com
Share several of their more than 40 tapas dishes, order up a bottle of wine or a pitcher of sangria, sit back, chat and enjoy an adventurous and romantic dining experience.

Best Place for Coffee and Dessert
Mike's Pastry
300 Hanover St., Boston
(617) 742-3050 • www.mikespastry.com
Mike's is practically a Boston institution, serving up the

most delectable homemade desserts in the city. Order a cappuccino and the signature homemade cannoli — luscious!

Best Place for a Laugh
Improv Asylum
216 Hanover St., Boston
(617) 263-6887 • www.improvasylum.com

Laugh until your stomach hurts at this interactive comedy theater. Stop by for a show or a special dinner theater package — just make sure the wine doesn't spurt through your nose!

Best Creative Date
Waterside, Boston

Pick any place along the water and pack a picnic and books. You can read individually or take turns reading to each other. It's close, comfy and revealing!

Best Club
Parris (entry through Ned Devine's)
250 Quincy Market Bldg., Faneuil Hall, Boston
(617) 248-9900 • www.parrisboston.com/parris

Weekdays this posh palace is filled with business execs sipping martinis and shooting the breeze; on weekends its gymnasium-sized dance floor really sizzles.

Best After Hours Place
News
150 Kneeland St., South Station, Boston
(617) 426-6397

Your imagination is just about the only menu limitation here — it's huge. You can get anything from burgers to Japanese, and all points in between, as well as libations.

Best Special Occasion Restaurant
The Capital Grille
359 Newbury St., Boston
(617) 262-8900 • www.thecapitalgrille.com

Your special occasion needs great steaks, a warm ambiance and the impeccable service you'll find here. Their wine list has won national awards, and the desserts are fantastic!

Best Place To Buy a Gift
Bliss Home
121 Newbury St., Boston
(617) 421-5544 • www.blisshome.com

They showcase eclectic home furnishings, accessories, textiles, glassware and much, much more. You'll find the perfect gift at Bliss.

Top Five Dates

#1. What's In Your Future?
South End Psychic Studio
552 Columbus Ave., Boston
(617) 970-8593 • www.bostonpsychic.com

Regardless of whether you and your date believe in the mystical, a psychic reading will provide enough conversation for many dates to come. Get your palms read, have your astrological charts mapped, or get a tarot card reading. Have fun, keep an open mind, and you never know — you just might learn something new about yourselves and each other!

#2. Take Me Out To the Ballgame
Fenway Park, Boston
(617) 267-9440 • http://boston.redsox.mlb.com

Take the T down to Kenmore and get ready for a fun-filled tour through history. After watching the Red Sox knock 'em out of the park from this historical stadium, you've no doubt already scored the next date. Just make sure you plan ahead and get a seat with a clear view.

#3. Finding Nemo
New England Aquarium
Central Wharf, Boston
(617) 973-5200 • www.neaq.org

Have some good old-fashioned fun together at the New England Aquarium. Watch your inner 5-year-olds rise to the surface as you delight in the waddling penguins, fascinating sharks and illuminated jellyfish. You can also board the Voyager III for a whale watching tour, or sit back and enjoy an exploratory 3-D IMAX film.

#4. *Meeting of the Minds*
    Museum of Fine Arts
    465 Huntington Ave., Boston
    (617) 267-9300 • www.mfa.org

    For starters, the Boston Museum of Fine Arts has the finest Monet collection in the country. Add that to hands-on fine art classes and workshops, Friday night events with jazz and wine and an auditorium featuring live music, foreign films and cutting-edge theater — it's a date made in intellectual heaven.

#5. *Wrap Yourselves in Luxury*
    Daryl Christopher
    37 Newbury St., Ste. 4, Boston
    Other locations: Waltham, Wayland
    (617) 424-0250 • www.dchristopher.com

    Daryl Christopher offers a full-service, all-natural spa menu delivered within an unpretentious, clean-feeling atmosphere. Craft your own day around his and hers massages, facials, manicures and even hairstyles. Then hit the town with your new looks and rejuvenated spirits!

Charlotte

Best Restaurant for Lunch or Brunch First Date
Upstream (Brunch)
6902 Phillip's Place Court, Charlotte
(704) 556-7730 • www.upstreamseafood.com
Named by Esquire magazine as "Best New Rest of 2001." Offering Pan-Asian seafood cuisine in a beautiful atmosphere by the water. Also awarded Charlotte Magazine's "Best Seafood."

Best Restaurant for First Dinner Date
Red Star Tavern
East Blvd., Charlotte
(704) 333-3393
www.redstartavern.net/charlotte/homeCNC.html
Upscale version of comfort food with a large beer selection in an urban, "clubby" atmosphere around an open fireplace.

Best Cheap Date
The Penguin
1921 Commonwealth Ave., Charlotte
(704) 375-6959 • www.coldfury.com/Penguin
Ice cream parlor turned café and bar. A '50s soda shop serving beer and liquor. White-collar to body-art-painted diners come here. Tried the fried pickles or banana pudding.

Best Restaurant for a Second Dinner Date
Solé
1608 East Blvd., Charlotte
(704) 343-9890 • www.solespanishgrille.com
A selection of traditional Spanish, Latin and Mediterranean dishes in a cozy, intimate atmosphere, with live Spanish guitar music on Wednesday nights.

Best Place for Coffee and Dessert
Dean & Deluca Marketplace Café
Stonecrest Shopping Ctr., 201 S. Tryon, Charlotte
(704) 377-0037
The latest by Dean & Deluca offers a terrific house-roast cof-

fee and scrumptious desserts. Try the white chocolate quiche with a cup of java. Open till 10:00 A.M. on weekends.

Best Place for a Laugh
The Comedy Zone
516 N. College St., Charlotte
(704) 348-HAHA

A favorite stop for national comedians on tour, this venue also serves fantastic food and drinks.

Best Creative Date
Mint Museum of Craft & Design
220 North Tryon St., Charlotte
(704) 337-2000

If you're more of a "hands on" person, you can enjoy the displays as well as participate in a variety of workshops and watch demonstrations by visiting artists.

Best Club
Coyote Joe's
4612 Wilkinson Blvd., Charlotte
(704) 399-4946 • http://350m.com/coyotejoes

Catch major country stars, such as Merle Haggard, as well as lesser-known up and comers — plus free dance lessons, country karaoke and great drink specials.

Best After Hours Place
Skyland Family Restaurant
4544 South Blvd., Charlotte
(704) 522-6522

Greek-owned with lots of pictures of Greek gods and Olympians. It's inexpensive, but with good Greek desserts and huge portions. Open 24 hours.

Best Special Occasion Restaurant
Latorre's
118 W. Fifth St., Charlotte
(704) 377-1312

For a mid-week celebration, try the Tuesday night four-course wine dinner, where Spanish wines, pan-seared duck breast and Catalonian chocolate custard are on the menu.

Best Place To Buy a Gift
Cottage Chic
1232 East Blvd., Charlotte
(704) 374-1888

You can find everything from Kate Spade bags and lotions to Oprah's favorite pajamas in this house off of East Boulevard.

Top Five Dates

#1. *Take a trip to Paradise*
Paradise Island Divers
2317 South Blvd., Charlotte
(704) 525-9234 • www.paradisedivers.com

Before you take your first vacation together, why not take scuba diving lessons at Paradise Island's on-site indoor pool? This 'buddy sport' is perfect for a date — and once you get certified — you can take the trip to Hawaii you've been dreaming about.

#2. *"A bottle of wine and thou..."*
Dean & Deluca Marketplace Café
Stonecrest Shopping Ctr., 201 S. Tryon, Charlotte
(704) 377-0037

Stop by this New York style deli/café and pick up a selection of fabulous foods to take to your favorite outdoor location. A bottle of wine and a blanket will turn this picnic into a lovely, romantic interlude.

#3. *Take a trip for two to the Voci Spa*
Stonecrest/ South Charlotte, Rea Rd. @ I-485, Charlotte
2620 E. 7th St., Charlotte
(704) 752-8030 • www.vocispa.com

Spend the afternoon in this "total body renewal center" then try a wine flight at one of Charlotte's local night spots. You'll be more relaxed than you ever imagined — and it's the perfect way to release your inhibitions so your hot date will be even hotter.

#4. *McGill Rose Garden*
940 N. Davidson St., Charlotte
(704) 333-6497
http://features.aroundcarolina.com/mcgill/

Romance is in bloom at this seasonal garden retreat. Stroll the grounds hand-in-hand and luxuriate in the beautiful sights and scents of roses, roses, roses!

Take a camera to capture the beauty of these beautiful flowers for your scrapbook — maybe even have a joint photo taken while you pose amidst the spectacular floral displays.

#5. *Fondue for two*
   901 S Kings Dr., Charlotte
   Other location: 230 E WT Harris Blvd., Ste. C-1, Charlotte
   (704) 334-4400
   What could be more romantic than fondue for two? With three-course pre-selected specialty dinners, you can focus on each other rather than the menu.

Chicago

Best Restaurant for Lunch or Brunch First Date
Nookies
1747 Wells St., Chicago
Call for other locations.
(312) 337-2454

The lunches are quick and filling — try the apple and cheddar cheese omelet — and if you have time for dessert, splitting one is a guilt-free way to enjoy Nookie on a first date.

Best Restaurant for First Dinner Date
Orso's Restaurant
1401 N. Wells, Chicago
(312) 787-6604 • www.orsosrestaurant.com

The lighting and pianist make this the perfect place for romance. The filet mignon is a must. Save room to share a dessert. The summertime patio is Chicago's most beautiful.

Best Cheap Date
Movie in the Park Millennium Park
Millennium Park, Chicago
www.cityofchicago.org

Every Tuesday night in the new Millennium Park one classic movie is shown after sun down. Pack some lawn chairs and a picnic. Admission is free.

Best Restaurant for a Second Dinner Date
Govnor's Pub
207 N. State, Chicago
(312) 236-3696 • www.govnors.com

The drinks are really good and the food is great at this extremely popular pub located in close proximity to the Chicago Theatre.

Best Place for Coffee and Dessert
Millennium Perk
79 E. Madison, Chicago
(312) 384-1270 • www.millenniumperk.com

Madison at Michigan — how great it is to seen an independent coffee shop thriving in the high-rent Loop. This adorable little spot has great coffee and makes sandwiches to order.

Best Place for a Laugh
The Elevated
Cherry Red Bar, 2833 N. Sheffield (back room), Chicago
(773) 477-3661

You never know who'll stop by this comedy showcase. Up-and-coming performers present comedy ranging from standard club comedy to the avant-garde.

Best Creative Date
Kayak/Tandem Rides
Rentals at North Pier on Ogden Slip, Chicago
(630) 336-7245 • www.kayakchicago.com

In the summer you and your date can paddle through the rivers of Chicago beneath the city's looming skyscrapers. If you're not seasoned kayakers, lessons are available.

Best Club
Excalibur Night Club
632 N. Dearborn St., Chicago
(312) 266-1944 • www.excaliburchicago.com

This medieval castle-themed club has three floors of entertainment. Pool tables and HDTV are available if you don't feel like dancing to some of the best DJs in the country.

Best After Hours Place
Lakeview Lounge
5110 N. Broadway, Chicago
(773) 769-0994 • www.lakeviewlounge.com

This place is a hoot. The house band, Night Watch, plays every Thursday through Saturday from 10 p.m to 4 A.M.. There's no cover and drinks are cheap.

Best Special Occasion Restaurant
Tru
676 N. Saint Clair, Chicago
(312) 202-0001 • www.trurestaurant.com

Enjoy progressive French cuisine in a whimsical setting. For a truly special occasion, book a private party with a custom menu created by Tru's chefs.

Best Place To Buy a Gift
T-Shirt Deli
1739 N. Damen Ave., Chicago
(773) 276-6266 • www.tshirtdeli.com

Visit Bucktown's T-Shirt Deli and design a personalized made-to-order T-shirt. Or two.

Top Five Dates

#1. The Oprah Winfrey Show
Harpo Studios, 1058 W. Washington
(312) 630-0808 • www.oprah.com

Have you ever watched Oprah? Women idolize her and men admire her. What a great place for a date to start. How could it possibly not end well? Call Harpo Studios and reserve space in the audience to experience this phenomenal Chicago icon first hand.

#2. Navy Pier Romantic
Navy Pier, Chicago
www.navypier.com

Want the perfect summer date? Try strolling along Navy Pier at sunset. Grab some ice cream from the Haagen Dazs café. Then, ride the Ferris wheel and check out the skyline while the fireworks show begins. There are also actual pyrotechnic displays on Wednesday and Saturday nights summer through fall.

#3. Out of the Frying Pan, into the Fire
The Chopping Block
4747 N. Lincoln Ave., Soldier Field, Chicago
(773) 472-6700, • www.thechoppingblock.net
The Chicago Fire
(888) MLS-FIRE • www.chicago.fire.mlsnet.com

Balance out your masculine and feminine sides. Start off the evening with a cooking class and end with sports. Everybody ends up happy.

#4. *The 21st Century's Yesterday*
Sony Gallery of Consumer Electronics
663 N. Michigan Ave., Chicago
(312) 943-3334 • www.sony.com
Museum of Contemporary Art
220 E. Chicago Ave., Millennium Park, Chicago
(312) 280.2660 • www.cityofchicago.org
See all that is shiny and futuristic in the city. Imagine you're the Jetsons on their first date.

#5. *Unleash Your Inner Tiger*
Sydney R. Marovitz Golf Course
3600 N. Recreation Dr., Chicago
(312) 742-7930 • www.chicagoparkdistrict.org
Golf is for lovers. Okay, we made that up. But golf is a great couple's activity and if you're already a fan this might be a way to get your date hooked on you and the game.

Cincinnati

Best Restaurant for Lunch or Brunch First Date
Palomino Restaurant, Rotisseria & Bar
505 Vine St., Cincinnati
(513) 381-1300 • www.r-u-i.com

Nestled above Tiffany's and overlooking Fountain Square, this is a fabulous choice for a first date. Be sure to request a table by the window.

Best Restaurant for First Dinner Date
La Petite France
3177 Glendale-Milford Rd., Evendale
(513) 733-8383 • www.lapetitefrance.biz

This very classy, yet quiet French restaurant is more country French than Paris, with all the right romantic charm. No visit would be complete without dessert.

Best Cheap Date
Zip's Cafe
1036 Delta Ave., Mt. Lookout
(513) 871-9876

Zip's Café is one of the city's best-known places to get an inexpensive, quick and tasty burger. The mood is clubby, and you're sure to look "hip," rather than "cheap."

Best Restaurant for a Second Dinner Date
Iron Horse Restaurant
40 Village Sq., Glendale
(513) 771-4787 • www.ironhorseinn.net

You'll find great steaks, burgers, fresh fish, creative pastas and vegetarian specialties along with nightly specials in this historic eatery, established in the 1800s.

Best Place for Coffee and Dessert
The Grand Finale
3 E. Sharon Rd., Glendale
(513) 771-5925 • www.grandfinale.info

Look no further for fabulous Sunday brunches, special

occasion dining and ladies lunches. The delectable desserts, however, could well be the biggest draw.

Best Place for a Laugh
Go Bananas
8410 Market Place Lane, Montgomery
(513) 984-9288 • www.gobananascomedy.com

Cincinnati's premiere comedy club, Go Bananas features national and regional comedians. Reservations are required, and seating is first-come, first-served.

Best Creative Date
The Dude Ranch
3205 Waynesville Rd., Morrow
(513) 421-DUDE • www.TheDudeRanch.com

Is your date the adventurous type? How do horseback riding, paintball, ATV riding and cattle drives sound? Be sure to book ahead, as this place fills up fast.

Best Club
Red Cheetah
1133 Sycamore St., Cincinnati
(513) 684-9500

A new addition to the Cincinnati scene, Red Cheetah features a combination of techno, rap and hip-hop. This spacious club features numerous bars.

Best After Hours Place
The Warehouse
Jail Alley, Main and 12th Streets
(513) 684-9313

Not hungry and not ready to go home yet? Head to the Warehouse, Cincinnati's late-night club, and dance your heart out to hip-hop music until 4 A.M..

Best Special Occasion Restaurant
Jag's Steak & Seafood
5980 West Chester Rd., West Chester
(513) 860-5353 • www.jags.com

Jag's is where Chicago turf meets Boston surf. Be assured that you will have a fine dining experience in one of their seven individually themed dining rooms.

Best Place To Buy a Gift
One in a Million
222 Wooster Pike, Terrace Park
(513) 248-9080 • www.oneinamillionllc.com

Find one-of-a-kind jewelry, furs and gifts from local, national and international designers and artists.

Top Five Dates

#1. The Lights of the City and Theater for Two
Cincinnati Playhouse in the Park
962 Mt. Adams Dr., Mt. Adams
(513) 345-2242 • www.cincyplay.com

Your date will be impressed with this classy choice! Enjoy a live theatrical performance in an establishment that has received top national honors. Be sure to book in advance, as performances sell quickly. Beer, wine and sandwiches are served in the foyer area. This place is sure to satisfy your cultural appetite, as well.

#2. Serious Sports Spectacular!
Paul Brown Stadium or Great American Ballpark
Pete Rose Way, Cincinnati
(513) 621-8383 or (513) 381-7337
www.bengals.com • www.cincinnatireds.com,
www.tickets.com

Cincinnati is the proud home of the Bengals and the Reds. If your date has a sweet spot for sports, a day or evening at the ballpark or stadium is sure to be a huge hit. The Bengals play eight regular-season home games, and the Reds play 81. Don't just take him or her out... take him or her out to the ballgame!

#3. Almost Vegas!
Belterra Casino Resort & Spa
777 Belterra Dr., Florence
(888) BELTERRA
www.belterracasino.com

Las Vegas in Indiana? Believe it. Belterra is a perfect getaway for the adventurous. Located less than an hour from Cincinnati, the hotel and casino offer exciting gaming, relaxing pools, comfortable rooms and fine dining. Be sure to pamper yourself and your date at the luxurious spa and salon.

#4. *Walk, Ride or Rollerblade!*
   Little Miami Scenic Trail
   69-mile paved byway beginning in Milford.
   www.dnr.state.oh.us/parks
   www.sierraclulb.org/miami/outings

   If you want your date to "work out," try the ultimate workout! Take your date on a scenic trip of the Little Miami Scenic Trail. How you take this trip is up to you. Walk, jog, Rollerblade or bike the 69-mile paved, multiuse byway that spans four Ohio counties! Be sure to take some energy bars and drinks on this exciting adventure!

#5. *South of the Border Eating, Drinking and Dancing*
   La Tradicion Mexican Restaurant
   106 4th St., Covington
   (859) 261-6700

   Caliente! This authentic Mexican restaurant is open for lunch and dinner seven days a week, but the real excitement begins Fridays and Saturdays after 10 A.M. That's when the live salsa bands open, followed by furious dancing. Put your salsa moves to the test, as you and your date prepare to party till dawn!

Cleveland

Best Restaurant for Lunch or Brunch First Date
Heck's Café
2927 Bridge Ave., Cleveland
(216) 861-5464

Come sit in the porch-like garden room and enjoy Cajun cooking. It's just like being in New Orleans.

Best Restaurant for First Dinner Date
Vivo
347 Euclid Ave. at E. 6th St., Cleveland
(216) 621-4678 • www.vivo-cleveland.com

Like a candle-lit night at the finest place in Rome with great music playing in the background, Vivo has the best Italian dishes Cleveland has to offer.

Best Cheap Date
Cleveland Museum of Art
11150 East Blvd., Cleveland
(216) 421-7340 • www.clevelandart.org

Admission is free to see some of the greatest art in the world on permanent display. Other charges apply for special events and exhibitions so be sure and call ahead.

Best Restaurant for a Second Dinner Date
Pickwick & Frolic Restaurant and Club
2035 E. Fourth St., Cleveland
(216) 241-7425 • www.pickwickandfrolic.com

Local and professional talent is showcased on stage in the dining room; sit near the stage if you don't want to talk. Follow dinner with a show in the cabaret. Valet parking.

Best Place for Coffee and Dessert
Presti's Bakery
12101 Mayfield Rd., Cleveland
(216) 421-3060

Homemade butter cookies, fruit tortes, and fresh cannoli give this coffee house its competitive edge. Pull up a chair and enjoy people watching with your coffee and pastry.

Best Place for a Laugh
Howl at the Moon Saloon
2000 Sycamore St., Cleveland
(216) 861-4695 • www.howlatthemoon.com/

Howl at the Moon is a sing-along piano club that provides an incredible opportunity for people watching and belly laughing. Crowd ranges from college-age to 80+.

Best Creative Date
Power Play Room
2000 Sycamore St., Cleveland
(216) 696-7664

Test your competitive instincts on 44 video games at Cleveland's premiere video arcade. It's usually adults only after 9 A.M. and alcoholic drinks are available.

Best Club
Mirage on the Water
2510 Elm St., Flats
(216) 348-1135 • www.mirageonthewater.com

Mirage on the Water has a 7,500-square foot marbled dance floor with enough room for hundreds to show off their greatest hip-hop dances moves.

Best After Hours Place
Panini's Bar & Grill
1290 W. 6th St., Cleveland
Call for other locations.
(216) 523-7070 • www.paninisgrill.com

Where everyone goes after the bars close for overstuffed sandwiches, pizza and french fries.

Best Special Occasion Restaurant
Lockkeepers
6190 Canal Rd., Cleveland
(216) 524-9404 • www.lockkeepers.com

With opulence worthy of any special occasion, Lockkeepers has a proficient, amiable waitstaff and in-house sommelier to anticipate your every whim.

Best Place To Buy a Gift
Lion and Blue
15106 Detroit Ave., Lakewood
(216) 529-2328

A lovely boutique with his and hers trinket boxes, this is a wonderful place to find beautiful things to share with someone special.

Top Five Dates

#1. Patterson Fruit Farm
11414 Caves Rd., Chesterland
(440) 729-1964 • www.pattersonfarm.com

Even if it is too cold to pick your own fruit, stop in and enjoy warm apple cider and a slice of fresh baked pie. Maybe you can steal a kiss on one of the hayrides.

#2. Cleveland Museum of Art
11150 East Blvd., Cleveland
(216) 421-7350 • www.clevelandart.org

After enjoying one of the many special exhibits at this top museum, stop into The Still Lifes Café and enjoy a snack, lunch, dinner, wine, or dessert.

#3. Lunch at the West Side Market
W. 25th St. & Lorain Ave., Cleveland
(216) 664-3387 • www.westsidemarket.com

Depending on your preference, you can enjoy a stroll through the open-air market or take a walk through the enclosed market. Afterwards, you and your date can head over to W. 25th St. for lunch at one of the many local restaurants.

#4. Mario's International Spas
35 E. Garfield Rd., Aurora
(330) 562-9171

Whether you're looking to spend one day or an entire weekend at the spa, Mario's could be the cement a new couple is looking for. The pampering and relaxation will do you both good.

#5. *Mayfield Drive-In*
   Rt. 322 at Mayfield Rd., Cleveland
   (440) 286-7173 • www.drive-ins.com/detail/ohtmayf
   You can still go to the drive-in for a weekend date. Only this time you don't have to tell your parents where you are going. This is a blast from the past.

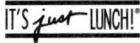

Columbus

Best Restaurant for Lunch or Brunch First Date
Basi Italia
811 Highland St., Columbus
(614) 294-7383

Basi Italia offers a cozy atmosphere, with seating for only 26 in their dining room. They offer a wide variety of Italian and Mediterranean dishes that are simply delicious.

Best Restaurant for First Dinner Date
Trattoria Roma
1447 Grandview Ave., Columbus
(614) 488-2104

This is a truly romantic restaurant with superb Italian cuisine and great service. You will enjoy getting to know your date at Trattoria Roma.

Best Cheap Date
Barley's Smokehouse and Brewpub Ale House No. 2
1130 Dublin Rd., Columbus
(614) 485-0227 • www.barleysbrewing.com

Barley's has been named the "Best Wings in the City" by a local radio station. Come on a Monday evenings and enjoy their famous wings for just 33 cents each.

Best Restaurant for a Second Dinner Date
The Ocean Club
4002 Easton Station, Columbus
(614) 416-CLUB • http://www.cameronmitchell.com/restaurants/ restaurantinformation/index.cfm?rid=19

The Ocean Club gets rave reviews for its seafood dishes. One of the top ten restaurants in Columbus, The Ocean Club has a well-trained staff and offers exceptional service.

Best Place for Coffee and Dessert
Coffee Table
731 High St., Columbus
(614) 297-1177

This location has outdoor tables where you can enjoy your

choice of many different delicious pastries and coffees. As a bonus, they offer free dog treats.

Best Place for a Laugh
Funny Bone Comedy Club and Café
145 Easton Town Ctr., Columbus
(614) 471-JOKE • www.gofunnybone.com

This is the best comedy club in the Columbus area. They have featured Drew Carey, Jerry Seinfeld, Paul Reiser, Chris Rock, Ellen Degeneres and other top comedians.

Best Creative Date
Extreme Croquet Tournament
Barley's Smokehouse and Brewpub Ale House No. 2
1130 Dublin Rd., Columbus
(614) 485-0227 • www.barleysbrewing.com

Enter yourself and your date in an Extreme Croquet Tournament offered by Barley's, as you enjoy their handcrafted brews.

Best Club
Red Zone Night Club
303 S. Front St., Columbus
(614) 621-0416 • www.redzone-club.com

Red Zone is the top nightclub in Columbus. They offer many special events and guest DJs. This is the best in upscale, metropolitan nightlife.

Best After Hours Place
Bristol Bar
132 E. 5th Ave., Columbus
(614) 291-0552 • www.bristolbar.com

Bristol bar is a sophisticated bar with valet parking. They have 11 different martinis to choose from including a chocolate martini.

Best Special Occasion Restaurant
Buca di Beppo
343 N. Front St., Columbus
(614) 621-3287 • www.bucadibeppo.com

Plan your next special event from the convenience of your own home. Buca di Beppo allows you to reserve space and place your order for Italian cuisine online.

Best Place To Buy a Gift

Baskets by Bonnie
721 N. High St., Columbus
(614) 228-8700 • www.basketsbybonnie.com

Come to Baskets by Bonnie for that perfect gift. They will custom design a gift basket for any occasion. You can browse on-site or online for your convenience.

Top Five Dates

#1. Life is a Cabaret
2Cos Cabaret
790 N. High St., Columbus
(614) 437-2267 • www.shadowboxcabaret.com

Take your date to a show at 2Cos Cabaret. They offer a mix of theater and acoustic music in a cabaret setting. Order the hand-made pizza and be served by the performers! This is an amusing way to spend an evening.

#2. Just be a Kid
Six Flags Wyandot Lake
10101 Riverside Dr., Powell
(614) 889-9283 or (800) 328-9283
www.sixflags.com/parks/wyandotlake

Grab your swimsuit and your date and head to Six Flags Wyandot Lake! They offer 45 different rides, slides and attractions. They have an old-fashioned wooden roller coaster, wildly spinning rides, live shows and plenty of water slides to get you wet and cool you down.

#3. Relax Together
Mukha Custom Cosmetics and Skin Salon
980 N. High St., Columbus
(614) 294-SKIN

If dating tends to stress you out, then this is the date for you. Mukha Custom Cosmetics and Skin Salon offers Thermastone massages. This is a deep tissue relaxation massage that uses warm and cool basalt stones. Get yourself and your date a Thermastone massage and relax together.

#4. Do the Gallery Hop
27 East Russell Street Gallery
27 E. Russell St., Columbus
(614) 464-4000

For 20 years on the first Saturday of each month, The Short North area offers The Gallery Hop. There are 26 galleries that participate in this event. You can start with the 27 East Russell Street Gallery, which is filled with works from local artists. Then 'Hop' over and see the other 25 galleries. This will be a fun-filled date with plenty of culture.

#5. Go on a Skiing Adventure
Snow Trails
P.O. Box 1454, Mansfield
(419) 774-9818
(800) OHIO-SKI • www.snowtrails.com

If you enjoy skiing, or would just like to learn, take a drive to Snow Trails. They guarantee snow and have beautifully groomed slopes for all ability levels. They offer instructors who can teach you to ski as well as snowboard. After spending some time on the slopes, you can warm up with your date over a cup of hot chocolate.

IT'S *just* LUNCH!®

Dallas

Best Restaurant for Lunch or Brunch First Date
Ferre Ristorante e Bar
3699 McKinney Ave., Dallas
(214) 522-3888 • www.ferredallas.com

Here you'll find contemporary Tuscan cuisine in a casual, yet sleek setting. The best date tables are along the windows, numbers 61 through 64.

Best Restaurant for First Dinner Date
Steel
3102 Oak Lawn Ave., Dallas
(214) 219-9908. • www.steeldallas.com

This trendy Japanese hotspot offers up much more than just sushi and sake. Call ahead for reservations and ask for table 43; it's a little quieter and has a lovely view! \

Best Cheap Date
Lakewood Theater
1825 Abrams Pkwy., Dallas
(214) 526-8077 • www.lakewoodtheater.com

This restored 1938 art deco theater shows classic movies all year round. The best part? The 15-cent admission!

Best Restaurant for a Second Dinner Date
Tei Tei Robata Bar
2906 N. Henderson, Dallas
(214) 828-2400 • www.teiteirobata.com

Sushi lovers listen up! This Asian-chic bar serves super-fresh sashimi and delectable grilled plates. Sip sake and snuggle up on the black couches while you wait for a table.

Best Place for Coffee and Dessert
Bread Winners Café
3301 McKinney Ave., Dallas
Other location: Inwood Village
(214) 754-4940 • www.breadwinnerscafe.com

Featuring yummy selections of fresh breads, pastries and

desserts, this uptown location wins out for its tranquil patio garden dining.

Best Place for a Laugh
Ad-Libs
2613 Ross Ave., Dallas
(214) 754-7050 • www.ad-libs.com

Nothing can pull you out of a weekend rut like a show at Ad-Libs. Prepare yourself for a belly-full of laughs from this improvisational comedy troupe.

Best Creative Date
Studio Movie Grill
5405 Beltline Rd., Dallas
(972) 991-6684
Other locations: Plano • www.studiomoviegrill.com

Dinner and a movie — together at last! This unique spot offers a variety of flicks (that you won't find in mainstream theatres) while enjoying a sampling of the upscale bar fare. This may not be the thing to do for cinema purists, but for a date it's the right ticket. We recommend arriving a little early to secure better seating and getting your order in before the film starts.

Best Club
Minc
813 Exposition Ave., Dallas
214.370.4077 • www.minclounge.com

Welcome to the red light district of clubs. With sexy mood lighting, unique hut-styled seating and fabulous drinks, this is one of the hottest clubs in Dallas.

Best After Hours Place
Café Brazil
2815 Elm St., Dallas
(214) 747-2730
Call for other locations • www.cafebrazil.com

With various locations across Dallas, this is a great place to strike up frothy conversation over a cup of Brazil's finest coffee. The food's eclectic, as is the lively clientele.

Best Special Occasion Restaurant
Il Mulino
2408 Cedar Springs Rd., Dallas
(214) 855-5511

Delicious veal chops, homemade porcini-stuffed raviolis and more are served in this incredibly decadent and romantic Old-World setting. You'll feel like Italian royalty.

Best Place To Buy a Gift
Stanley Korshak
500 Crescent Ct., Ste. 100, Dallas
(214) 871-3600 • www.stanleykorshak.com

This is one of America's leading shopping destinations and has something for everyone, as long as you want only the best.

Top Five Dates

#1. *Sky Helicopters*
(214) 349-7000 • www.skyhelicopters.com

Fly out of Addison airport and see the Dallas skyline. Land at the Crescent hotel and have dinner at Capital Grill or an afternoon brunch at Beau Nash.

#2. *Massage This*
Four Seasons Spa & Salon
4150 N. MacArthur Blvd., Irving
(972) 717-2555 • www.fourseasons.com

Spending a day being pampered at the spa is pure luxury, and it's even more memorable if you share it with someone you really like. Ask for a couple's retreat, which often includes a candlelit champagne privacy soak. Or, try the Four Seasons' signature Texas Two Step, an exfoliating treatment and luxurious sagebrush-oil massage.

#3. *Dinner and Dancing*
Medici
2404 Cedar Springs, Ste. 400, Dallas
(214) 855-0202

A night of dancing at Medici's is fun by itself, but you can make this date extra-memorable by starting off with a wild game dinner at George. (www.georgerestaurant.com 214-366-9100).

#4. *Highland Park Village Stroll*
Patrizio's
25 Highland Park Village, Dallas
(214) 522-7878

Lunch at Patrizio's and take a stroll through Highland village. Window shop (or more) at the many upscale shops, including Christian Dior and Chanel. End your date sweetly with ice cream at Paciugo next door.

#5. *Picnic by the Water*
White Rock Lake
8300 Garland Dr., Texas
(214) 670-8243

A great date doesn't have to break the bank. It can simply be a quiet get-together that allows for stimulating conversation. Get innovative and spice up the date with a Spanish theme, make a big bowl of paella, bring plenty of sangria, and stick the Gypsy Kings on your portable CD player. Olé!

Denver

Best Restaurant for Lunch or Brunch First Date
Cherry Creek Grille
184 Steele St., Cherry Creek
(303) 322-3524 • www.houstons.com

At this fantastic Cherry Creek mainstay, the food is outstanding with wood-fired rotisserie chicken, to-die-for cornbread, and a friendly warm atmosphere.

Best Restaurant for First Dinner Date
Sambuca Jazz Cafe
1320 15th St., Denver
(303) 629-5299 • www.sambucajazzcafe.com

Jazz up the night. After a night at Sambuca, the senses will surely be satisfied.

Best Cheap Date
Films on Fillmore
Fillmore Plaza, Cherry Creek
(303) 595-3456 • www.denverfilm.org

Thursdays in July and August, enjoy an evening under the stars with a great film. Bring a blanket and splurge on a picnic — the film itself is free!

Best Restaurant for a Second Dinner Date
Sushi Den
1487 S. Pearl St., Denver
Call for other locations.
(303) 777-0826 • www.sushiden.net

This sushi marvel is known throughout the world. The best thing besides the food is the staff; they're charming and they remember regulars by name.

Best Place for Coffee and Dessert
Sweet Rockin' Coffee
414 E. 20th Ave., Denver
(303) 318-9788

Fun and interesting people, good coffee, great desserts, and open-mic nights — it doesn't get any better than this.

Best Place for a Laugh
Bovine Theater
1527 Champa St., Denver
(303) 758-4722 • www.bovinemetropolis.com

In the style of "Whose Line is it Anyway?" four actors and a moderator use audience suggestions to make a hilarious night of fun and laughter.

Best Creative Date
Mataam Fez Moroccan Restaurant
2226 Pearl St., Colorado Springs
(303) 440-4167 • www.mataamfez.com

Enjoy belly dancing while being treated to Moroccan hospitality at its finest.

Best Club
Rise
1909 Blake St., Denver
(303) 383-1909 • www.rise-nightclub.com

Probably the hippest thing to hit Denver. A trip to Rise is like stepping back in time to New York's Studio 54. It's the place to see and be seen.

Best After Hours Place
Denver Diner
740 W. Colfax Ave., Denver
(303) 825-5443

At two-thirty A.M.. just about every type of partier drops in here. So say hello and compare notes on the nightlife.

Best Special Occasion Restaurant
Opus Restaurant
2575 W. Main St., Littleton
(303) 703-6787

When making the best impression matters, try the subtle elegance of Opus, a fine dining experience without all the fuss.

Best Place To Buy a Gift
Chocolate Foundry
2625 E. 3rd Ave., Denver
(303) 388-7800 • www.chocolatefoundry.com

Sometimes the best way to impress is to give one of Chocolate Foundry's artful delicious creations.

Top Five Dates

#1. *Art Movie Night*
Landmark Mayan
110 Broadway, Denver
(303) 352-1992
"So, what's your favorite movie?" It's always s a great question to ask someone. Share an old movie together and let the magic flow. It's also a great place to stroll around before and after the show.

#2. *Walk on the Wild Side*
Denver Zoo
2300 Steele St., Denver
(303) 376-4800 • www.denverzoo.org
Nothing beats a stroll through the zoo for excitement or for an opportunity to learn more about each other through some easy-going conversation.

#3. *How much was that?*
Stanley & Co. Auction Rooms, Ltd.
395 Corona St., Denver
(303)-355-0506
From the speed talking to the final bang of the gavel, going to a high-end auction brings out the "Antiques Roadshow" in all of us. Educational, spellbinding, and always a fun thing to do, going to an auction can help spark mutual interests.

#4. *Paint Something to Share*
Get Fired Up
105 Broadway, Denver
(303) 744-1595
Pick a ceramic plate, cup, or figurine to paint. Then let the laughter fly as you check out each other's artistic skills. It's easy to set up another date for a few days later—you have to come back for your masterpiece after its fired in the kiln.

#5. *Getting to Know You*
Washington Park
Louisiana Ave., S. Downing St., Virginia Ave. and S. Humboldt St., Denver
www.washpark.org
Sometimes the simplest things are the ones that

become treasured memories. The Park has an amazing view, beautiful scenery surrounded by world class architecture, and there's plenty of food and places to visit nearby. Bring a blanket, some wine, and let future memories abound.

Des Moines

Best Restaurant for Lunch or Brunch First Date
Basil Prosperi Bakery
407 E. Fifth St., Des Moines
Other locations: Skywalk and Locust Mall
(515) 243-9819

Fresh bread, crisp salads and delicious pasta make this a noontime favorite.

Best Restaurant for First Dinner Date
Splash Seafood Bar & Grill
303 Locust St., Des Moines
(515) 244-5686 • www.splash-seafood.com

Fresh seafood is flown in daily and prepared with an island influence. Their wine list is extensive, so you're sure to find the perfect wine to complement your dinner.

Best Cheap Date
Baratta's
2320 S. Union, Des Moines
(515) 243-4516

This locally owned Italian eatery welcomes customers like family. Savor the chicken amaggio and old-fashioned cannolis.

Best Restaurant for a Second Dinner Date
Chat Noir Café
644 18th St., Des Moines
(515) 244-1353

Chat Noir — the black cat — is a cozy hideaway, known for European influenced cooking. Not to be missed is the house specialty: crepes.

Best Place for Coffee and Dessert
Java Joes
214 4th St., Des Moines
(515) 288-5282 • www.javajoescoffeehouse.com

Enjoy fresh-roasted coffee while satisfying your sweet

tooth. Choose from a wide selection of freshly baked biscottis, cakes, pies and cookies.

Best Place for a Laugh
Ingersoll Dinner Theater
3711 Ingersoll Ave., Des Moines
(515) 274-4686 • www.dinnertheater.org

Share a laugh while dining at this charming theater. Check the website for upcoming shows.

Best Creative Date
Effigy Mounds
Office of the State Archaeologist
The University of Iowa
700 Clinton St. Building, Iowa City
(319) 384-0732

For something completely different, take a trip back in time by visiting ancient mounds in Iowa. Learn about the culture, rituals and society of the Native American Woodlanders.

Best Club
The Garden
112 E. 4th St., Des Moines
(515) 243-3965

Dance the night away at the best dance club in Des Moines. They're also known for foam parties (for when you're feeling a little bit wild).

Best After Hours Place
Mannings Bar & Grill
202 Indianola Ave., Des Moines
(515) 288-0030

This south-side bar features a late night happy hour from 1 A.M.. to 2 A.M.. They serve appetizers until the wee hours as well.

Best Special Occasion Restaurant
Bistro Montage
2724 Ingersoll Ave., Des Moines
(515) 557-1924 • www.bistromontage.com

A blend of American and French cuisine, the risotto is exquisite; the duck divine. For a special treat, try the Banana Brule.

Best Place To Buy a Gift
Chocolate Storybook
1000 Grand Ave., W. Des Moines
(515) 226-9893

Featuring decadent, homemade chocolates and creative gifts, Chocolate Storybook is a shopping (and chocolate lover's) dream!

Top Five Dates

#1. Adventureland Park
305 34th Ave., NW, Altoona
(515) 266-2121 • www.adventurelandpark.com
Imagine a day filled with magic shows, live music, great food and roller coasters! Feel like a kid again at this exciting adventure park.

#2. Varsity Theater
1207 25th St., Des Moines
(515) 277-0404
Dinner and a movie doesn't have to include the current blockbuster. Take a chance and enjoy an independent film or documentary at this great, old-fashioned theater.

#3. The Salisbury House
4025 Tonawanda Dr., Des Moines
(515) 274-1777
Tour historic Salisbury House, an English-style mansion with lovely gardens. It's the perfect place to take a walk and get to know each other better.

#4. Des Moines Botanical Center
909 E. River Dr., Des Moines
(515) 323-8900
Spend a quiet afternoon enjoying the Bonsai collection, a vast array of tropical and desert plants and watching the free-flying birds in the dome.

#5. Iowa Cubs Baseball
One Line Dr., Des Moines
(515) 243-6111 • www.iowacubs.com
Catch a ballgame, and maybe even a foul ball! This excellent AAA ball club (an affiliate of the Chicago

Cubs) provides tons of excitement from energetic, young baseball players.

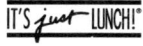

Detroit

Best Restaurant for Lunch or Brunch First Date
The Grill at the Ritz-Carlton
300 Town Center Dr., Dearborn
(313) 441-2100 • www.ritzcarlton.com
Sunday's Champagne Brunch features made-to-order omelets and fresh seafood salads. Saturday afternoon tea offers cucumber sandwiches, scones and raspberries with cream.

Best Restaurant for First Dinner Date
Rochester Chop House
306 N. Main St., Rochester
(248) 651-2266 • www.kruseandmuerrestaurants.com
This is an elegant downtown restaurant with an extensive menu, from premium steaks to fresh seafood, as well as live piano music to add a bit of ambience.

Best Cheap Date
Local Wine Events
www.localwineevents.com
This website lists local wine-tasting events throughout the year, many paired with lovely dinners. Paesano's patio, for instance, holds fabulous tastings throughout the summer.

Best Restaurant for a Second Dinner Date
The Gandy Dancer
401 Depot St., Ann Arbor
(734) 769-0592 • www.muer.com
In the Michigan Central Depot train station, this quiet romantic spot has four separate dining rooms and is renowned for its fine seafood.

Best Place for Coffee and Dessert
Café de Troit
1260 Library St., Detroit
(313) 962-8050 • www.cafedetroit.com
This neighborhood coffee shop offers soup, sandwiches and a variety of sweets. You can even see their resident chiropractor on Tuesday and Thursday mornings!

Best Place for a Laugh
Chaplin's Comedy Club
34244 Groesbeck, Clinton Township
(586) 792-1902 • www.chaplinscomedyclub.com

Along with Whoop It Up Thursdays, Chaplin's has a variety of special events and headliners. You can even hire a comic for your own event or fundraiser.

Best Creative Date
Michigan Star Clipper Dinner Train
840 N. Pontiac Tr., Walled Lake
(248) 960-9440 • www.michiganstarclipper.com

Enjoy five-course meals prepared on board during your three-hour journey. The trip includes a performance of a musical or a murder mystery.

Best Club
The Cavern Club and Millennium
210 S. 1st, Ann Arbor
(734) 332-9900

Three clubs in one! The Cavern Club books the best in R&B bands; in Millennium, high-energy techno flows from the DJ; and the Circus Bar is brand-new sports bar.

Best After Hours Place
Crave Lounge Restaurant & Sake Bar
22075 Michigan Ave., Dearborn
(313) 277-7283 • www.cravelounge.com

For sensual dining in a luxurious setting, this newly opened lounge offers gourmet sushi with a Mediterranean twist — and draws singles of all ages.

Best Special Occasion Restaurant
The Palm
5600 Crooks Rd., Troy
(248) 813-7256

For huge lobsters, this is the place. Feast on surf and turf and a bowl of lobster bisque while you see how many caricatures of local celebrities you can identify.

Best Place To Buy a Gift

Blossoms Floral Design
34200 Woodward Ave., Birmingham
(248) 644-4411 • www.blossomsbirmingham.com

Beautiful floral arrangements appear as natural as if they just came in from the garden. Blossoms can also create gift baskets.

Top Five Dates

#1. Greektown
Monroe St., Detroit

Can't make it to Greece for an evening's entertainment? Feel like you're in Greece for the price of parking. Food, music and a casino line this street — a wonderful way to get away from it all and never leave Detroit.

#2. Comerica Park
2100 Woodward Ave., Detroit
(313) 967-4000 • http://detroit.tigers.mlb.com

This home of the Detroit Tigers is no ordinary stadium: it combines theme park, ballpark and a baseball museum with huge statues of tigers, a Ferris wheel, a carousel (with tigers of course) and a fountain that celebrates each home run with a display of colored lights and music.

#3. Hazel Park Raceway
1650 E. 10 Mile Rd., Hazel Park
(248) 398-1000 • www.hazelparkraceway.com

An entertainment complex has replaced the original grandstand and now you can enjoy the excitement of harness racing and a wonderful dining experience, as well as bands, BBQ and more.

#4. Wine Creation
31049 Dequindre Rd., Madison Heights
(248) 307-9463 • www.winecreations.com

Come taste the wonderful Chiantis, merlots and Rieslings produced by this winery. Then, make your own labels to create your own private-label wine.

#5. New Detroit Science Center
   5020 John R St., Detroit
   (313) 577-8400 • www.sciencedetroit.org
   Go on a trip to the stars and beyond at the New Detroit Science Center's IMAX dome or planetarium, or just by watching the stars in the park. Romance and adventure lie just beyond the doors.

East Bay

Best Restaurant for Lunch or Brunch First Date
La Tapatia
1802 Willow Pass Rd., Concord
(925) 685-1985

With over 125 tequilas and a terra-cotta patio surrounded by flower-filled planters, this is a one of a kind lunch spot.

Best Restaurant for First Dinner Date
Jordan's at the Claremont Resort
41 Tunnel Rd., Berkeley
(510) 843-3000
www.claremontresort.com

Romantic views of the Bay and the San Francisco skyline combined with the incredible entrees available make this the top spot on the Bay for dinner and more.

Best Cheap Date
Zachary's Chicago Pizza
5801 College at Oak Grove, Berkeley
Other locations: Berkeley
(510) 655-6385

This is the Bay's best stuffed pizza and calzones in an interesting setting.

Best Restaurant for a Second Dinner Date
Garibaldis
5356 College Ave. at Manila Ave., Oakland
(510) 595-4000

Wonderful, California-Mediterranean food, infused vodkas, tempting desserts, and celebrity sightings make this one of your 'can't miss' destinations.

Best Place for Coffee and Dessert
Fatapple's Restaurant and Bakery
1346 Martin Luther King Jr. Way, Berkeley
(510) 526-2260

Fatapple's Restaurant and Bakery offers inviting cakes,

cookies, pastries, great coffee, and also a nice place to sit and get to know one another.

Best Place for a Laugh
Mingles Martini and Champagne Lounge
370 Embarcadero, Jack London Sq., Oakland
(510) 835-3900

This is more than just a comedy club. This is a fun locale with a great crowd, a sultry setting, and a full bar to enjoy.

Best Creative Date
Rooster T. Feathers Comedy Club
157 W. El Camino Real, Sunnyvale
(408) 736-0921 • www.roostertfeathers.com

They have courses for comics of any level that want to learn about the business of stand-up as well as performance improvement.

Best Club
Eli's Mile High Club
3629 Martin Luther King Jr. Way, Oakland
(510) 655-6161 • www.elisblues.com

This is a true West Coast roadhouse full of great blues music and people who love to dance and party.

Best After Hours Place
Pring's
15015 E. 14th St., San Leandro
(510) 351-3266

This is a quiet haven in which to kick back, talk, and explore each other after a busy night out.

Best Special Occasion Restaurant
The Purple Plum
4228 Park Blvd., Oakland in Oakland's Glenview Village
(510) 336-0990 • www.thepurpleplum.com

A changing, seasonal menu of California 'soul' food such as seafood, vegetarian specials, coconut cream pie, or choco-brownie cookies ensure that you'll have a great meal.

Best Place To Buy a Gift
Happy Trails
1354 Park St., Oakland
(510) 864-BANG • www.shophappytrails.com

This is a great store for fun toys, interesting gifts, and a wide variety of T-shirts from retro to rock and roll.

Top Five Dates

#1. Floating Fantasy
Gondola Servizio
568 Bellevue Ave., Oakland
(510) 663-6603
www.gondolaservizio.com

Imagine you're in Venice aboard an authentic gondola hand built in Venice. These private, romantic cruises come complete with serenading gondoliers. Mama mia!

#2. Rafting and Rolling
Wilderness Adventures
(530) 926-6282
(800) 323-RAFT

Experience an adventure in a white-water raft on some of California's best rivers. Rafting gives you the chance to work, get wet, laugh, and see natural beauty together.

#3. Bye-Bye Biplane
Golden Gate Biplane Adventures
(650) 325-3253
www.flySF.com

Take that special person up for a spin in an open cockpit biplane and see the world from a totally different view. You'll never regret or forget this fantastic flight!

#4. A Pair in the Park
Tilden Park
Grizzly Peak Blvd. at Shasta Rd., Berkeley
www.EBParks.org

Tilden Park has something for everyone: horseback riding, great views, and places to feed the ducks. Wander the trails together and enjoy a sweet day in the park.

#5. *Small Boat Sailing At the Berkeley Marina*
Cal Sailing Club
Berkeley Marina, 201 University Ave., Berkeley
www.cal-sailing.org

Spend a lazy day on the water enjoying the great views and calm breezes. Pack a picnic basket and make sure you stay for the sunsets. The view is the best in the Bay.

Greenville / Spartanburg

Best Restaurant for Lunch or Brunch First Date
Italian Market & Grill
534 Woods Lake Rd., Greenville
(864) 234-8464
http://www.italianmarketandgrill.com/img-sc/index.html
They have so many good lunch items that you just might be there until dinner! It's a nice place to sit, drink wine, nibble on wonderful Italian foods and get to know each other.

Best Restaurant for First Dinner Date
Portofino's Italian Restaurant
3795 E. North St., Greenville
(864) 268-9432
Candlelight, a subtle décor, fantastic food, an extensive wine list, incredible garlic rolls and a cozy atmosphere for conversation make this an ideal first dinner date location.

Best Cheap Date
Beacon Drive-In
255 Reidville Rd., Spartanburg
(864) 585-9387 • www.beacondrivein.com
This is the most fun for the money around: They claim to serve more iced tea than any restaurant, have the best chili-cheeseburger you'll ever eat and offer curb service!

Best Restaurant for a Second Dinner Date
Ellis An American Bistro
148 West Main St., Spartanburg
(864) 948-9333
Whatever you're in the mood for it's here, whether it's Mediterranean, Middle Eastern, French or American, they do it well. Add pianos, jazz, and a cigar bar and it's complete!

Best Place for Coffee and Dessert
Strossner's Bakery
21 Roper Mountain Rd., Greenville
(864) 233-3996 • www.strossners.com

If you've got a sweet tooth, this is your place. Since 1947, Strossners has made bakery goodies that are delicate and delicious, like their Italian cream cake with amaretto.

Best Place for a Laugh
Café and Then Some
101 College St., Greenville
(864) 232-2287 • www.cafeats.com

Eat a great dinner here, then watch a hilarious comedy troupe that has been creating laughter since 1978. It's all original and it's all funny; it's a wonderful evening out.

Best Creative Date
Issaqueena Falls/Stumphouse Mountain Tunnel
Highway 28, Walhalla
(864) 638-4343

See one of the most beautiful falls anywhere, and visit a Civil War-era tunnel where Clemson University used to make blue cheese. You'll have plenty to talk about, too.

Best Club
Handlebar
304 E. Stone Ave., Greenville
(864) 233-6173 • http://www.handlebar-online.com

Whatever your musical tastes, you'll find it right here — it's always exciting. You can eat, drink, listen to a live band, take lessons and meet many eligible people.

Best After Hours Place
Friends
112 N. Main St., Anderson
(864) 231-0663

You've got to try Friends for their late-night menu of 'food with flair.' It's well worth your time and is a very short drive. Check out their weekend entertainment.

Best Special Occasion Restaurant
33 Liberty
33 Liberty Lane, Greenville
(864) 370-4888 • www.33liberty.com

Owned by a married pair of nationally known chefs, 33

Liberty presents food that is beyond belief! The culinary creativity and eclectic menus are exquisite.

Best Place To Buy a Gift
Ayers Leather Shops
201 N. Main St., Greenville
(864) 232-9463 • www.ayersleather.com

If you can't find a gift for someone here, you won't find one anywhere! They offer a fantastic variety of leather and other items from around the world, and will ship, too!

Top Five Dates

#1. To the Max
33 Liberty
33 Liberty Lane, Greenville
(864) 370-4888 • www.33liberty.com

For a night you'll never forget, make a reservation at 33 Liberty. It's the way you've always thought a restaurant should be, especially when you really want it to be incredible. Owned by a married pair of nationally known chefs, 33 Liberty presents food that is beyond belief! The culinary creativity and eclectic menus are exquisite.

#2. Meet Your Relatives
Greenville Zoo
150 Cleveland Park Dr., Greenville
(864) 467-4300 • www.greenvillezoo.com/menu.htm

It's great fun to walk along, hand in hand, and try to figure out what people you know look (or act) like that chimp (silly), that lion (haughty) or that orangutan (bewildered). You'll find plenty to talk about, laugh about and think about. It's great fun!

#3. Talking and Listening
Handlebar
304 East Stone Ave., Greenville
(864) 233-6173 • http://www.handlebar-online.com/

If you both like music, just check the calendar at Handlebar and pick your date. They have an extraordinary range of musical types and talents from which to choose. And you can sit, sip a drink and talk outside the Listening Room. You're sure to have a great time!

#4. Home is Where the Heart Is
Dinner for Two
Your Place

If you want to show that special someone a special time, prepare dinner at home. He or she really will appreciate it. It's a great chance to talk without interruptions. And if you're attentive enough to think of champagne, candles and good music, it can be a night neither of you will ever forget!

#5. Get Out, Get Out
The mountains, foothills, lakes and rivers

You're in a gorgeous area, so go see it. It's a great way to spend an afternoon or weekend. You've got more lakes, rivers, waterfalls, mountains and beautiful views than you'll ever get around to seeing. Take two hours or two days — it's just the two of you in the car, talking, looking, commenting, questioning and getting to know each other!

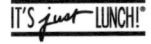

Harrisburg and Central Pennsylvania

Best Restaurant for Lunch or Brunch First Date
Raspberries Rotisserie — Hilton Harrisburg and Towers
One N. 2nd St., Harrisburg
(717) 233-6000

Raspberries Rotisserie — Hilton Harrisburg and Towers has casual American dining at moderate prices. It offers an elaborate lunch buffet for busy professionals on the go.

Best Restaurant for First Dinner Date
Fire House Restaurant
606 N. 2nd St., Harrisburg
(717) 234-6064

Fire House is located in the completely restored, original 1871 Harrisburg Firehouse. They specialize in American eclectic cuisine with moderate pricing.

Best Cheap Date
Select Medical IMAX Theatre
222 Market St., Harrisburg
(717) 214-ARTS • www.whitakercenter.org/imax

This IMAX Theatre has the largest floor to ceiling images and state of the art surround sound you will find in this area.

Best Restaurant for a Second Dinner Date
Fisaga's
201 N. 2nd St., Harrisburg
(717) 441-1556

This is an open air bar located on 2nd street. Glass garage doors close during the winter and will make you feel like you are always in the middle of the action.

Best Place for Coffee and Dessert
Cocoa Beanery and Hotel Hershey
Hershey
(717) 534-8800 • www.hotelhershey.com

Cocoa Beanery and Hotel Hershey offer specialty coffees, chocolate pastries, and Hershey hot chocolate. This is great place to start the day.

Best Place for a Laugh
Doc Holiday's — Harrisburg's Comedy Zone
Limekiln Rd., New Cumberland
(717) 920-3627 • www.harrisburgcomedyzone.com

This is a new comedy club which plans to attract the nation's best comedians on Friday and Saturday nights. It's a fun spot any night of the week.

Best Creative Date
Hershey Park
100 Hershey Park Rd., Hershey
(800) HERSHEY • www.hersheypark.com

Hershey Park offers year round entertainment. There are amusement park rides, top name act and a musical laser spectacular, "The Sweetest Parade on Earth."

Best Club
Dragonfly
234 N. 2nd St., Harrisburg
(717) 232-6940

Here is a taste of South Beach in Central Pennsylvania. This is Harrisburg's biggest nightclub. The first floor has a circular bar. The second features a glossy dance floor.

Best After Hours Place
Coyote Hardware Bar
240 N. 2nd St., Harrisburg
(717) 221-0530

Come and enjoy the wild and crazy atmosphere from the film Coyote Ugly. Enjoy music while pole dancing on the bar.

Best Special Occasion Restaurant
Parev
215 Pine St., Harrisburg
(717) 920-1800 • www.parevrestaurant.com

Parev offers a unique dining experience which features

European contemporary cuisine. They are also known for their excellent California and French wines.

Best Place To Buy a Gift
Strawberry Square
11 N. 3rd St., Harrisburg
(717) 236-8975

There are many shops available at this convenient, popular downtown Harrisburg location. Strawberry Square is great for the busy professional.

Top Five Dates

#1. Penn State Games

Pack up the car and plan on a day of tailgating prior to the Penn State Games. This is a great way to introduce some of your friends. Go with a group or meet friends later. After the game, enjoy the excitement of the Allen Street and College Avenue area in State College. Choose from one of the many restaurants and go for the nightlife.

#2. Name a Star

A great date doesn't have to break the bank. Pick a romantic spot to look at the sky and name your star together and wish on it forever. You will melt her heart. The International Star Registry, at www.star-registry.com, is a star naming resource that allows you to name an actual star.

#3. Sitting on Top of the World

Enjoy the beauty and tranquility of a balloon ride with your date. The Great American Hot Air Balloon Ride starts with watching the inflation of the beautiful balloon. This is followed by a gentle ascent up to between 500 and 1000 feet After landing, champagne.

#4. Create Your Own Amusement

Spend a day at Hershey Park or Kneobel's Amusement Park in Elysburg. Release your inner child and have a great time. Go for a spin on the Ferris wheel, scream your head off on the roller coaster, or become an instant hero and win a teddy bear. Kneobel's and Hershey Park offer many opportunities for exciting dates throughout the year.

#5. *Winter Skiing*

We're lucky enough to be within driving range of a variety of ski resorts that can be a perfect winter wonderland date. Enjoy the breathtaking view together from the top of the mountain and the exhilarating run down the slope. Relax by the fire in the lodge.

Hartford / New Haven

Best Restaurant for Lunch or Brunch First Date
The Saybrook Point Inn and Spa
2 Bridge Street, Saybrook
(860) 395-2000
http://www.saybrook.com/saybrook_point_inn.html

With its laid-back atmosphere and superior hospitality, the Inn is the place to get to know each other over brunch. Excellent food and service with a beautiful view of the water.

Best Restaurant for First Dinner Date
Bella Nadia
764 East Main Street, Branford
(203) 481-5170

Bella Nadia is a great secret hideaway that no one knows about! Romantic and reasonable!

Best Cheap Date
Close Harbor Seafood
959 Meriden Waterbury Turnpike, Plantsville
(860) 621-7334

It's actually a fish and seafood market, but also has eat-in or takeout meals. Really fresh seafood, cooked to perfection! Great, reasonable daily specials.

Best Restaurant for a Second Dinner Date
Bee & Thistle Inn
100 Lyme Street, Old Lyme
(800) 622-4946 • www.beeandthistleinn.com

Impress your date with a wondrous dinner at the Bee & Thistle. Superb cuisine, attentive service, lovely surroundings and extremely romantic!

Best Place for Coffee and Dessert

Daybreak Coffee Roasters, Inc.
2377 Main Street, Glastonbury
(860) 657-4466 • www.daybreakcoffee.com

Daybreak roasts its own coffee in small batches to ensure quality and freshness. Nibble on a homemade pastry at the espresso bar with a cup of coffee, tea or an espresso.

Best Place for a Laugh

City Steam Brewery
942 Main Street, Hartford
(860) 525-1600 • www.citysteam.com

Offering a pleasant change, City Steam presents a comedy club that hosts some of today's hottest comics. These weekend performances are popular, so reservations are advised.

Best Creative Date

Dinosaur State Park
400 West Street, Rocky Hill
(860) 529-8423 • www.dinosaurstatepark.org

Beneath the dome, there's an exceptional display of early Jurassic fossil tracks that were made 200 million years ago. Outside are more than two miles of nature trails.

Best Club

The Midnight Sun Cafe
7 Water Street, Torrington
(860) 489-3116

There is a cool little hole in the wall up in Torrington. They have live Rock music on weekends and no cover charge. Just around the corner from the Warner Theatre.

Best After Hours Place

Gotham Citi
130 Crown Street, New Haven
(203) 498-2484

Gotham is the hottest and most dependable club by far and it stays open the latest. The place to be after everything else closes. Drop-dead hipness!

Best Special Occasion Restaurant
Cavey's
45 E. Center Street, Manchester
(860) 643-2751

Owned by the same family for several generations, Cavey's French restaurant is simply the best in cuisine and ambiance. Marriage proposals often take place here. Divine.

Best Place To Buy a Gift
Honore Gallery
995 Farmington Ave # B, West Hartford
(860) 232-3306

The unusual is usual at Honore. There is something for everyone here and whatever it is, you won't see it anywhere else. The service is delightful. They make shopping fun.

Five Great Dates

#1. *Abbott's Lobster in the Rough*
  117 Pearl Street, Groton
  (860) 536-7719
  Lunch or dinner outdoors on the Mystic River, sit at a picnic table and watch the boats go by. The freshest lobster. Bring your own champagne, breathe deeply and relax.

#2. *The West Hartford Reservoir*
  Farmington Avenue, West Hartford
  1.5 miles from West Hartford Center
  Not very far from downtown Hartford lies a beautiful getaway spot. Pack a picnic, meander the trails, sit by the water and watch the sun set. Serenity and beauty.

#3. *The Carousel in Bushnell Park*
  Bushnell Park, downtown Hartford
  (860) 585-5411
  On a beautiful day, spend time riding on the jewel of downtown Hartford. The most you'll ever get for 50 cents. Then see what's showing at the Pump House Gallery.

#4. *Mark Twain House*
  351 Farmington Ave., Hartford
  (860) 247-0998
  Admit it, you've never been there. It's a great date

place. No worries about creating conversation; the house itself will give you lots to talk about. Guided tours are offered.

#5. *The Peabody Museum of Natural History*
170 Whitney Avenue, New Haven
(203) 432-5050 • http://www.peabody.yale.edu

A glorious adventure on a winter's afternoon. A big museum with a cozy feeling. A place to wander around and whisper into each other's ear. Then have pizza at Pepe's or Sally's.

Honolulu

Best Restaurant for Lunch or Brunch First Date
Hoku's at the Kahala Mandarin Oriental Hotel
5000 Kahala Ave., Honolulu
(808) 739-8780 • www.mandarinoriental.com/kahala

Sip champagne and nibble local style poke for brunch. Afterwards, go and hang out at the dolphin pool.

Best Restaurant for First Dinner Date
Don Ho's Island Grill
101 Ala Moana Blvd., Honolulu
(808) 528-0807 • www.donho.com

Yes, the Tiny Bubbles man himself has a casual place to hang at the Aloha Tower Marketplace. The memorabilia on the walls always makes for a good conversation starter.

Best Cheap Date
Iolani Palace
364 S. King St., Honolulu
(808) 538-1471 • www.iolanipalace.org

Take a guided or self-guided tour and show your date the home of ancient Hawaiian royalty. Every Friday during lunch hour, the Royal Hawaiian Band plays for free.

Best Restaurant for a Second Dinner Date
Sarento's Top of the "I"
1777 Ala Moana Blvd., Honolulu
(808) 955-5559

If you can divert your attention from the mind-boggling views of Diamond Head and the Honolulu skyline from the top of the Ilikai Hotel, try the Osso Bucco or lobster ravioli.

Best Place for Coffee and Dessert
Leonard's Bakery
933 Kapahulu Ave., Honolulu
(808) 737-9951 • www.leonardshawaii.com

Leonard's is famous for its malasadas (Hawaiian doughnuts). The cream-filled one is really good; just be prepared for a bit of a sugar overload.

Best Place for a Laugh
Society of Seven at the Outrigger Waikiki Hotel
2335 Kalakaua Ave., Honolulu
(808) 923-0711

This popular ensemble puts on a fast-paced show featuring show tunes, local songs, impersonations and hilarious comedy skits.

Best Creative Date
Snorkel at Hanauma Bay
7455 Kalanianaole Highway, Honolulu
(808) 395-2211 • www.hanaumabay-hawaii.com

Follow the signs to one of the most beautiful natural marine reserves in the world. Hint: venture around the left-side to the "blowhole," but watch your step!

Best Club
Esprit Lounge in the Sheraton Waikiki
2255 Kalakaua Ave., Honolulu
(808) 944-4422 • www.sheraton-waikiki.com

As popular as the Waikiki Beach it overlooks, Esprit is lively, upscale and jamming with DJs as well as live rock and hip-hop acts.

Best After Hours Place
Liliha Bakery
515 Kuakini St., Honolulu
(808) 531-1651

Open all hours Tuesday through Sunday, Liliha Bakery offers local home-style grub like stew bowls. Step back into the '60s with countertop service.

Best Special Occasion Restaurant
La Mer at the Halekulani Hotel and Resort
2199 Kalia Rd., Honolulu
(808) 923-2311 • www.halekulani.com

La Mer is very sophisticated, very romantic and very French. And the panoramic view of Diamond Head is a perfect setting for any special intimate occasion.

Best Place To Buy a Gift

The Little Hawaiian Craft Shop
2201 Kalakaua Ave., Honolulu
(808) 926-2662

This shop in the Royal Hawaiian Shopping Center has lots of little knick-knacks, but the koa woodcarvings by local artists are the best.

Top Five Dates

#1. Chill Out
Ice Palace
4510 Salt Lake Blvd., Aiea
(808) 487-9921 • www.icepalacehawaii.com

There aren't too many chances to see ice in Hawaii — well, except in drinks. Even if you don't like to skate, or simply can't, the Ice Place is a great place to keep cool on blistering summer days.

#2. Swim with Flipper
The Kahala Mandarin Oriental Hotel
5000 Kahala Ave., Honolulu
(808) 739-8888 • www.mandarin-oriental.com

Take your date for a swim with six bottlenose dolphins in this twenty-six thousand-square foot natural lagoon. You will never look at dolphins the same again after swimming up close with them.

#3. Go See Pali
The Pali Lookout, Windward Oahu
www.hawaii-guide.com/oahu

The breathtaking lookout provides a spectacular view of the Koolau mountain range. But grab your date on hold on tight; it is so windy that adults are actually advised to hold the hands of children.

#4. Follow the Whales
Wild Side Specialty Tours,
Waianae Boat Harbor, Slip A-11, Honolulu
(808) 306-7273 • www.sailhawaii.com

See the whales up close December through March. It's absolutely mind-boggling to see animals this smart and this big swim this fast and jump completely out of the water.

#5. Be Tourist for a Day
Take a day trip to another island. Go to Kauai and tour the Na Pali coast. Or, visit Maui and take a long walk through Lahaina. It's not a cheap date, but it's a lot of fun to see how completely unique each island is.

Indianapolis

Best Restaurant for Lunch or Brunch First Date
Loughmiller's Pub & Eatery
301 W. Washington St., Indianapolis
(317) 638-7380

Loughmiller's is a great, independent pub, and they serve a succulent English Beef Sandwich that makes a perfect lunch.

Best Restaurant for First Dinner Date
Agio
635 Massachusetts Ave., Indianapolis
(317) 488-0359

Mediterranean and Italian fare is even more enjoyable when you dine alfresco at any time of the year. Agio has a covered, heated patio! Reservations recommended.

Best Cheap Date
El Sol de Tala Mexican Restaurante y Cantina
2444 E. Washington St., Indianapolis
(317) 635-8252

Dine on homemade tortillas and tender, pulled pork and beef. On weekends, sit back with a margarita while listening to the live mariachi band.\

Best Restaurant for a Second Dinner Date
Rick's Café Boatyard
4050 Dandy Trail, Indianapolis
(317) 290-9300

It may be the perfect Indy surf and turf restaurant, but it's the quiet conversation as the sun sets over Eagle Creek Reservoir that will make a lasting impression.

Best Place for Coffee and Dessert
Shapiro's Delicatessen
808 S. Meridian St., Indianapolis
(317) 631-4041

Let the layered cakes, cookies and pies tempt your sweet

tooth at this city landmark. Be sure to try the house specialty, The Hoosier Mud Pie — a chocolate dream.

Best Place for a Laugh
Mystery Café
231 S. College Ave., Indianapolis
(317) 684-0668 • www.themysterycafeindy.com

Who knew a four-course meal could be such "killer" fun? This interactive dinner show is sure to keep you guessing and laughing through the night.

Best Creative Date
The Fountain Room
1103 Shelby St., Indianapolis
(317) 685-1959

Who says dressing up is just for kids? Dress your 40s best and head to The Fountain Room and have a great time swing dancing to the big band on Saturday nights.

Best Club
The Vogue
6259 N. College Ave., Indianapolis
(317) 259-7029

Get up and dance at this Indy hotspot. Locals swear the Wednesday Night Retro Rewind is not to be missed. And the live acts vary from local bands to major headliners.

Best After Hours Place
The Mirage Nightclub
4514 S. Emerson Ave., Indianapolis
(317) 782-3300

Dine, dance and drink the night away. Open until 3 A.M., The Mirage has great live music on Fridays and Saturdays.

Best Special Occasion Restaurant
Keystone Grill
8650 Keystone Crossing, Indianapolis
(317) 848-5202

Savor the pecan-crusted salmon as you enjoy the sophisticated ambiance of the Keystone Grill. They also offer a spectacular wine list for whatever you wish to celebrate.

Best Place To Buy a Gift
Circle Center
49 W. Maryland St., Indianapolis
(317) 681-8000

Circle Center has it all, including major retailers and many independent shops. You're sure to find the perfect gift for anyone in this downtown shopping center.

Top Five Dates

#1. Holcomb Observatory
Butler University
4600 Sunset Ave., Indianapolis
(800) 368-6852

Take a closer look at the stars at the Holcomb Observatory, one of the largest public observatories in the world. You'll never look at the night sky the same way again.

#2. Indianapolis Civic Theatre
Marian College
3200 Cold Spring Rd., Indianapolis
(317) 923-4597

Do something completely different — spend an evening at the theatre. Whether you laugh at a farce or cry at a tragedy, be sure to experience the thrill of live entertainment.

#3. Indianapolis Zoo & White River Gardens
1200 W. Washington St., Indianapolis
(317) 630-2001

Spend an afternoon monkeying around at the zoo or stroll through the lush gardens on more than a mile and a half of beautiful pathways. And be sure to say "hi" to Brutus the Walrus.

#4. Clermont Deluxe
10310 E. Hwy. 136, Indianapolis
(317) 291-1560

Why not do something different and see a movie at the drive-in? Go back in time, cuddle up in the car and pretend you're on your very first date — ever!

#5. The Backwards Date
Be silly and order everything backwards. Order

dessert first and ask for the salad last. Or better still, meet your date for dessert, head to a matinee, and then dinner.

Houston

Best Restaurant for Lunch or Brunch First Date
Back Street Café
1103 South Shepherd Dr., Houston
(713) 521-2239 • www.backstreetcafe.net

Sante magazine awarded them Best Bistro Wine List in the U. S. A. — that's impressive! If you're not in the mood for wine, try their Jazz Brunches on Saturdays and Sundays.

Best Restaurant for First Dinner Date
La Colombe D'Or
3410 Montrose Blvd., Houston
(713) 524-7999

The most romantic dining destination in Houston has a modern French-inspired menu, superlative food, and impeccable service.

Best Cheap Date
Café Caspian
12126 Westheimer Rd. #100, Houston
(281) 493-4000 • www.cafecaspian.com

Try exotic Persian foods in a bistro-like décor. Try the kabobs if it's your first time. Don't order appetizers; they offer a complimentary feta cheese plate with taftoon bread.

Best Restaurant for a Second Dinner Date
Rouge
812 Westheimer Rd., Houston
(713) 520-7955 • www.rougehouston.com

The fare is a bit exotic here — duck breast, rabbit, and stuffed calamari for example. But if you're willing to be a little adventurous, it's really quite delicious!

Best Place for Coffee and Dessert
King Biscuit Patio Cafe
1606 White Oak Dr., Houston
(713) 861-2328
http://www.kingbiscuitcafe.com/about_us.html

What could be better than enjoying a spectacular view of

the white oak greenbelt while you sample the delights of Neapolitan cheesecake?

Best Place for a Laugh
Great Caruso Dinner Theatre
10001 Westheimer Rd., Houston
(713) 780-4900 • www.houstondinnertheatre.com

A sophisticated venue with Victorian antiques, crystal chandeliers, and marble staircases that offers a three-course meal with a musical comedy show.

Best Creative Date
Texas Air Adventures
Meets at West Oak Mall, Houston
(281) 379-3165 • www.texasaa.com

Enjoy a sunrise champagne brunch after you fly over western Texas in a balloon. Neither of you will ever forget this experience. E-mail Info@TexasAA.com for details.

Best Club
Hush Club
15625 Katy Frwy., Houston
(713) 330-4874 • www.hushonline.com

Without questions, this is the best club in the west side of town, with over 48 plasma TVs and four levels in which to roam. The fun never stops.

Best After Hours Place
Chachos Mexican Restaurant
6006 Westheimer Rd., Houston
(713) 975-9699

You've got to try this wonderful 24-hour Mexican restaurant that offers great margaritas, sizzling fajita platters, and some very cheesy quesadillas.

Best Special Occasion Restaurant
Vargo's International
2401 Fondren Rd., Houston
(713) 782-3888

With eight acres of plush lakeside garden, this gorgeous establishment can accommodate every request from birthdays to a marriage proposal.

Best Place To Buy a Gift
The Chocolate Bar
1835 W. Alabama St., Houston
(713) 520-8599

They have chocolate covered everything: fruit, potato chips, popcorn, ice cream, and fortune cookies. The chocolate flower makes a lovely gift.

Top Five Dates

#1. Lost in Space
Space Center Houston
1601 NASA Rd. 1, Houston
(281) 244-2100 • www.spacecenter.org/hours.html

There was a time when every little boy (and some little girls) wanted to be an astronaut when they grew up. Come to the Space Center and help your date to a small taste of what it would really be like. Direct the space shuttle and use the Excursion Module trainer used by Apollo space explorers. There are tons of things to do here, even an Imax movie theater. As a fun romantic date, this one is to the moon and back!

#2. That's Entertainment!
Theatre Under The Stars
800 Bagby St., Suite 200, Houston
(713) 558-8887 • www.tuts.com

Nobody can resist a good musical, and Theater Under the Stars brings you some of the best. Hold hands with your date while the actors sing love songs to each other. And if it's summer, see one of their shows for free at Miller Outdoor Theatre in Hermann Park.

#3. Whose Line Is It Anyway?
ComedySportz Houston
901 Town & Country Blvd., Houston
(713) 868-1444 • www.comedysportzhouston.com

There's one sport everybody loves: ComedySportz. Two teams of improvisers battle for laughs and points through scenes, games, and songs based on audience suggestions. The real winners? You and your date as you laugh together, of course.

#4. *Set Sail*
   Port of Houston and Ship Channel
   7300 Clinton Dr., Houston
   (713) 670-2609

   See Houston from the water. Enjoy the gentle rocking of the boat, try to see where you live, smell the salt air, and enjoy the grandeur and majesty that Houston offers from the sea.

#5. *Kids For a Day*
   Six Flags Astroworld
   9001 Kirby Dr., Houston
   (713) 799-1234
   www.sixflags.com/parks/astroworld/index.asp

   When's the last time you screamed your head off? Grab some cotton candy, your date's hand, and go to Six Flags Astroworld. Get wet at the Waterworld, or dizzy rushing through the air on SWAT (it looks like a giant fly swatter). Let loose and be a kid again. Your date will love seeing this side of you!

Jackson

Best Restaurant for Lunch or Brunch First Date
Nick's Restaurant
1501 Lakeland Dr., Jackson
(601) 981-8017 • www.nicksrestaurant.com

Known as one of the best restaurants in Jackson for the last fifteen years. Phenomenal lunch specials in an elegant setting make this the perfect spot for a first date.

Best Restaurant for First Dinner Date
Steam Room Grille
5402 I-55 North East Frontage Road, Jackson
(601) 899-8588 • www.steamroomgrille.com

You will not go home hungry after eating here. You can be rock inside or step onto the outside deck for a more intimate gathering. Tuck in that bib if you're having the lobster.

Best Cheap Date
Smith Robertson Museum & Cultural Center
528 Bloom St., Jackson
(601) 960-1457 • www.city.jackson.ms.us

Five bucks gets you an intimate look at the cultural significance of this beautiful city. Check out the history of the state's slavery and Civil War records.

Best Restaurant for a Second Dinner Date
Bravo!
Highland Village — Upper Level
I-55 North and Northside Dr., Jackson
(601) 982-8111 • www.bravobuzz.com

Step it up a notch if you get that chance for a second date. Be sure to brush up on your wine knowledge before perusing their extensive wine list.

Best Place for Coffee and Dessert
Flashbacks Espresso Café
5620 I-55 South (Siwell Road) Byrum
(601) 372-3220 • www.flashbacksespressocafe.com

Not only do they have gourmet espresso drinks and great desserts, they offer live entertainment.

Best Place for a Laugh
Rascals
Headliners Entertainment Resort
6107 Ridgewood Road, Jackson
(601) 957-6946 • www.rascalscomedyclub.com

Open Thursday, Friday and Saturday with reasonable ticket prices and hilarious live acts. Book your tickets online for your convenience.

Best Creative Date
Robert C. Davis Planetarium/Ronald E. Mcnair Space Theater
201 E Pascagoula St., Jackson
(601) 960-1550 • www.thedavisplanetarium.com

If you've never been to a planetarium/space theater, you have to check this place out. Extremely interesting exhibits and laser light shows are set to contemporary music.

Best Club
Rufus Restaurant & Lounge
1154 N Mill St., Jackson
(601) 354-0174

Get ready to get down and dirty, the Rufus way. Don't worry, there's always time to sleep tomorrow.

Best After Hours Place
Amerigo
6592 Old Canton Rd., Ridgeland
(601) 977-0563 • www.amerigo.net

Casually upscale contemporary Italian cuisine is served until 10:30 A.M. on weekends. Reservations not needed.

Best Special Occasion Restaurant
Fairview Inn
734 Fairview St., Jackson
(601) 948-3429 • www.fairviewinn.com

Chosen one of the Top 10 Most Romantic Inns by American Historic Inns, Inc., The Fairview lends elegance and style to any special occasion.

Best Place To Buy a Gift

A Balloon Basket &Gift Garden Downtown
206 W Pearl St., Jackson
(601) 969-6482 • www.myfsn.com/aballoonbasket

Specializes in flower arrangements for special occasions. Don't miss out on the gift baskets with fruits and cheeses!

Top Five Dates

#1. *It's America's Favorite Pastime!*
Jackson Generals
1200 Lakeland Dr., Smith-Wills Stadium
(601) 981-4664

Ok, so this isn't the Major Leagues, but it's close. Come eat hot dogs, drink beer and watch the Houston Astros' AA farm team. It's the only pro ball in Mississippi!

#2. *Add a little culture to your life*
Mississippi Symphony Orchestra
Mississippi Arts Center
201 E. Pascagoula St., Jackson
(601) 960-1565 • www.msorchestra.com

Do something a little unusual and take your date to the orchestra. Call for schedules that include touring orchestras and chamber music.

#3. *Spend an afternoon in the garden*
Mynelle Gardens
4736 Clinton Blvd., Jackson
(601) 960-1894 • www.city.jackson.ms.us.com

Astounding beauty and tranquility make this an attraction for artists and environment buffs from all over the world. Very romantic, indeed.

#4. *Shake off those Blues*
The Delta Blues Museum
(601) 627-6820 • www.deltabluesmuseum.org

This takes a few hours of driving, so you get a bonus road trip! One of the most culturally significant and insightful museums in the South.

#5. *See it from the sky*
    Balloon Promotions Incorporated
    Highway 82 E, Greenwood
    Enjoy another little road trip as you drive to Greenwood for a sky journey unlike anything you've ever experienced.

Jacksonville

Best Lunch or Brunch Date
b.b.'s
1019 Hendricks Ave., Jacksonville
(904) 306-0100

A casual yet first-rate place for that first date, b.b.'s offers a wide variety of outstanding food — from salads to pizza to seafood. The casual atmosphere let's you relax and talk, too.

Best First Dinner Date
First Street Grille
807 N. First St., Jacksonville Beach
(904) 246-6555

Enjoy great seafood and steaks on their patio overlooking the ocean. They've been rated one of Florida's Top 500 Restaurants—try them out and you'll understand why.

Best Cheap Date
Chowder Ted's
5215 Hecksher Dr., Jacksonville
(904) 714-6900

Enjoy delicious seafood, burgers, chowder (of course), and a variety of appetizers. Ted's has a great view of the water and it's easy on your wallet, too.

Best Restaurant for a Second Date and Beyond
Gene's Seafood
4000 Saint Johns Ave., Jacksonville
(904) 381-1414
Call for other locations

A great choice anytime, Gene's has some of the best seafood in the area plus large portions, friendly service, and scrumptious appetizers. Try the fried alligator and shrimp combo.

Best Place for Coffee and Dessert
Café Carmon
1986 San Marco Blvd, Jacksonville
(904) 399-4488

Whether your heart is set on the key lime tart or the crème brulee, you are sure to have a mouth watering dessert with great coffee at Café Carmon.

Best Place for a Laugh
The Comedy Zone
The Ramada Inn, 3130 Hartley Rd., Jacksonville
(904) 268-8080 • www.comedyzone.com

You can always count on the Comedy Zone for good laughs; they feature some of the best comedians around. The second and fourth Mondays are when the locals get to show off!

Best Creative Date
Diamond D Horse Stables
5901 Solomon Rd., Jacksonville
(904) 289-9331

Mosey along, talk, and enjoy the outdoors on horseback! It's the perfect way to spend a couple of hours, an afternoon, or if you're really adventurous, an overnight pack trip.

Best Club
Art Bar
1261 Kings St., Jacksonville
(904) 381-0686

The music ranges from indie rock to vintage Sinatra and there's artwork everywhere! This is a fun place where you can show your best moves on the lighted dance floor or just chill in the courtyard.

Best After-Hours Place
Crazy Horse Saloon
5800 Philips Hwy., Jacksonville
(904) 731-8892

This is more than just a country-western club with a mechanical bull; you can learn the two step, polka, and waltz here! They always have specials going on, especially for the ladies.

Best Special-Occasion Restaurant
Matthew's at San Marco
2107 Hendricks Ave., Jacksonville
(904) 396-9922

Delight in this four-star, four-diamond restaurant for any special occasion; you will be glad you did. Try the five course tasting menu paired with the appropriate wine.

Best Place to Buy a Gift
The Bombay Company, Regency Square Mall
9501 Arlington Expwy. Ste. #590, Jacksonville
(904) 721-4859 • www.bombayco.com
Call for other locations

The biggest problem here is the amount of time you spend browsing — there's so much to look at. They have a tremendous selection, in all price ranges and categories, for men and women.

Top Five Dates

#1. See you at the seaside
(904) 242-0024 • www.jacksonvillebeach.org
You're truly surrounded by water here, both freshwater and saltwater. Pick a spot, any spot, and just go walking. It's a great chance to talk without interruption, enjoy the fresh air, and really get to know your date. You can plan an activity or just play it by ear – you can't lose either way!

#2. You animal you!
Jacksonville Zoological Gardens
8605 Zoo Pkwy., Jacksonville
(904) 757-4462 • www.jaxzoo.org/home.asp
Like the song said, "it's all happening at the zoo," and this zoo is constantly busy. In addition to all of the wonderful Florida wildlife, like the jaguars, panthers, and alligators, you can see African animals galore — from birds and meerkats to great apes and elephants. With the recently added Australian exhibits, you get a look at some of the best from Down Under too.

#3. *Cure those two left feet*
First Coast Shag Club
P.O. Box 551424, Jacksonville
http://bellsouthpwp.net/j/a/janismylod/page6.html
Learn the true dance of the South — the Carolina Shag. These are the people who can really teach you — for free. Just check out their website for their schedule; most lessons are Wednesday and Sunday nights at the Marriot on Salisbury Road. What better way to spend an evening than holding your date's hand?

#4. *Charlie and the Chocolate Factory*
Whetstone Chocolate Factory
2 Coke Rd., St. Augustine
(904) 825-1710
Chocolate is for lovers. Take a forty-five minute tour of Whetstone Chocolate Factory and see how they make it. Smell the pralines and the fudge as you walk through the plant. You'll feel like a kid in a candy store. If you want to keep that feeling, drive ten minutes north on U.S. 1 and ride the carousel at Davenport Park (behind the library on San Carlos Rd).

#5. *Resorting to a restaurant*
The Grill Room
The Ritz-Carlton, 4750 Amelia Island Pkwy., Amelia Island
(904) 277-1100
www.ritzcarlton.com/resorts/amelia_island/
Take your time and enjoy this treat! One of only four AAA Five Diamond restaurants in the state, The Grill Room is about as close to perfection as you're going to come. Choose from over 500 wines, fresh seafood, choice meats, and wild game flown in daily to the island. While you're delighting your taste buds, you can also delight your eyes looking out over the Atlantic.

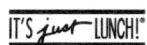

Kansas City

Best Restaurant for Lunch or Brunch First Date
Blue Bird Bistro
1700 Summit St., Kansas City
(816) 221-7559
www.kansascitymenus.com/bluebirdbistro

Blue Bird is like finding a twenty dollar bill in an old jacket; a pleasant surprise. The menu will please vegetarians and carnivores alike.

Best Restaurant for First Dinner Date
J. Alexander's
11471 Metcalf Ave., Shawnee Mission
(913) 469-1995

The service here is as remarkable as the food. Be sure and save room for dessert. The carrot cake is the best in Kansas City.

Best Cheap Date
Boulevard Drive-In
1051 Merriam Ln., Kansas City
(913) 262-0392 • www.boulevarddrivein.com

This isn't your parents' drive-in. The hundred-foot screen and state-of-the-art sound streaming from six hundred speakers helps make you feel like you're right in the action.

Best Restaurant for a Second Dinner Date
Stroud's
1015 E. 85th St., Kansas City
Other location: Northland
(816) 333-2132 • www.stroudsrestaurant.com

Forget about your waistline and live a little. Stroud's is home cookin' at its finest.

Best Place for Coffee and Dessert
LatteLand Espresso
318 W. 47th St., Kansas City
(816) 931-7477

A hip coffee shop with a diverse crowd featuring your typical coffee selections, wonderful baked goods and much more. Lots of outdoor seating.

Best Place for a Laugh
Red Balloon
10325 W. 75th St., Shawnee Mission
(913) 962-2330

Advertising the largest, cheapest, coldest beers in the city, karaoke is the staple here with singers crooning from open to close. The diverse crowd adds to the atmosphere.

Best Creative Date
Tasso's Greek Restaurant
8411 Wornall Rd., Kansas City
(816) 363-4776

Sure to leave a smile on your face. Break a plate, sing along with the live entertainment and admire the belly dancer.

Best Club
The Club at Plaza III
4749 Pennsylvania Ave., Kansas City
(816) 753-0000

A wonderful place to bring your date and cozy up while listening to amazing jazz, this would be a perfect night for any special occasion.

Best After Hours Place
IHOP
8701 Shawnee Mission Pkwy., Merriam
Call for other locations
(913) 362-8663 • www.ihop.com

IHOP: International House of Pancakes or Incomparable Hotbed of single People? Definitely the latter, after the bar crowd makes IHOP its last stop of the evening.

Best Special Occasion Restaurant
The American Restaurant
25th St. & Grand Blvd., Kansas City
(816) 426-1133

"Flawless" is how to describe this elegant restaurant. With more than thirty years in business, their consistency in remaining one of the top restaurants in town is impressive.

Best Place To Buy a Gift
Westport District Shops
Westport Rd. and Pennsylvania, Westport
(816) 756-2789

From classic candles to quirky furniture, you're sure to find a gift for that special someone at one of the unique gift shops in the historic Westport District.

Top Five Dates

#1. Dance Dance Dance
Kansas City Swing Dance Club
6101 Martway St., Shawnee Mission
(913) 831-7964

Grab your partner and get in on America's hottest craze, swing dancing. Enjoy the mood, music and fun that was the '40s. Do the Lindy in a great setting that you'll both enjoy.

#2. Make Something Beautiful
Bearden's Stained Glass
7600 Metcalf, Overland Park
(913) 381-4527

Take a chance and create something beautiful together. Have fun, learn the ancient art of stained glass and make something you'll treasure for years to come.

#3. Wine for Lovers
Wines by Jennifer
405 Main St., Parkville
(816) 505-WINE • www.winesbyjennifer.com

Wine is the drink of love, but do you know why? Find out with that special someone, and learn what goes into the making of fine wines — and maybe a little about love.

#4. Sing for your Supper
Red Balloon
10325 W. 75th St., Shawnee Mission
(913) 962-2330

"What's your favorite song?" is always a great question to ask a date, and now you can hear the answer. Both of you can belt out your faves here and shed your inhibitions!

#5. *Shakespeare, Anyone?*
   Theatre in the Park
   7900 Renner Rd., Shawnee
   (913) 631-7050 • www.theatreinthepark.org
   Look up and you see twinkling stars in the sky. Look out, and you see thespian stars on the stage. Maybe, beside you, your date will have stars in their eyes, only for you!

Las Vegas

Best Restaurant for Lunch or Brunch First Date
Z'Tejas Southwestern Grill
3824 S. Paradise Rd., Las Vegas
Other locations: 9560 W. Sahara (Summerlin)
(702) 732-1660

A casual restaurant; offers an outstanding menu that fuses flavors from Louisiana, Native American, Mexico and Pacific Rim cuisines.

Best Restaurant for First Dinner Date
Little Buddha (Palms Hotel)
4321 W. Flamingo Rd., Las Vegas
(702) 942-7778 • www.littlebuddhalasvegas.com

Trendy, attractive restaurant; Asian-inspired dishes, including sushi. Delectable, gorgeous bits of sushi are almost too sexy for a first dinner date — but not quite!

Best Cheap Date
The Coffee Pub
2800 W. Sahara Ave., Las Vegas
(702) 367-1913

This quaint coffee shop has been in business for 20 years. Casual seating indoors or outdoors with great baked goods, homemade meals, and outstanding coffee.

Best Restaurant for a Second Dinner Date
Viaggio
11261 S. Eastern Ave., Henderson
(702) 492-6900

Worth the drive to the Seven Hills/Anthem area. This upscale, quaint restaurant has an outstanding view, fabulous Italian entrees, and a separate wine bar.

Best Place for Coffee and Dessert

Chocolate Swan (Mandalay Place)
3930 Las Vegas Blvd. S., Las Vegas
Other locations: Two locations in Mandalay Place
(702) 632-9366 • www.chocolateswan.com

Romantic, creative, and tasteful. Browse the candy display downstairs, then head upstairs for dessert: homemade frozen custard, bite-sized cheesecakes, and fabulous coffee.

Best Place for a Laugh

Comedy Stop at the Trop (Tropicana)
3801 Las Vegas Blvd. S., Las Vegas
(702) 739-2411 • www.thecomedystop.com

Your $19.95 admission includes two cocktails and three different stand-up comedians. Small venue without a bad seat. Two shows nightly, at 8:00 and 10:30.

Best Creative Date

Helicopter Ride to Grand Canyon
6075 Las Vegas Blvd. S., Las Vegas
(702) 261-0007 • www.maverickhelicopter.com

Try the Wind Dancer tour, a three-and-a-half hour trip that takes you from Vegas to the canyon floor for champagne and hors d'oeuvres. Ends with a bird's-eye view of the Strip.

Best Club

Rain Las Vegas (The Palms)
4321 W. Flamingo Rd., Las Vegas
(702) 940-7246

"Rain in the Desert" has VIP skyboxes, cabanas, and water booths you can reserve- not to mention go-go dancers and a light show that looks like fire, fog, rain on the dance floor.

Best After Hours Place

Mr. Lucky's 24/7 (Hard Rock Hotel)
4455 Paradise Rd., Las Vegas
(702) 693-5000

This 24-hour diner has the best breakfast in town. Lively, great people-watching, loud music. If it's dinnertime, ask for the "local surf-n-turf" (not on the menu).

Best Special Occasion Restaurant
Renoir (Mirage)
3400 S. Las Vegas Blvd, Las Vegas
(702) 791-7223

This small, intimate restaurant is truly a work of art, in terms of the ambiance, artwork, and menu. Dine amongst authentic Renoirs. This restaurant is pricey, but worth it.

Best Place To Buy a Gift
Virgin Megastore
3500 Las Vegas Blvd. S., Las Vegas
(The Forum Shops at Caesars)
(702) 696-7100 • www.virgin.com

This huge store has a fantastic collection of CDs, in addition to books, games, movies, and more. A great place to find a thoughtful gift that won't break the bank.

Top Five Dates

#1. Sittin' On Top of the World
   Exhilarate your date by bringing him or her to the highest points in Las Vegas. Visit the Eiffel Tower Restaurant in the Paris Hotel, Top of the World at the Stratosphere, the VooDoo lounge at the Rio, or the ghostbar at the Palms — especially at night. Bring a disposable camera and take lots of pictures, then agree to meet up the following week to look at them.

#2. A Day at Lake Mead
   Head out to Lake Mead when you want to get away from hot Las Vegas. If you don't have a boat, don't worry — you can rent one when you get there. Enjoy water sports like water skiing, wakeboarding, jet skiing, and swimming; or just relax on the beach.

#3. Create Your Own Amusement
   Bring out your inner five-year-old: visit the new Star Trek Borg 4-D at the Hilton, the roller-coaster at New York, New York, and finish with the free-fall ride at Flyaway Indoor Skydiving. The couple that plays together stays together!

#4. Just For Laughs
   Laughter is a natural aphrodisiac, so why not check out one of the comedy clubs or visiting comedians,

laugh yourselves silly, and get ready for a whole lot of loving? A regular favorite is the Second City at the Flamingo.

#5. *Unleash Your Inner Tiger*

Golf is for lovers. Well...okay, I made that up. But golf is a great couple's activity, and if you're already a fan, this might be a good opportunity to get your date hooked (on you and the game). Las Vegas has over 30 courses to choose from, so just take your pick.

Little Rock

Best Restaurant for Lunch or Brunch First Date
Ashley's at The Capital
111 West Markham Street, Little Rock
www.thecapitalhotel.com

Elegant, but retains a touch of the casual. They offer an extensive, creative menu. Make sure you try the macadamia-crusted snapper with Thai curry sauce.

Best Restaurant for First Dinner Date
Best Impressions
Interstate 30 & Ninth Street, Little Rock
www.arkarts.com/restaurant

Located in the beautiful Arkansas Arts Center, this elegant spot lets you enjoy works of art on your plate and on the walls. Try the pork medallions with the bleu cheese slaw garnish!

Best Cheap Date
Murry's Dinner Playhouse
6323 Asher Ave., Little Rock
(501) 562-3131 • www.murrysdinnerplayhouse.com

Where else can you get dinner and a show without leaving your seat? Less than $20 and buffet style, so bring your appetite.

Best Restaurant for a Second Dinner Date
Sonny Williams Steakroom
500 East Markham Street, Suite 100, Little Rock
(501) 324-2999 • www.sonnywilliamssteakroom.com

After you get to know each other, this is the place to go when you're willing to spend a little more. Afterward, or even before, you can relax at the bar and listen to the piano.

Best Place for Coffee and Dessert
Brave New Restaurant
2300 Cottondale Lane, Little Rock
(501) 663-2677 • www.Bravenewrestaurant.com

One of the few places willing to create dessert specials

according to the availability of fresh fruits. Perfect for the toppings on their excellent cheesecakes.

Best Place for a Laugh
The Loony Bin Comedy Club
10301 North Rodney Parham Road, Little Rock
(501) 228-5555 • http://www.loonybincomedy.com

Most of the funny people you see on TV today have been through the Loony Bin. This place has been featured on Comedy Central and FOX. Call ahead for a schedule of performers.

Best Creative Date
Shakespeare Festival of Arkansas
Center Stage Theatre
616 Center St., Little Rock
(501) 376-PLAY

Transport yourself back into time and watch people in funny costumes act out the plays they forced you to learn in high school. Inexpensive, as well.

Best Club
Noa-Noa Night Club
2657 Pike Ave N., Little Rock
(501) 758-5359

If you're looking for late-night fun where the pumping music makes you hungry for more action, the Noa-Noa Club has your beat.

Best After Hours Place
Vino's
923 W 7th, Little Rock
(501) 375-8466 • www.vinosbrewpub.com

Live music keeps the ears entertained after hours, while the pizza and fresh-brewed beer takes care of the stomach. Call ahead for performance schedule.

Best Special Occasion Restaurant
The Villa Italian Restaurant
12111 West Markham, Little Rock
(501) 219-2244

Typically huge portions for an Italian restaurant are offered here. Excellent salads. Save room for crème brulee.

Best Place To Buy a Gift

All Star Gifts & Card
11121 North Rodney Parham Road, Little Rock
(501) 223-1100

Specializes in balloon-themed gifts, but not the cheesy, state-fair variety. Great for showing you're thinking of your sweetheart but without being too obtrusive.

Top Five Dates

#1. It's Roller Coaster Time!
Magic Springs & Crystal Falls
1701 Highway 70 E
Hot Springs, AR 71901
(501) 624-0100 • www.magicsprings.com

It's a short drive and it's worth it! Scream like children again, and if it's a hot day, jump in the water park to cool off.

#2. Take a deep breath of fresh air
Pinnacle Mountain State Park, Roland
(501) 868-5806

This is for the moderate hiker, so don't worry about tiring out. Killer views of the Arkansas River atop the most visible point in Central Arkansas. Make sure you bring a picnic lunch!

#3. Smell the Daffodils
Annual Wye Mountain Daffodil Festival, Wye Mountain
(501) 330-2403

The second weekend in March is a big one here. Seven acres of nothing but daffodils! Stroll around and enjoy the barbecue. Nothing says romance like seven acres of flowers.

#4. Soar with the Birds
Wind Dancer Balloon Adventures
P.O. Box 13096, Maumelle
(501) 851-4405

Don't forget the champagne as you lift off and hear nothing but the wind and the birds. Can seat up to 10, which makes for an intimate adventure.

#5. *Take a day trip to Hot Springs*
   53 miles west of downtown Little Rock
   (501) 321-2277 • www.hotsprings.org

   "Chill" in the 147-degree natural hot springs or watch the horses run at Oaklawn Park. A nice day trip, or, if you're far enough along in your relationship, a weekend getaway.

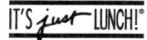

Los Angeles

Best Restaurant for Lunch or Brunch First Date
Polo Lounge
9641 Sunset Blvd., Beverly Hills
(310) 276-2251 • www.beverlyhillshotel.com

The best brunch, in the most romantic setting, is found here inside the Beverly Hills Hotel. Be sure to make reservations for seating on the lush outdoor patio.

Best Restaurant for First Dinner Date
Maple Drive
345 N. Maple Dr., Beverly Hills
(310) 274-9800 • www.mapledrive.com

On this quiet tree-lined street in Beverly Hills you'll find an L. A. dining institution that attracts the top players in town. The scene is timeless chic with a California flare.

Best Cheap Date
Glen Ivy
25000 Glen Ivy Rd., Corona
Other location: Brea
(888) 258-2683 • www.glenivy.com

A short drive from Los Angeles is the better of the two locations. Soak all day long in red clay baths, numerous spas, and pools for one low price. Both genders are welcome.

Best Restaurant for a Second Dinner Date
Katana
8439 Sunset Blvd., West Hollywood
(323) 650-8585 • www.katanarobata.com

The traditional Robata and Sushi menu is as notable as the hip clientele. Whether you dine under the stars or inside next to them, the food and the experience are truly the best.

Best Place for Coffee and Dessert
King's Road Café
8361 Beverly Blvd., Los Angeles
(323) 655-9044

The young and hip adorn this café seven days a week. It

may be the location that brings them back, but of course it may also be the best cup of coffee in town.

Best Place for a Laugh
Groundlings
7307 Melrose Ave., Los Angeles
(323) 934-4747 • www.groundlings.com

For thirty years this comedy troop has been churning out the hits. Many Groundlings have gone on to Saturday Night Live fame. See them before they make it big!

Best Creative Date
Universal Studios
100 Universal City Plaza, North Hollywood
(818) 622-3801 • www.universalstudios.com

Unleash your inner-child, and spend the day at this movie-based theme park. The ride of your life is closer than you think!

Best Club
XES
1716 N. Cahuenga Blvd., Hollywood
(323) 461-8190 • www.xeshollywood.com

XES is a sexy addition to the neighborhood. Strong drinks and polls on the dance floor make for a fun night.

Best After Hours Place
Berri's Pizza Café
8410 W. Third St., Los Angeles
(323) 852-0642

When you pull up at three in the morning and the valet is jam-packed, you know you're at Berri's. This late night eatery has some of the best New York-style pizza in L.A.

Best Special Occasion Restaurant
Patina
141 S. Grand Ave., Los Angeles
(213) 972-3331 • www.patinagroup.com

Downtown dining just got better with the addition of Patina, located in the Walt Disney Concert Hall. It's the perfect locale for a classical night of fine dining.

Best Place To Buy a Gift
Fred Segal
8100 Melrose Ave., Los Angeles
(323) 651-4129

Inside this cluster of trendy boutiques is where you'll find the most current 'must have' urban clothing, shoes, sunglasses and beauty items.

Top Five Dates

#1. *Spa Day In 90210*
   Sea Mountain Spa Beverly Hills
   9960 L. Santa Monica Blvd., Beverly Hills
   (877) 928-2827
   Nothing says, "I care about you" like a massage for both of you. Start with twin facials, some mud, a little champagne, then let the masseuses have you purring like kittens. It's a date, it's a gift, and it's a special thing to enjoy together.

#2. *A Ride to Nowhere*
   Hollywood Stars Limousine Service
   1110 S. Catalina Ave. Ste 211, Redondo Beach
   (323) 456-9333
   Tour Los Angeles, Hollywood style, in a stretch limo. Turn up the music a little, pop some fine wine or champagne, and do a little sightseeing. Make the whole evening a really decadent event, by just enjoying the ride until it's over.

#3. *Catch a Rising Star*
   The Groundlings
   7303 Melrose Ave., Los Angeles
   (323) 934-3737 • www.groundlings.com
   Where does Saturday Night Live find its talented writers and stars? The Groundlings! Masters of sketch comedy and improv, this group has been the home to Lisa Kudrow and Pee-Wee Herman among others. Catch the next rising star, or go to the late Friday show where you might see alumni like Will Ferrell and Cheri Oteri join in the fun.

#4. *Hey, I'm on TV!*
   Audiences Unlimited
   100 Universal City Plaza, Universal City
   (818) 506-0043

   The magic of TV is tamed a little when you go see a live taping of a show. Nonetheless, it's fun to see how it all comes together. Enjoy the bloopers and laugh a lot!

#5. *Doggie Double Date*
   Runyon Canyon
   Mulholland Dr. and Fuller Ave., Hollywood
   www.runyon-canyon.com

   Introduce your schnauzer to his or her pug on this one-hour hike where dogs are welcome. Humans love the panoramic view at the top, which includes the Hollywood sign and downtown L.A. Surprisingly, Runyon Canyon is also a great place for spotting a celebrity — with his or her dog in tow.

Louisville

Best Restaurant for Lunch or Brunch First Date
City Cafe
1250 Bardstown Rd., Louisville
(502) 589-1797 • www.citycafelunch.com
Call for other locations.

Try a table in the loft and feast on a turkey, roast beef or portabella mushroom sandwich. Stroll to Ehrman's Bakery for ice cream.

Best Restaurant for First Dinner Date
Jack Fry's Restaurants
1007 Bardstown Rd., Louisville
(502) 452-9244 • www.jackfrys.com

This four-star restaurant offers live piano jazz. Artfully presented dishes include roasted organic chicken and salmon encrusted with almonds and pistachios.

Best Cheap Date
Baxter Ave. Theatres
1250 Baxter Ave., Louisville
(502) 459-2288

Make this haven for independent film lovers your special spot. Then, window-shop along the avenue.

Best Restaurant for a Second Dinner Date
Bristol Bar & Grille
614 Main St., Louisville
Call for other locations.
(502) 456-1702

Their green chili wontons are known citywide. Spice up the night with hot 'n spicy Thai chicken.

Best Place for Coffee and Dessert

Heine Brother's Coffee
2714 Frankfort Ave., Louisville
Call for other locations.
(502) 899-5551 • www.neinebroscoffee.com

Pair a "Lucky in Kentucky" cookie and a Yemen Mocha Matri coffee for a date with international flavor.

Best Place for a Laugh

Molly Malone's Irish Pub & Restaurant
(933) Baxter Ave., Louisville
(502) 473-1212 • www.mollymalonesirishpub.com

Their Tuesday night trivia contest is a winner for laughs. Plus, they offer 29 beers, Irish whiskey and great chicken wing specials.

Best Creative Date

Sugar & Spice Scrapbooks
9457 Westport Rd., Louisville
(502) 423-0208

Preserve the memories you've made together. A large studio, thousands of stamps and an expert staff await your creative efforts.

Best Club

Phoenix Hill Tavern
644 Baxter Ave., Louisville
(502) 636-0405

Four stages, each rocking with a different band. Male and female hotties populate the club on weekends.

Best After Hours Place

Twig & Leaf
2122 Bardstown Rd., Louisville
(502) 451-8944

Personalities blend in this small landmark diner, where breakfast is served 24/7. Dig into large portions of French toast, egg dishes and Twig Taters (hash browns).

Best Special Occasion Restaurant

Lilly's Restaurant
1147 Bardstown Rd., Louisville
(502) 451-0447 • www.lillyslapeche.com
Call for other locations.

This celebrated restaurant is romantic, hip and known for

its fresh fish and veal. Choose blackberry pudding for dessert. Check out the half-price wine tastings.

Best Place To Buy a Gift
Nanz & Kraft Florists
141 Breckenride Ln., Louisville
(502) 897-6551

Show how much you care with artistic floral presentations, gift baskets and plants. Refrigerated trucks deliver love three times a day.

Top Five Dates

#1. *La Relais*
2815 Taylorville Rd., Louisville
(502) 451-9020 • www.lerelaisrestaurant.com

Take a "Romance in the Air" plane ride at this restaurant, situated at historic Bowman Field. Remember to make reservations for your flight. Then sit on the deck to watch small aircraft coming and going as you enjoy fine French cuisine.

#2. *Wheel Fun Rentals*
439 W. Ohio St., Louisville
(317) 767-5072 • www.wheelfunrentals.com

Pedal side by side when you rent a Deuce Coupe (a tricycle built for two) and head downtown to historic Old Louisville, one of the largest Victorian preservation districts in the United States. Stop at the Conrad Calwell House for a mansion tour and take photos at the St. James Court fountain.

#3. *Belle of Louisville*
Moored at 4th St. and River Rd., Louisville
(502) 574-2355 • www.belleoflouisville.org

One classic date is a sunset dinner cruise on this historic paddlewheel steamboat. Then, stroll on the romantic and paved (good for heels) Riverwalk to Waterfront Park and the Louisville Extreme Park (for skaters and skateboarders). Nearby is E. Main Street, home of the Louisville Ballet, Slugger Field and many art and antique stores.

#4. Churchill Downs
 700 Central Ave., Louisville
 (502) 636-4400 • www.churchilldowns.com

Inject some of the excitement and pageantry of the greatest two minutes in sports into your date. Daily races (in season), walking tours and a backstretch breakfast tour are all exciting options. Walk to the Kentucky Derby Museum, where you can pretend to be a jockey and ride in a race. Eat trackside or at the museum's Derby Cafe (weekdays).

#5. Palace Theatre
 625 S. 4th St., Louisville
 (502) 583-4555 • www.louisvillepalace.com

Dress up and step out in the style this venue demands. Cats, Tony Orlando, Sinbad, Franki Valli and the Trans-Siberian orchestra are among the top names this venue attracts. The theater's ceiling features 100 carved faces and the auditorium looks like a village courtyard. You'll have plenty to talk about during intermission.

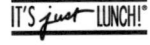

Maine

Best Restaurant for Lunch or Brunch First Date
Little's Lad's Basket Bakery
128 Maine St., Bangor
(207) 942-5482

The incredibly healthy vegan food here is a real conversation starter, and to sweeten you both up and put you in a good mood, the ice cream is a perennial favorite.

Best Restaurant for First Dinner Date
The White Barn Inn
37 Beach Ave., Kennebunkport
(207) 967-2321 • www.whitebarninn.com/rest.html

This is one of the best and most romantic restaurants in Maine, with its classic cuisine. They have received the AAA Five-Diamond Award for 11 consecutive years.

Best Cheap Date
Acadia National Park
www.nps.gov/acad/

Not only is it cheap, it's great exercise and one of the most beautiful ways to get to know that special someone hiking by your side.

Best Restaurant for a Second Dinner Date
The Deckhouse Restaurant and Cabaret Theater
11 Apple Lane, Southwest Harbor
(207) 244-5044 • www.thedeckhouse.com/deck_main.htm

There is no better way to make a perfect a date than with great food and great entertainment, and this locale provides the best of both.

Best Place for Coffee and Dessert
David's Creative Cuisine
22 Monument Sq., Portland
(207) 773-4425
www.davidsrestaurant.com/MenuDessert.html

Any place that serves this many delicious, creative

desserts, with cognac if you choose, has to impress your date and put you both in a wonderful mood.

Best Place for a Laugh
Comedy Connection
8 Custom House Wharf, Portland
(207) 774-5554 • www.mainecomedy.com

There's no end to the laughs at this joke machine, which features some of the funniest stand-up comedians in Maine.

The Best Creative Date
Shakti Yoga Studio
44 Emery Mills Rd., Lebanon
(207) 457-2298

This very tranquil yoga studio, in a country locale, sets the mood for a very relaxing, intimate way to get to know your date spiritually and personally.

Best Club
Big Easy Blues Club
55 Market St., Portland
(207) 871-8817 • www.bigeasybluesclub.com

Here's the place for live entertainment and dancing in the heart of Portland's Old Port; it's also a great place to meet like-minded singles early or late at night!

Best After Hours Place
Brian Boru
57 Center St., Portland
(207) 780-1506 • www.bboru.com

One of the most popular after-hours spots in town, Brian Boru's showcases live fiddlers and flute players, and an astounding array of national and international brews.

Best Special Occasion Restaurant
The White Barn Inn
37 Beach Ave., Kennebunkport
(207) 967-2321 • www.whitebarninn.com/rest.html

With its European and American cuisine, impeccable service, and its national ranking (AAA Five-Diamond Award for 11 consecutive years), this is the special place.

Best Place To Buy a Gift
Portland Public Market
Located between Preble and Elm Streets on Cumberland

Avenue in Portland, this market offers everything including specialty food items, spices, wine, beer, cookies and cakes!

Five Great Dates

#1. Oh, Say Can You Sea?
Maine Sport Outfitters
Rte. 1, P.O. Box 956, Rockport
(888) 236-8797 • www.mainesport.com
There's nothing like paddling around in a sea kayak to help you relax and talk to your partner. You'll know pretty quickly if they're willing to contribute half the fun and half the work! Choose the length of your trip, from mere hours to days, and your destination. It's great fun, a learning experience, and you'll know more about your date quickly.

#2. A Perfect Way to Start the Day
Poulet Rouge
106 N. Sixth St., Boise
(208) 343-8180
Sleep a little late, then head out for Poulet Rouge (Red Chicken) for a perfect brunch — especially if you can grab a chair and dine outdoors. The menu lets you indulge whatever suits your fancy. Then, after a gourmet coffee and a pastry, you're ready for whatever comes your way. You and your date have a thousand choices after a great start!

#3. Laugh All Over the Place
Duff
(207) 832-6688 • http://duffcomedy.com
Duff has been marked by some publications as a real up-and-comer. He bases his humor on everyday life and keeps you rolling through the whole show. A Maine native, Duff started out in theater and dance while at the University of Maine-Orono. As he says, "You neva know what you're gonna get" — except you know he'll keep you laughing.

#4. Get Out of Town
The Kennebunk Inn
45 Maine St., Kennebunk
(207) 985-3351 • www.thekennebunkinn.com
Just 80 minutes north of Boston and 25 minutes

south of Portland is one of the most romantic inns and restaurants in Maine, The Kennebunk Inn. Surrounded by nature preserves, museums, galleries, antique shops and the beautiful natural environs of Kennebunk, this is one dinner establishment that is sure to please.

#5. Exploring Ain't Boring

One of the best ways to get to know people is to spend a few hours with them in a car. You're in one of the most beautiful states in the nation and you can go from seaside to mountainside, and all the gorgeous spots in between. It's a great chance to talk without interruption. You can go where you want, and stop and share the local delicacies!

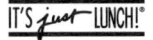

Memphis

Best Restaurant for Lunch or Brunch First Date
Paulette's
2110 Madison Ave., Memphis
(901) 726-5128

This is *the* place for a quiet, conversational lunch or incredible brunch where you can get to know each other. The food is outstanding and the atmosphere is elegant, but casual.

Best Restaurant for First Dinner Date
Erling Jensen Restaurant
1044 South Yates, Memphis
(901) 763-3700 • http://www.ejensen.com/menu.htm

For a super first dinner date, you can't beat Erling Jensen's; he is the chef and owner. He creates unique, fantastic dishes. Everything here is perfect: mood, food and service.

Best Cheap Date
Huey's
1927 Madison Ave., Memphis
(901) 726-4372

The absolute best burgers, graffiti on the walls and a chance to shoot a toothpick through a straw into the ceiling make this the most fun cheap date you'll find anywhere!

Best Restaurant for a Second Dinner Date
Houston's
5000 Poplar Ave., Memphis
(901) 683-0915 • http://www.banderarestaurants.com

The roomy booths, subdued lighting, and brass, wood and brick décor make this a perennial favorite. Expect a good menu, great food, large portions and fine desserts.

Best Place for Coffee and Dessert
Chez Phillipe
The Peabody Hotel, 149 Union Ave., Memphis
(901) 529-4000 • http://www.peabodymemphis.com

You can't miss this one: Incredibly rich and delicious

French desserts, elegant atmosphere, impeccable service, and, of course, the ducks waddling through the lobby!

Best Place for a Laugh
Memphis Improvisational Theatre
3024 Keats Road, Bartlett
(901) 213-0331 • www.memphisimprov.com

Not only will you laugh from this group's antics, they will train you to do comedy and improv! Visit their website for events and classes.

Best Creative Date
The Pink Palace
3050 Central Ave., Memphis
(901) 320-6320 • www.pigglywiggly.com

The home of the very first self-service grocery store is right here in Memphis. The Pink Palace is a unique, pink-marbled mansion that is sure to fascinate and entertain!

Best Club
BB King's Blues Club
143 Beale St., Memphis
(901) 524-5464 • http://memphis.bbkingclubs.com

Without question the best club in Memphis, BB's has great music, a dance floor, good food and an interesting crowd. They even set up a bar on Beale Street on weekends!

Best After Hours Place
Club 152
152 Beale St., Memphis
(901) 544-7011
www.bealestreet.com/clubsshops/club152.shtml

This place became so popular they had to open up two new floors! They feature local bands and DJs. It's the spot for after-hours clubbing until the wee hours.

Best Special Occasion Restaurant
Cielo
679 Adams Ave., Memphis
(901) 524-1886

A beautiful restaurant located in a turn-of-the-century mansion in the Victorian Village, Cielo serves a delicious assortment of international cuisines that are all exquisite!

Best Place To Buy a Gift

Elephant's Trunk Zoo Shop, Memphis Zoo
2000 Prentiss Place, Memphis
(901) 333-6776 • www.memphiszoo.org

There is truly something for everyone here. You can get goodies from around the world, including toys, clothes, stuffed animals, jewelry and artwork. You can shop online, too!

Top Five Dates

#1. Return to the Old World
Paulette's
2110 Madison Ave., Memphis
(901) 726-5128

The old-world elegance and style displayed in a mansion full of antiques makes it very romantic, and the food is extraordinary. It was voted 2003's Most Romantic restaurant! Once you dine there, you'll understand why, and you'll go back again and again. It's a classic that will help make your evening truly special.

#2. It's All Happening at the Zoo
Memphis Zoo
2000 Prentiss Place, Memphis
(901) 333-6776 • www.memphiszoo.org

You'll have plenty to talk about here. You can get to know your date and your natural neighbors at the same time. It relaxes you and brings back memories and feelings of childhood — for the both of you.

#3. Talking, Walking and Listening
Beale Street, Memphis

Take a walk down Beale Street and fill your eyes and your ears. Dance to the bands that play in Handy Park, visit any (or all) of the great clubs along the street, and learn a little about the Blues — which was born right here in Memphis. There's also the Blues Museum, the Police Museum, the Orpheum Theatre and the New Daisy Theater to enjoy!

#4. Out With the Birds and the Bees
Memphis Botanic Garden
750 Cherry Rd., Memphis
(901) 685-1566
http://www.memphisbotanicgarden.com/
Delight in 96 acres of beautiful gardens, including the famous Japanese Garden of Tranquility and Sensory Garden. There's nothing like strolling hand in hand through millions of gorgeous flowers or stunning autumn leaves to create a romantic mood. There are lakes, woodlands, formal plots and enough beauty to keep your eyes busy for hours!

#5. Just the Two of Us
If you want to show someone you care, invite him or her to your place for a home-cooked meal — even if you hire someone else to actually cook it. This is an opportunity to set a warm, intimate atmosphere with candles, flowers and champagne. Add the right music and comfort to the mix and you never know where it will go from there! To find a chef, go to www.personalchefsearch.com.

Milwaukee

Best Restaurant for Lunch or Brunch First Date
Lake Park Bistro
3133 E. Newberry Blvd., Milwaukee
(414) 962-6300 • www.lakeparkbistro.com

This bistro offers authentic French cuisine and a commanding view of Lake Michigan. It's a local favorite for lunch, dinner and a champagne brunch.

Best Restaurant for First Dinner Date
Tula's Restaurant
117 E. Wells St., Milwaukee
(414) 276-7575 • www.tulasrestaurant.com

Enjoy Tula's seasonally inspired menu with an international flair. Dine inside in a contemporary atmosphere, or dine outside on the Rine-or-Shine Deck.

Best Cheap Date
Holy Hill National Shrine of Mary
1525 Carmel Rd., Hubertus
(262) 628-1838 • www.holyhill.com

Enjoy a relaxing drive out to Holy Hill National Shrine of Mary, where the view of Kettle Moraine will take your breath away.

Best Restaurant for a Second Dinner Date
Coquette Café
316 N. Milwaukee St., Milwaukee
(414) 291-2655 • www.coquettecafe.com

Nestled in the Landmark Building in the historic Third Ward, Coquette Café serves up authentic bistro fare in warm, casual surroundings.

Best Place for Coffee and Dessert
Simma's
817 N. 68th St., Milwaukee
(414) 257-0998 • www.simmasbakery.com

Simma's received the International Award of Excellence and was voted Best of Milwaukee from 1993 to 2003. They feature a full-service bakery, where everything is made from scratch.

Best Place for a Laugh
Comedy Sportz
420 S. First St., Milwaukee
(414) 272-8888 • www.comedysportzmilwaukee.com
Laugh to your heart's content with improvisational comedy on Wednesdays, Thursdays, Fridays and Saturdays.

Best Creative Date
Cedar Creek Winery
N70 W6340 Bridge Rd., Cedarburg
(262) 377-8020 • www.cedarcreekwinery.com
Take a tour of the winery and old village and relish in complimentary wine tasting. After you've identified your favorite wine, purchase a bottle or two for that upcoming special occasion.

Best Club
Have A Nice Day Café
1103 Old World Third St., Milwaukee
(414) 270-9650 • www.cafemilwaukee.com
They serve up the most popular music from the '70s, '80s and '90s, with a great dance floor straight out of Saturday Night Fever.

Best After Hours Place
The Knick
1030 E. Juneau Ave., Milwaukee
(414) 272-0011
A casual bar and restaurant with a great menu of appetizers, salads, sandwiches and burgers. They're open late for dancing and sport one of the city's best patios.

Best Special Occasion Restaurant
Bacchus
925 E. Wells St., Milwaukee
(414) 765-1166 • www.bartolottas.com
This gem is one of Milwaukee's newest high-end restaurants, offering a contemporary American menu featuring beef, seafood, pasta, among others dishes.

Best Place To Buy a Gift

Things Remembered
2500 N. Mayfair Rd., Wauwatosa
Other locations: Brookfield, Greendale
(414) 258-1360 • www.thingsremembered.com

This is *truly* the place to find personalized gifts from the heart. Too busy to go out? Shop online and have that special gift delivered.

Top Five Dates

#1. *Weekend Away*
Lake Geneva Resort
7036 Grand Geneva Way, Lake Geneva
(262) 248-8811 • www.grandgeneva.com

Get away for the weekend at the gorgeous resort in beautiful Lake Geneva. Indulge yourself in the lavish spa, play golf, or enjoy a night of entertainment and fantastic dining.

#2. *Night At The Theater*
Milwaukee Repertory Theater
108 E. Wells St., Milwaukee
(414) 224-9490 • www.milwaukeerep.com

Enjoy live theatrical performances at the Milwaukee Rep. Create a memorable night with dinner and a show. Go online to see what shows are now playing.

#3. *Let Your Imagination Soar*
House on the Rock
5754 Highway 23, Spring Green
(608) 935-3639 • www.thehouseontherock.com

The House on the Rock is a 14-room house that is an extraordinary complex of rooms, streets, buildings and gardens covering over 200 acres. A must see!

#4. *Beer Tour*
Miller Brewery Factory Tour
4251 W. State St., Milwaukee
(414) 931-BEER • www.millerbrewing.com

Witness each step of the brewing process during one of Miller's free daily tours. Tours are offered every Monday through Saturday. And, for the best part: Sample the brews at the end of the tour!

#5. *Gamble the Night Away*
   Potawatomi Bingo Casino
   1721 W. Canal St., Milwaukee
   (414) 645-6888 • www.paysbig.com
   Enjoy more than 256,000 square feet of casino fun. With more than 1,000 slot machines, 32 gaming tables and bingo, there's something for everyone. Catch a show or dine in one of the world-class restaurants.

Montana

Best Restaurant for Lunch or Brunch First Date
John Bozeman's Bistro
125 W. Main St., Bozeman
(406) 587-4100 • www.johnbozemansbistro.com
This downtown institution is well known for its fresh food served with local flair. For a true taste of Montana, order the Fancy Flank Steak Burger, served with beer-battered fries.

Best Restaurant for First Dinner Date
Walkers American Grill and Tapas Bar
2700 1st Ave., Billings
(406) 245-9291 • www.walkersgrill.com
The gourmet-style Southwestern cuisine served at this romantic locale keeps locals and celebrity diners coming back for more. Stay for dessert — the crème brulee begs for it.

Best Cheap Date
American Classic Pizzeria Co.
1425 Broadwater Ave., Billings
(406) 248-4700 • www.americanclassicpizzeria.com
For a delicious and filling meal, try their Tailgate Buffet: It's only $7 for all you can eat. They also have great salads, sandwiches, pasta, calzones and desserts!

Best Restaurant for a Second Dinner Date
MacKenzie River Pizza Co.
222 E. Main St., Bozeman
Call for other locations
(406) 587-0055 • www.mackenzieriverpizza.com
Now that you're more comfortable with each other, it's time to bring out the big guns with the best pizza and beer in the state. Be sure and try the Hot Hawaiian.

Best Place for Coffee and Dessert
City Brew
2228 Grand Ave., Billings
Call for other locations
(406) 652-0877

City Brew is quickly becoming one of the largest chains in Montana — and with their impressive selection of rich, homemade coffee blends and goodies, it's really no wonder.

Best Place for a Laugh
Brewery Follies
H. S. Gilbert Brewery, Virginia City
(800) 829-2969 • www.breweryfollies.com

Enjoy a night of cabaret entertainment and big laughs. Sit back and sip a few locally made microbrews while you watch, but be forewarned: You might be asked to participate!

Best Creative Date
Picnic in the Park

A picnic is truly a great way to talk, listen and get to know someone. There's no loud music, sound effects or screen action to distract you from your date. It's just you two!

Best Club
The Carlin Martini Bar & Nightclub
2501 Montana Ave., Billings
(406) 245-2503 • www.thecarlin.com

This nightclub, located in the classic Carlin Hotel, serves up exotic beats and fabulous martinis to a hot singles scene — it doesn't get any better than this!

Best After Hours Place
The Carlin Hotel/Club Carlin
2501 Montana Avenue, Billings
(406) 245-7515 • www.carlinhotel.com

You can eat a good dinner, have a few drinks, listen to live music or DJs and dance well into the night. They have a lot of martini and draft beer specials, too.

Best Special Occasion Restaurant
Walkers American Grill and Tapas Bar
2700 1st Ave., Billings
(406) 245-9291 • www.walkersgrill.com

The menu covers everything from chicken to brulee, and

you can't go wrong with any of it. It's cozy, romantic and a great place for any special occasion.

Best Place To Buy a Gift
Gainan's
502 N. 30th, Billings
Call for other locations
(406) 245-6434 • www.gainans.com

So much more than your average florist, Gainan's is also a premier destination for fine gifts for him and her. Be sure to check out their remarkable holiday selection.

Top Five Dates

#1. Dinner and a Movie
The Roxy Theater
718 S. Higgins, Missoula
(406) 728-9380 • www.wildlifefilms.org

Enjoy a classic night out at the movies. The historic Roxy Theater will give you plenty to discuss, from the architectural décor to the film offerings. They play environmentally themed films designed to stimulate conversation. You'll see great wildlife and scenery! Check their website for current film listings.

#2. Boot Scootin' Boogie
Montana Chad's
3953 Montana Ave., Billings
(406) 259-0111

Slither into your Wranglers and don your favorite boots, it's time to line dance! Montana Chad's offers free dancing lessons for you and your sweetie on Tuesday nights. Learn a few moves, then step, turn and slide the night away.

#3. The Great Outdoors
Gallatin Valley Trails
Greater Bozeman
www.gallatindesign.com/websites/gvtrails/

Montana is known for its great outdoors, so why not get out there and enjoy it? There are several opportunities throughout the state for hiking, biking, skiing, horseback riding and more. In Bozeman alone there are several National forests and parks within

10 miles of the city limits. Check their website for trail information. And pack a picnic!

#4. *Romance Lessons from the Master*
Montana Shakespeare in the Parks
Montana State University Strand Union Theatre, Bozeman
Call for other locations.
(406) 994-3310 • www.montana.edu/shakespeare
Who knew romance better than William Shakespeare himself? Montana Shakespeare in the Parks puts on nearly 100 different productions in 50 different locations throughout Montana, and they're all free! Pack a picnic lunch, a bottle of wine, a warm blanket and enjoy a night of Shakespeare under the starry Montana sky.

#5. *Rest and Relaxation*
Chico Hot Springs Resort and Day Spa
One Chico Rd., Pray
(406) 333-4933 • www.chicohotsprings.com
From whitewater rafting to cross-country skiing, intimate massages to dips in the open-air hot springs pools, there's always something romantic in store at Chico Hot Springs, no matter the season. Bring your sweetheart for a weekend packed with spirit and rejuvenation!

Naples, Ft. Myers and Sarasota

Best Restaurant for Lunch or Brunch First Date
The Dry Dock Waterfront Grill
412 Gulf of Mexico Drive, South Longboat Key
(941) 383-0102

The Dry Dock is all about atmosphere. It offers a stunning waterfront view, and you may opt to dine dockside while watching the boats come and go.

Best Restaurant for First Dinner Date
BICE Ristorante
300 5th Ave. S., Naples
Call for other locations
(239) 262-4044 • www.bicenaples.com

This place serves up wonderful northern Italian food. Once the weather cools, request a table in the private outdoor brick terrace for a romantic evening.

Best Cheap Date
St. Armand's Circle
St. Armand's Key, off John Ringling Blvd., Sarasota
www.starmandscircleassoc.com

Home to several one-of-a-kind shops, boutiques and restaurants, this shopping destination is known throughout the country as a smaller Rodeo Drive.

Best Restaurant for a Second Dinner Date
Roy's
26831 South Bay Dr., Bonita Springs
(239) 498-7697 • www.roysrestaurant.com

This upscale casual Hawaiian fusion is known for its Euro-Asian entrees such as the pot roast, rib eye and the rack of lamb — but our favorite is the butter fish. Aloha!

Best Place for Coffee and Dessert
Pastry Art Bakery
1508 Main St., Sarasota
(941) 955-7545

Ooo-la-la, French pastries, delectable coffees, and more but we definitely recommend the iced mocha latte — it's made to perfection!

Best Place for a Laugh
Gecko's Grill & Pub
4870 Tamiami Tr. S., Sarasota
(941) 923-8896

This fun and casual bar also offers Sunday night stand-up comedy, with a "Premium Happy Hour," which includes 2 for 1 on any drink after 10:30 A.M.

Best Creative Date
Captain Bob's Excellent Adventure Air Boat Ride
Fort Myers Beach
Call for other locations
(239) 437-2095 • www.excellentadventure.org

Enjoy a daylong safari in the Everglades. Bob's van will pick you up at your desired location, and take you through a day of nature walking, airboat rides, food and fun.

Best Club
Dolce Vita
1244 Periwinkle Way, Sanibel Island
(239) 472-5555

Be entertained by dueling pianos every night in the Dolce Notte bar and lounge, or enjoy a drink from the International Champagne Bar.

Best After Hours Place
Mona Lisa Italian Restaurant Pizza and Lounge
7091 College Pkwy, Fort Myers
(239) 939-5344

This is the best place in Fort Myers to go for late-night pizza and cocktails. For your (and perhaps others') entertainment, Mona Lisa offers karaoke every night.

Best Special Occasion Restaurant
Hayeloft Dessert Bar & Lounge
5540 Gulf of Mexico Dr., Longboat Key
(941) 383-3633 • www.euphemiahaye.com

Upscale bar with a breathtaking view of the Gulf, serving gourmet desserts, complemented by a full bar menu. Hayeloft offers live entertainment Wednesday through Saturday nights.

Best Place To Buy a Gift
Sharper Image
10801 Corkscrew Rd., Suite 303, Estero
Call for other locations
(239) 949-6959 • www.sharperimage.com

From practical home goods to car accessories, Sharper Image carries gift ideas featuring the latest technology.

Top Five Dates

#1. Biking Sanibel Island

Get your bikes out or rent one on the island. Sanibel offers over 25 miles of paved bike paths. Meander busy streets and bike along Periwinkle Way with its quaint shops and restaurants. Pick up a bike map at the chamber of commerce and take your camera for those perfect sunsets. Then you can get together again after the photos are developed.

#2. Sunset over the Gulf of Mexico
The Ritz Carlton
280 Vanderbilt Beach Rd., Naples
(239) 598-3300 • www.ritzcarlton.com/resorts/naples

Since we're lucky enough to be within driving distance of the Gulf of Mexico, it's a perfect date location. Everyone feels relaxed walking by the Gulf, and it's so romantic. Afterward, go for a plate of calamari and a few Mai Tais — you'll feel like you took a mini-vacation. The Gumbo Limbo restaurant at the Ritz offers excellent views.

#3. Miniature Golf
Smugglers Cove Adventure
2000 W. Cortez Rd., Bradenton
(941) 756-0043

There are few better ways to impress your date than

by sinking an uphill, 25-foot putt that goes through a lion and around an alligator, by way of an abandoned ship. Just think of the possibilities.

#4. *Dining In*
Carolina Catering
(239) 285-6102

They say the way to a man's heart is through his stomach. Well, We've got news for you: It works with women too. Kick it up a notch with a gourmet dinner prepared by a fine cuisine chef right in your own kitchen. Ask Lisa Resch to prepare crispy fried oyster salad with mint rosemary dressing, garnished with roasted pine nuts, lamb and black bean ragout.

#5. *Picnic on Siesta Key*
(First go to Morton's Gourmet Market)
1924 S. Osprey Ave., Sarasota
(941) 955-9856

Morton's offers a multitude of deli items, specialty sandwiches, fresh salads, fresh-baked pastries and desserts. A great date doesn't have to break the bank. It can simply be a quiet get-together that allows for stimulating conversation. Get innovative and spice up the date with a Spanish theme — make a big bowl of Paella, bring plenty of sangria, and stick the Gypsy Kings in your portable CD player. Olé!

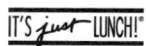

Nashville

Best Restaurant for Lunch or Brunch First Date
Café Nonna
4427 Murphy Rd., Nashville
(615) 463-0133 • www.cafenonna.com

The golden earth tones and wooden furniture set the stage for a warm, welcoming meal here. The menu is Italian, the food is fresh and excellent and the service is great!

Best Restaurant for First Dinner Date
Margot
1017 Woodland St., Nashville
(615) 227-4668 • www.margotcafe.com

Their menu changes daily to get the best and freshest items for their wonderful French- and Italian-inspired menu. The atmosphere is cozy, and they have a great wine list.

Best Cheap Date
The Family Wash
2038 Greenwood Ave., Nashville
(615) 226-6070 • www.familywash.com

This is a cool, quirky little place that used to be a Laundromat! You'll get good, inexpensive food, more than 35 different beers, wine by the glass and live music.

Best Restaurant for a Second Dinner Date
Wild Iris
127 Franklin Rd., Brentwood
(615) 370-0871

Not only do you find fantastic food here, you get to see ever-changing works by local artists. Dinner is always intriguing and delicious, and the atmosphere is friendly.

Best Place for Coffee and Dessert
Provence Breads & Cafe
1705 21st Ave. S., Nashville
(615) 386-0363

Billed as Tennessee's premier French bakery, Provence

will tickle your sweet tooth like no other! Everything from the chocolate marquise to the fruit tarts is outstanding.

Best Place for a Laugh
Zanies
2025 8th Ave. S., Nashville
(615) 269-0221 • www.nashville.zanies.com

Zanies has been making people laugh for 20 years; they book the best national and local comedians consistently. Call or check their website for show schedules and reservations.

Best Creative Date
Grand Ole Opry Museum
2802 Opryland Dr., Nashville
(615) 889-6611

Take a fascinating tour through the history of country music and see exhibits honoring all the legends. The audio and video effects let you see and hear it all — and it's free!

Best Club
Wild Horse Saloon
120 2nd Ave. N., Nashville
(615) 902-8200 • http://wildhorsesaloon.com/new

Whether you're a country music fan or not, you'll have a great time here! They have top entertainers performing live, plus food, drinks, dancing and plenty of pretty people.

Best After Hours Place
Café Coco
210 Louise Ave., Nashville
(615) 321-2626 • http://www.cafecoco.com

They're open 24 hours, have good food, great coffee and live music most evenings. The menu includes sandwiches, pasta, salads, breakfast and more.

Best Special Occasion Restaurant
The Wild Boar
2014 Broadway, Nashville
(615) 329-1313 • www.wildboarrestaurant.com

This is one of the very few places in the world to have won Mobil Four Stars, AAA Four Diamonds, DiRoNA, and 2003 Wine Spectator's Grand Award; that says it all.

Best Place To Buy a Gift
Pangea
1721 21st Ave. S., Nashville
(615) 269-9665

Pangea defines interesting, funky and international gifts. Along with women's clothing you'll find trinkets, house wares and other appealing items.

Top Five Dates

#1. *Music, Music, Music*
Ryman Auditorium
116 Fifth Ave. N., Nashville
(615) 889-3060 • www.ryman.com

Ryman used to be the home of the Grand Ole Opry, but it has become one of the foremost live music venues in Nashville. You can see and hear a variety of artists including the Nashville Symphony Orchestra. Go early and learn a little of the history of this fascinating place, which has been a catapult for so many stars.

#2. *Cruising Down the River*
General Jackson Showboat
2812 Opryland Dr., Nashville
(615) 871-6100 • www.generaljackson.com

Take your pick of evening (dinner), midday (lunch), morning or special occasion cruises aboard this 300-foot-long paddleboat that will take you back to the 1800s. There's plenty of room for dining, dancing, star-gazing and watching the scenery. It's a great chance to slow down and talk with each other — top speed is only 13 miles per hour!

#3. *Sing Little Blue Bird*
Bluebird Café
4104 Hillsboro Rd., Nashville
(615) 383-1461 • www.bluebirdcafe.com

Where else can you sit in a small, intimate 21-table café and listen to the greats and soon-to-be-greats in music? You might even be on the TV show that is broadcast from here. But you can't talk during the performances — their motto is "ssshhh" — but you'll have plenty to talk about between sets. You can eat and drink, too, while you're listening.

#4. *Fine Dining Extraordinaire*
   The Wild Boar
   2014 Broadway, Nashville
   (615) 329-1313 • www.wildboarrestaurant.com

   When you're in a restaurant that is one of the very few places in the world to have won Mobil Four Stars, AAA Four Diamonds, DiRoNA and 2003 Wine Spectator's Grand Award, you're in a very special place. The menu changes according to the season, as does the availability of the delicacies Chef Robert Price prepares. It's all exquisite!

#5. *Rub It In, Rub It In*
   Adagio Massage & Spa Co.
   The Gulch, 1205 Pine St., Nashville
   (615) 777-0602 • www.adagiomassageco.com

   What better way to relax and enjoy your date than with any one of three different kinds of massages, aromatherapy, reflexology, a massage specifically for the face, a hot and cold stone massage or a "Duo Massage?" The Duo simply means you both get a massage at the same time. What a way to spend the day together!

New Hampshire

Best Restaurant for Lunch or Brunch First Date
Jack's Coffee
207 Main St., New London
(603) 526-8003 • www.jackscoffee.com

Much more than just a coffee joint, this charming breakfast and lunch café offers cozy winter seating by the fireplace or breezy summer dining out on the patio.

Best Restaurant for First Dinner Date
The Woodshed
128 Lee Rd., Moultonboro
(603) 476-2311

Voted one of the Best Places to Kiss by *The Romantic Travel Guide*, The Woodshed offers gourmet fare and decadent desserts served inside a rustic 19th Century farmhouse.

Best Cheap Date
Ceres Bakery
51 Penhallow St., Portsmouth
(603) 436-6518

It's amazing how good the food is, given the low prices. They always have great soup, sandwiches, and bakery items. Plus, you get to see original artwork on the walls!

Best Restaurant for a Second Dinner Date
Home Hill French Inn & Restaurant
River Road, Plainfield
(603) 675-6165 • www.homehillinn.com

This intimate inn offers award-winning provincial cuisine with contemporary flair. Dine inside by the fire or order their signature picnic lunch and take it on a day's adventure.

Best Place for Coffee and Dessert

Awakenings Espresso Café
62 Canal St., Laconia
(603) 524-1201 • www.awakeningsespressocafe.com

Grab a table by the large windows or out on the patio and delight in a steaming cup of macadamia-nut coffee and a fresh, home-baked dessert at this upbeat, bright location.

Best Place for a Laugh

Funspot
Rte. 3, Weirs
(603) 366-4377 • www.funspotnh.com

All the fun to be had here, from arcade games to miniature golf, bingo to bowling, is sure to put a smile on your face. Afterward, catch a flick at the nearby Weirs Drive In.

Best Creative Date

Treehouse Toys
143 Market St., Portsmouth
(888) 560-TOYS • www.treehousetoys.com

Take a date to this toy store and take yourselves back in time! As you wander around amazed at how toys have changed, you'll laugh, talk and remember your own childhood.

Best Club

The Stone Church Music Club
5 Granite St., Newmarket
(603) 659-6321 • www.thestonechurch.com

The biggest headliner acts and local mainstays stop by this newly reopened historical mecca. A warm crowd really packs it in, especially during the Sunday gospel brunches.

Best After Hours Place

The Capitol Grille
1 Eagle Square, Concord
(603) 228-6608 • www.capitol-grille.com

Their Philly cheese steak sandwich won the Best in New Hampshire in 2003, and that's just one item! From the salads to the steaks, you'll be glad you came by.

Best Special Occasion Restaurant
Café Mirabelle
64 Bridge St., Portsmouth
(603) 430-9301 • www.cafemirabelle.com

One visit will show you why it was named Yankee Magazine's Editor's Choice for 2004! You can experience exquisite French country cuisine in a beautiful, relaxed atmosphere.

Best Place To Buy a Gift
Artisan's Workshop
186 Main St., New London
(603) 526-4227

Browse through their selection of creative and unique fine art, pottery, glassworks and much, much more. It's all created by the area's most talented artists.

Top Five Dates

#1. Fun in the Sun
Hampton Beach
(603) 926-8717 • www.hamptonbeach.org
Pack a picnic, grab your suits, and head to the beach for a day of sand and surf. During the summer months, be sure to take advantage of Hampton Beach's free live entertainment, fireworks displays and sporting events.

#2. An Evening Under the Stars
Christa McAuliffe Planetarium
Two Institute Dr., Concord
(603) 271-7827 • www.starhop.com
Gazing up at the night's sky always makes for a romantic date. Attend an informational show at the planetarium, such as Tonight's Sky. After the show and a night on the town, you can step outside and point out the "real" stars together. Make sure to check out the Super Star Fridays, special events held both in the theater and outside on the lawn.

#3. Small Town Charm
Historic Meredith
(603) 279-6121 • www.meredithcc.org
Spend an exciting day exploring historic Meredith. This charming little town located on Lake Win-

nipesaukee offers several opportunities for a romantic getaway, whether it's for a weekend or just a day. Get pampered at the Cascade Spa, eat at one of several fine restaurants or take an intimate walk on the lake's sandy beaches.

#4. *Arts & Culture*
Currier Museum of Art
201 Myrtle Way, Manchester
(603) 669-6144 • www.currier.org

Spend a day taking in and discussing the fine works of Picasso, Matisse, Monet, O'Keefe and others. Before you go, make a reservation to tour the museum's Zimmerman House, the only residence in New England designed by Frank Lloyd Wright. The museum also offers various fine art classes. Check the website for a current schedule.

#5. *Dining In*
Bedford Farmers' Market
Riley Field, County and Nashua Rds., Bedford
(603) 493-4665 • www.bedfordfarmersmarket.com

They say that the way to a person's heart is through their stomach. Take a trip through the farmers' market's aisles of fresh organic produce, dairy products and free range meats and pick up your favorite ingredients to create a romantic meal at home. Don't forget the wine and homemade candles!

New Orleans

Best Restaurant for Lunch or Brunch First Date
BACCO
310 Charles St., New Orleans
(504) 522-2426 • www.bacco.com

This establishment was Southern Living Magazine's top pick for lunch for its gutsy fusion of Italian and Creole dishes and romantic setting. For lunch, try lobster ravioli.

Best Restaurant for First Dinner Date
Commander's Palace
1403 Washington Ave., New Orleans
(504) 899-8221 • www.commanderspalace.com

Impeccable table service eases your romance along at this New Orleans landmark. Popular dishes are shrimp cognac with grits and chicory-flavored quail.

Best Cheap Date
St. Charles Ave. Streetcar
St. Charles Ave. and S. Carrollton Ave., New Orleans
(504) 242-2600 • www.norta.com
Call for other locations.

Flirt shoulder to shoulder from Canal Street to S. Carrollton Avenue for only a $1.25 per rider.

Best Restaurant for a Second Dinner Date
Uglesich
1238 Barrone St., New Orleans
(504) 523-8571 • www.uglesichs.com

This lovable establishment serves the city's best po-boy, made with fresh trout and French bread. After dinner, stroll Canal Street for ongoing attractions.

Best Place for Coffee and Dessert
La Madeleine
601 S. Carrollton Ave., New Orleans
Call for other locations
(504) 861-8662 • www.lamadeleine.com

Strong, chicory-accented coffees will energize your date.

Share an amazing chocolate-chunk cookie or a melt-in-your-mouth napoleon.

Best Place for a Laugh
The Cat's Meow Karaoke Bar
701 Bourbon St., New Orleans
(504) 523-2788 • www.catsmeow-neworleans.com

Three for one happy hour plus karaoke singing equals lots of laughs. Like the worst of *American Idol*, but live.

Best Creative Date
The Bead Shop
4612 Magazine St., New Orleans
(504) 895-6161
Call for other locations

Trendy and thoughtful. String together memories and gifts for each other as you choose from thousands of beads. On-site experts and classes add that finishing touch.

Best Club
The Goldmine Saloon
705 Dauphine St., New Orleans
(504) 586-0745

The most cutting-edge music in town. Flaming Dr. Peppers encourage you to dance close and mingle with the large crowd.

Best After Hours Place
Cafe du Monde
800 Decatur St., New Orleans
(504) 525-4544 • www.cafedumonde.com

Steal a powdered sugar kiss at this New Orleans institution after eating their world famous beignet (powdered sugar and fried dough). Also famous for cafe-au-lait.

Best Special Occasion Restaurant
Bayona
430 Dauphine St., New Orleans
(504) 525-4455 • www.bayona.com

You can't go wrong taking your date here. Gourmet Magazine rated this the best restaurant in New Orleans. Quail salad and peppered lamb loin are signature dishes.

Best Place To Buy a Gift

Bourbon French Parfums
815 Royal St., New Orleans
(504) 522-4480 • www.neworleansperfume.com

Choose from one of 30 men's and women's scents, or create a custom blend!

Top Five Dates

#1. Tipitina's
501 Napoleon Ave., New Orleans
(504)895-8477 • www.tipitinas.com

Act like a local and rub the bust of jazz great Professor Longhair for good luck on your date. Dozens of the city's R&B artists call the big stage in this former brothel home. Kick up your heels at the Sunday night fais-do-do, a Cajun dance party.

#2. Jimmy Buffet's Margaritaville Cafe
1104 Decatur St., New Orleans
Call for other locations.
(504) 592-2655 • www.margaritaville.com

New Orleans is the home of Jimmy Buffet, and yes, he does stop in on tour. This is a parrothead's paradise with nonstop Buffet videos and tables that look like his album covers. Listen to live music in the Storyville Cafe bar or take your "The Who's To Blame" street-ready margarita and cheeseburger to go.

#3. Cookin' Cajun Cooking School
#1 Poydras St., Riverwalk Marketplace, New Orleans
(800) 786-0941 • www.cookincajun.com

Partner with your date for laughs and cook up a little romance at this hands-on cooking school. Relax as you crack eggs and spill flour to make southern dishes from gumbo to bread pudding with amaretto sauce. Food aficionados will like the largest selection of Cajun specialties anywhere. After class, window-shop Riverfront Marketplace.

#4. Rajun Cajun Swamp Tours
840 Poydras St, New Orleans
(504) 566-0703 • www.rajuncajuntours.com

Watch your date take air as you cruise in an airboat below ancient moss-covered cypress oaks in search of alligators. The best time of the year to go is September and October, but don't let that stop you from seeing a variety of animals other months. Expert guides share local lore and make sure you get good pictures.

#5. City Park
1 Palm Dr., New Orleans
(504) 483-9412 • www.neworleanscitypark.com

The best and largest park in the city contains endless dating ideas. For romance, follow a picnic with a canoe or pedal boat ride, and go antiquing on nearby Magazine St. Into fitness? Combine any of the park's many sport activities for an extreme date. Choose tennis, running, fishing, golfing and horseback riding.

New York City

Best Restaurant for Lunch or Brunch First Date
Sarabeth's Kitchen
1295 Madison Ave.
(212) 410-7335
Call for other locations • www.sarabethskitchen.com

Find great food, great people, and a great part of town on a Sunday. Their place at the Whitney Museum gives you a two-for-one location to get to know your date and talk art!

Best Restaurant for First Dinner Date
Isabella's
359 Columbus Ave.
(212) 724-2100

Their classic food is guaranteed good! This UWS restaurant caters to any taste and you'll feel comfortable here too.

Best Cheap Date
Gray's Papaya
402 Avenue of the Americas
Call for other locations
(212) 260-3532

Stop at this fun hot spot made famous in "Sex in the City". It's standing room only, no seats, but you and your date can share two hot dogs and a drink for under $3.

Best Restaurant for a Second Dinner Date
Ida Mae Kitchen 'N Lounge
1400 Broadway
(212) 704-0038

Dress casual and dig the menu that combines refined Southern soul food with French cuisine in comfy surroundings, and a midtown location. Share a dessert; it's more fun.

Best Place for Coffee and Dessert
Sticky Fingers
131 Ave. A
(212) 614-0560

Fresh pastries, brownies, and other sweets galore at this tiny Alphabet City haunt will keep attracting you. They're all finger-licking good.

Best Place for a Laugh
Dangerfield's
1118 First Ave.
(212) 593-1650 • www.dangerfields.com

You can count on the acts at Rodney's self-named comedy club to have a good time. Call to see who's on the bill that night.

Best Creative Date
Horseback Riding In Central Park
The Claremont Riding Academy
(212) 724-5100

This is another great way to see Central Park. Rent a horse at this venerable stable, trot around the park, and feel like you're at the Derby.

Best Club
Lotus
409 W. 14th St.
(212) 243-4420 • www.lotusnyc.com

The neighborhood's gone friendly upscale and it makes you want to come back again and again, especially to this high-profile club with a killer Pan-Asian menu.

Best After Hours Place
Dorian's
1616 Second Ave.
(212) 772-6660

This is the kind of place that never stops hopping! Even after 2:00 in the morning, this place gets packed. It's also crazy on Saturday night!

Best Special Occasion Restaurant

Tavern on the Green
1 W. 67th St.
(212) 873-3200
Other location: Broadway • www.tavernonthegreen.com

Set in the heart of Central Park, everything about this restaurant puts you in "romance central." Request seating in the Chandelier Room, which looks into the park.

Best Place To Buy a Gift

Tiffany & Co.
727 Fifth Ave.
(212) 230-6000
Call for other locations • www.tiffany.com

You can't go wrong at this jewelry store. Buy someone special a little something (even a silver key ring) wrapped in Tiffany's trademark blue box and they will be thrilled!

Top Five Dates

#1. Chinatown for dinner and Little Italy for coffee, or vice versa
Canal St.
www.chinatown-online.com • www.littleitalynyc.com

Canal Street officially divides Chinatown from Little Italy, and you'll never be as happy to see two cultures a block apart and doing their best to make you happy. There's so much to see you'll have a lot to talk about.

#2. Free movies at Bryant Park
42nd St. and Fifth Ave.

Not first-run flicks, but great oldies projected on a screen in the park on 42nd St. and Fifth Ave. They're free and a fun scene on a lovely night with a film buff at your side. Be forewarned: BYO popcorn.\

#3. An afternoon walk in Riverside Park
155th St. to 68th St.
http://nycgovparks.org

The East River has Lady Liberty but the Hudson has its magic too, especially a walk through Riverside Park, which follows the river. Everyone loves the intimacy of the park (only about a city block wide) and you will too, especially around the ultra-atmospheric boat basin at 79th St.

#4. *Any Indian restaurant anywhere along E. Sixth St.*
Treat a date to something new and exotic in any one of the dozens of great and cheap Indian restaurants on Sixth St. between and around First and Second Aves. The heady aromas of masala and curry are hypnotizing, as are those gauzy head-wrapped sitar-players in the windows!

#5. *Drinks at the Pen-Top Bar at the Peninsula Hotel*
55th St. and Fifth Ave.
(212) 956-2888 • www.peninsula.com
If you want to feel elegant, glam, like a player on top of the world, take your date to the bar at the top of this ultra-sophisticated hotel. The view says power and romance!

Northern New Jersey

Best Restaurant for Lunch or Brunch First Date
Andreotti's Viennese Café
1442 E. Rte. 70, Cherry Hill
(856) 795-0172 • www.andreottis.com

Explore this great little place for a continental brunch with excellent pastries and baked goods in an environment that feels European and very much like a café.

Best Restaurant for First Dinner Date
Don Pepe
844 McCarter Hwy., Newark
(973) 623-4662 • www.donpeperestaurant.com

A couple could find plenty to talk about by just perusing the endless Spanish menu. But sharing the perfection of the Paella Marinera is as romantic as it is delectable.

Best Cheap Date
Charlie's Hot Dogs
18 S. Michigan Ave., Kenilworth
(908) 241-2627

The Newark Hot Dog, deep-fried and served in a large circular Italian loaf loaded with ketchup and French fries, is much more interesting than McDonald's and crazy good.

Best Restaurant for a Second Dinner Date
Tropea
1251 Route 202/206, Bridgewater
(908) 658-3000 • www.tropearestaurant.com

Crab cakes and sweet monkfish served before a mural of Botticelli-like cherubs make this a lovely but not froufrou night to enjoy each others company.

Best Place for Coffee and Dessert
CoCoLuxe Fine Pastries
161 Main St., Peapack
(908) 781-5554 • www.cocoluxepastry.com

Legendary chocolatier Joanne Gusweiler brings her pastries and chocolates to a brand-new shop in beautiful Jersey horse country. Live the manored life for an afternoon!

Best Place for a Laugh
Rascal's Comedy Club
425 Pleasant Valley Way, West Orange
Other location: Ocean Township
(973) 736-2726

Dinner and show packages are available for well-known metro area Letterman regulars as well as first-timers. Smoke-free shows are available, too!

Best Creative Date
Have Balloon, Will Travel Inc.
57 Old Belvidere Rd., Phillipsburg
(800) 608-6359 • www.haveballoonwilltravel.com

Have Balloon ensures that you and your date will find adventure together high above the Garden State. Check them out for reasonable prices and seasonal excursions.

Best Club
Platinum Night Club
13 Paterson St., New Brunswick
(732) 937-6113 • www.clubplatinumonline.com

With two separate rooms and VIP bottle service tables, the Platinum was designed to create 'the New York atmosphere with New Jersey prices'.

Best After Hours Place
Mastoris
144 Highway 130-Rte 206, Bordentown
(609) 298-4650 • www.mastoris.com

Another Jersey landmark, Mastoris is considered the ultimate "gut-buster" of all the great diners. It's a real standout for its high-quality comfort food.

Best Special Occasion Restaurant
Marakesh
321 E. Rte. 46, Parsippany
(973) 808-0062 • www.marakesh.com

This Moroccan atmosphere rocks with soft couches, ornate pillows, and golden trays. The entertainment is not so bad either — think belly dancers!

Best Place To Buy a Gift
Princeton Record Exchange
20 S. Tulane St., Princeton
(609) 921-0880 • www.prex.com

This is the place to find a gift for the music lover.

Top Five Dates

#1. Oh, that Jersey Shore!
From Sandy Hook to Cape May
(800) 648-7263 • http://www.jerseyshore-online.com
Boardwalks, beaches, small town main streets, and lots of take-out picnic food. Any time of year is right for a romantic afternoon or evening at the Jersey Shore. There are dozens of beaches and each section has its own personality. There's no better way to get to know each other!

#2. Spend a Day in the Country
Frenchtown Inn
7 Bridge St., Frenchtown
(908) 996-3300 • www.frenchtowninn.com
Local produce enhances the French-American food at this historical inn. Spend a day combing the local farms or walking through the main drag, stopping at shops like French Country Pottery or Flemington Cut Glass Company. Then have a late lunch or early dinner at the Frenchtown Inn. Enjoy the outdoors in a quaint, beautiful atmosphere.

#3. Take the Hoboken/Sinatra Tour on the Palisades
Hudson River Walkway, 1st St., Hoboken
(201) 768-1360
Spend a day in Frank's world. Rent a kayak or grab a burger at the newly reopened Sinatra Park Café. A stone embankment leads you straight to the water's edge along a quiet beach scattered with driftwood.

Dine along the water or walk west from the river for two blocks to Washington Street where you can eat and club hop the rest of the night.

#4. Riding the Bulls at the Cowtown Rodeo
780 Rte. 40, Pilesgrove
(856) 739-3200 • www.cowtownrodeo.com
Cowtown Rodeo is a professional circuit stop for hundreds of cowboys and cowgirls from across the nation. The longest-running Saturday-night rodeo in the country, Cowtown is open May through September. It's a ride that makes for a really original date night!

#5. Act Like a Kid Again
Six Flags - Great Adventure
Rte. 537, Jackson
www.sixflags.com/parks/greatadventure/
An amusement park, animal safari habitat, and water park in one. Act like a kid all day and have a truckload of fun at Great Adventure. Those thrill rides get everyone's blood racing, right?

Northern Virginia

Best Restaurant for Lunch or Brunch First Date
Ritz-Carlton Grill
1250 S. Hayes St., Arlington
(703) 415-5000
www.ritzcarlton.com/hotels/pentagon_city

This is the spot to go if you are willing to spend a bit more for an intimate and rather luxurious meal. The Sunday brunch is exceptional.

Best Restaurant for First Dinner Date
The Cheesecake Factory
2900 Wilson Blvd., Arlington
Other locations: McLean
(703) 294-9966 • www.cheesecakefactory.com

A great first date place because it is incredibly low-stress fun in a comfortable environment and has excellent food. Save room for one of their amazing desserts.

Best Cheap Date
Cafe Deluxe
1800 International Dr., Tysons Corner
(703) 761-0600

An American Bistro with moderately priced food. It tends to get a bit noisy, but if you don't mind, it's an entertaining spot. The mussels in white wine sauce are great!

Best Restaurant for a Second Dinner Date
Mezza 9
Hyatt Arlington, 1325 Wilson Blvd., Arlington
(703) 276-8999

A Mediterranean restaurant with stylish decor and an extensive menu. This is a cool place to take a date and share some of their tasty appetizers before your meal.

Best Place for Coffee and Dessert
Palladio's Café Coffeehouse
2311 Wilson Blvd., Arlington
(703) 516-0003

Stop at Palladio's for a cup of java after catching a movie at the nearby Courthouse Theater.

Best Place for a Laugh
LaffTracks
Del Rio Mexican Restaurant, 701 E. Market St., Leesburg
(703) 777-9504

Eat some great Mexican food and laugh at the comedians.

Best Creative Date
Fredericksburg Cruises
468 Buzzard's Point Rd., Reedville
(804) 453-2628 • www.tangiercruise.com/index.html

Take your date on the river for dinner and dancing on a 100-foot paddle wheel boat. A romantic and unique way to spend an evening.

Best Club
The Shark Club
14114 Lee Hwy., Centreville
(703) 266-1888

An enormous club with bars, dance floors, pool tables, and a private room for VIPs. If you're in the mood for something different, this is the place to go.

Best After Hours Place
IHOP
3425-A Jefferson Davis Hwy., Alexandria
Other locations: Arlington, Falls Church
(703) 519 4220 • www.ihop.com

Open 24 hours, usually there's a wait, but it's the same old IHOP you've always known. After a night out on the town, try the Vive La French Toast platter.

Best Special Occasion Restaurant
The Greenbrier
300 W. Main St., White Sulphur Springs
(800) 852-5440 • www.greenbrier.com

Take your date on a weekend trip to The Greenbrier and drown yourselves in relaxation and romance. Dine in the Tavern Room for an intimate gourmet meal.

Best Place To Buy a Gift

Romance For The Senses
1102 King St., Alexandria
(703) 549-1102 • www.romanceforthesenses.com

A boutique for the romantic, featuring lingerie, chocolate, books, music, and jewelry

Top Five Dates

#1. Cruising Right Along
Potomac Riverboat Company
Alexandria City Marina, Cameron and
Union Sts., Alexandria
(703) 548-9000 • www.potomacriverboatco.com
How about a dinner cruise on the Potomac River? Leave from the Old Town Alexandria waterfront and enjoy a couple of hours on the water, drinking and eating. It's a great way to meet some new friends, dance and take in a beautiful view.\

#2. Steeeee-rike!
Falls Church Bowling Center
400 S. Maple Ave., Falls Church
(703) 533-8131
Go bowling! After all, who doesn't like putting on those cute bowling shoes and competing against each other? Consider setting the stakes that whoever loses buys dinner. It's a good way to loosen up and relax while getting to know each other.

#3. A Touch of Culture
Smithsonian Institution
Washington, D.C. • www.smithsonian.org
Take a picnic to the mall in Washington, DC. Sit on the grass in the midst of the Smithsonian Institution and have some lunch. Then take some time to walk around and explore some museums. This is an inexpensive date as well, as D.C. museums are free.

#4. A Recipe for Love
Whole Foods Market
2700 Wilson Blvd., Alexandria
Call for other locations
(703) 527-6596 • www.wholefoods.com
Prepare a special meal. Go to Whole Foods and pick

up the ingredients, along with a bottle or two of wine. Cook dinner for your date and set the table with some candles for an extra special touch. Soft jazz or classical music playing in the background is a great addition to a romantic atmosphere.

#5. *Get Away from It All*
The Greenbrier
300 W. Main St., White Sulphur Springs
(800) 453-4858 • www.greenbrier.com

Drive to The Greenbrier, where you can relax and enjoy a day or two away from the city. Enjoy some spa treatments together, play a little golf, take some walks through the woods and swim in the newly renovated pool. This is a great way to get away from the stress of the city for a short or long weekend.

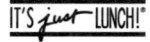

Oklahoma City

Best Restaurant for Lunch or Brunch First Date
Bellini's Ristorante and Grill
6305 Waterford Blvd., Oklahoma City
(405) 848-1065

Come to Bellini's Ristorante and Grill and eat in the vine-covered gazebo next to a picturesque duck pond. This is a beautiful location for a quiet, romantic date.

Best Restaurant for First Dinner Date
Zio's Italian Kitchen
12 E. California Ave., Oklahoma City
(405) 278-8888

Take your date on a romantic water taxi ride on the canal to Zio's Italian Kitchen. The food is excellent and the ambiance can't be topped at any other location.

Best Cheap Date
Remington Park
1 Remington Pl., Oklahoma City
(405) 424-1000 • www.remingtonpark.com

Come enjoy the excitement of thoroughbred horse races with your date and save a lot of money. Remington Park offers $1 admission each Monday.

Best Restaurant for a Second Dinner Date
Metro Wine Bar and Bistro
6418 N. Western Ave., Oklahoma City
(405) 840-9463

Metro Wine Bar and Bistro has daily seafood specials and a wide variety of American cuisine. They also offer a nice selection of wine to complement your meal.

Best Place for Coffee and Dessert
Uncommon Grounds
100 E. Main St., Oklahoma City
(405) 236-5282

Uncommon Grounds offers inside and outside seating in the Bricktown area. They have many different specialty coffees as well as cakes, cookies and biscotti.

Best Place for a Laugh
Bricktown Keys on the Canal
119 E. Oklahoma Ave., Oklahoma City
(405) 602-1494

At this local piano bar, the guests sing for their supper. Come wail along with this hot crowd on the canal and have a good laugh.

Best Creative Date
National Cowboy and Western Heritage Museum
Academy of Western Art Program
1700 N.E. 63rd St., Oklahoma City
(405) 478-2250 • www.nationalcowboymuseum.org

This museum sports very interesting exhibits about cowboys and the West. They also offer hands-on sculpture classes. Sign up for a class with your date and be creative.

Best Club
City Walk
70 N. Oklahoma, Oklahoma City
(405) 232-9255

City Walk has something for everyone! They offer seven clubs under one roof. There's a lot of loud music and big crowds at this local hotspot.

Best After Hours Place
Electro Lounge
5929 N. May Ave., Oklahoma City
(405) 843-8777

Electro Lounge draws a great night crowd. It is owned and operated by members of the younger generation. Lots of energy and enthusiasm can be found here.

Best Special Occasion Restaurant
The Mantel Wine Bar and Bistro
201 E. Sheridan Ave., Oklahoma City
(405) 236-8040

The Mantel is one of the country's best gourmet restaurants. They offer outdoor dining and private rooms. This is a super location for any special occasion.

Best Place To Buy a Gift
The Pine Shop
12020 N. E. I-35 Service Rd., Oklahoma City
(405) 478-0220 • www.pine-shop.com

The Pine Shop carries many unique and wonderful gifts. They offer an assortment of Mary Hadley pottery, Anri wood carvings and many local Oklahoma products.

Top Five Dates

#1. *Take in a Concert*
Bricktown Live
319 E. Sheridan, Oklahoma City
www.brewerentertainment.com/bricktownlive

Bricktown Live hosts many special events and concerts. They offer a full-service catering menu and bar service. This would be a delightful dinner/concert date. Check out their website to see what's playing now.

#2. *Come Monkey Around*
Oklahoma City Zoo
2101 N. E. 50th St., Oklahoma City
(405) 424-3344 • www.okczoo.com

You and your date will be busy checking out all the animal exhibits at the Oklahoma City Zoo. They're located on 110 acres and display 2,800 exotic animals. Come see the gorillas, orangutans, chimpanzees, dolphins, piranhas, sharks, sea lions and more! You're sure to have a memorable time together.

#3. *Try Boot Scootin'*
Cowboys
3034 Portland Ave., Oklahoma City
(405) 947-5978

Cowboys is an authentic country-western dance club. Show off for your date and ride the mechanical bull. Dust off your cowboy boots and do some line dancing on the large hardwood dance floor. Make sure you go to the 21-and-up dance club for an older, more seasoned crowd. You will have a boot scootin' good time!

#4. *Yee-Haw!*
International Professional Rodeo Association
P.O. Box 83377, Oklahoma City
(405) 235-6540 • www.iprarodeo.com

This is the real deal. You and your date will enjoy watching the team roping, bull riding, saddle bronc riding, bareback bronc riding, tie-down roping, cowgirls barrel racing and steer wrestling. This would be an exciting and very unique date to be remembered.

#5. *Take a Cruise Together*
Bricktown Brewery
1 N. Oklahoma Ave., Oklahoma City
(405) 232-2739

If it's not practical to go to the Caribbean, then try cruising down the canal. The Bricktown Brewery offers fun cocktail cruises. Enjoy the brewery's handcrafted ales, lagers and many beers. It will be a romantic, enjoyable evening for you both.

Omaha

Best Restaurant for Lunch or Brunch First Date
Wheatfields Eatery & Bakery
One Pacific Place
1224 S 103rd St., West Central Omaha
(402) 955-1485 • www.wheatfieldscatering.com

This laid-back, European-style cafe is well known for its crepes, omelets, casseroles and decadent desserts. Try one of the sumptuous cheese, meat or dessert fondues!

Best Restaurant for First Dinner Date
Café di Coppia
Regency Court
120 Regency Parkway, Central Omaha
(402) 392-2806

Café di Coppia's understated elegance and magnificent service will leave you feeling relaxed and comfortable as you dine on great Mediterranean and Asian specialties.

Best Cheap Date
Big Fred's Pizza Garden
1101 S. 119th St., West Central Omaha
(402) 333-4414

Pizza is made only one way here: a thin, hand-tossed crust, a touch of tomato, plenty of cheese and your favorite toppings. The menu also features sandwiches and prime rib.

Best Restaurant for a Second Dinner Date
Jams American Grill
7814 Dodge St., Central Omaha
(402) 399-8300

Amazing food and a fun atmosphere make this restaurant stand out in a very popular restaurant town. Make sure to enjoy an appetizer to get you started!

Best Place for Coffee and Dessert
Delice European Bakery & Coffee Bar
1206 Howard St., Downtown Omaha
(402) 342-2276

When you walk in the door, you can instantly see the wide

variety of luscious pastries, cakes, cookies and other treats on display.

Best Place for a Laugh
The Funny Bone Comedy Club & Restaurant
Village Pointe Center
17305 Davenport St. Suite 201, West Omaha
(402) 493-8036

Get ready to laugh with live national acts every Wednesday through Sunday. A tasteful selection of casual appetizers, entrees and desserts are an added bonus.

Best Creative Date
Carriage Ride and Dinner in the Old Market
M&J Carriage Services
(402) 453-6745 • www.mjcarriage.com

Magical Journey's Carriage Service has been providing carriage rides around the Old Market for more than 25 years.

Best Club
Nico's
11201 Davenport St., West Central Omaha
(402) 615-2582 • www.nicoomaha.com

Nico's has the best of both worlds, with its luxurious martini lounge and its lively dance club. The atmosphere is erotic and sensual featuring hip, high energy cocktails.

Best After-Hours Place
Stir
One Harrah's Boulevard, Council Bluffs, IA
(712) 329-6000 • www.harrahs.com

Not quite ready to go home? Extend your fun until 2 A.M.. Stir is the perfect mix of attitude and fun. We're talking high energy excitement with a Vegas twist!

Best Special-Occasion Restaurant
V'Mertz
1022 Howard Street, Downtown Omaha
(402) 345-8980 • www.vmertz.com

Whether you're celebrating a special occasion or just want to feel like you are, V'Mertz's warm and inviting ambience is only upstaged by its delectable food and world-class wine selections.

Best Place To Buy a Gift

Borsheims
120 Regency Parkway, Central Omaha
(402) 391-0400 • www.borsheims.com

Although they offer some of the world's most stunning jewelry pieces, an average shopper will find a trove of affordable trinkets and fine gifts as well as a bridal registry.

Top Five Dates

#1. *Joslyn Art Museum*
2200 Dodge St., Downtown Omaha
(402) 342-3300 • www.joslyn.org
First Friday JAM — Fall/ Winter

This popular after-work event features a diverse line-up of regional jazz, blues and alternative groups, with light fare and libations on the first Friday of each month from October through May. In addition, you can enjoy special exhibitions and Joslyn's collection of contemporary art on view in the Pavilion Galleries.

Jazz on the Green - Summer

Pack up your picnic basket and blanket and head out to the free summer jazz series held on six consecutive Thursdays beginning with the first Thursday after July 4. This is the place to see and be seen on those hot summer nights!

#2. *Omaha Community Playhouse*
6915 Cass St., Central Omaha
(402) 553-0800 • www.omahaplayhouse.com

Omaha is home to one of the largest community theaters in the United States. Actor Henry Fonda took this stage, as did Dorothy McGuire. Dorothy Brando also became a star here, influencing the Godfather himself, son Marlon Brando. The company stages 11 shows annually, including a holiday production of A Christmas Carol that is sure to please.

#3. *The Classy Gourmet Culinary Arts Center*
721 N. 98th St., Central Omaha
(402) 995.2665 • www.theclassygourmet.com

The Classy Gourmets cooking classes will not only inspire you, but educate you on the culinary arts and the ever-increasing role that food and wine play in our daily lives. Try the popular "Taste of the Orient

Series" with Chef Cory Guyer, who will create tasty Asian dishes and share some of his favorite recipes.

#4. Omaha's Henry Doorly Zoo
3701 S. 10th St., South Omaha
(402) 733-8401 • www.omahazoo.com

Feed the elephants or take a stroll into the jungle at the world-class Henry Doorly Zoo. The Lied Jungle is home of the world's largest indoor tropical rainforest. It encompasses three separate geographic zones. You can experience the sights, sounds and smells of the jungle as you meander through re-creations of Asian, African and South American rain forests.

#5. Heartland of America Park Gondola Ride
6th & Douglas St., Downtown Omaha
(402) 884-5677

Enjoy a romantic, relaxing cruise on a Venetian Gondola at Omaha's Heartland of America Park. Afterward, take a stroll down the Lewis & Clark Landing and grab a bite at Rick's Boatyard Café as you overlook the majestic Missouri River.

Orange County

Best Restaurant for Lunch or Brunch First Date
Ritz Carlton Laguna Niguel
1 Ritz-Carlton Dr., Dana Point
(949) 240-2000 • www.ritzcarlton.com

The fanciest Sunday brunch in Orange County can get a quick answer to whether or not that special someone is ready for a commitment.

Best Restaurant for First Dinner Date
Rouge Bistro and Bar
327 Newport Center Dr., Newport Beach
(949) 640-2700

David Wilhelm, Orange County's most noted restaurateur, continues to prove his worthiness in French gourmet cuisine with this new bistro and bar.

Best Cheap Date
Gypsy Den Grand Central Cafe
125 N. Broadway, Santa Ana
(714) 835-8840

Located in the trendy Santora Arts District of Santa Ana, Gypsy Den offers a cheap and cheerful dining experience with vegetable lasagna, quiches, and tamale pies.

Best Restaurant for a Second Dinner Date
Bandera
3201 E. Pacific Coast Hwy., Corona Del Mar
(949) 673-3524 • www.banderarestaurant.com

Elegant and refined, Bandera takes Spanish-American influences to produce some of the most flavorful and generously portioned steaks in the southland.

Best Place for Coffee and Dessert
Haute Cakes Caffe & Bakery
1807 Westcliff Dr., Newport Beach
(949) 642-4114

Paintings from local artists, a freestanding flower store, and a salon are but a few of the reasons to visit Haute Bakery, if not just for the delectable sweets themselves.

Best Place for a Laugh
Irvine Improv
71 Fortune Dr., Suite 841, Irvine
(949) 854-5455
www.symfonee.com/Improv/Irvine/home/index.aspx

Orange County's top comedy scene lures professionals and TV personalities from their regular LA gigs to weekend performances and midweek comedy nights.

Best Creative Date
Fairview Park
2501 Placentia Ave., Costa Mesa
(714) 754-5069 • www.cmfairviewpark.org

Adventurous types look to Fairview Park for action-packed dates that include gliding, horseback riding, and trail jumping.

Best Club
Rain
1700 Placentia Ave., Costa Mesa
(949) 548-3533

Don't let the Tiki-Bar ambiance lead you astray. Rain is where locals congregate almost every night of the week for DJ promotions, singles nights, and club-style dancing.

Best After Hours Place
Bungalow Restaurant
2441 E. Coast Hwy., Corona del Mar
(949) 673-6585 • www.thebungalowrestaurant.com

Specialty martinis and oversized velvet booths surrounded by dark cherry woods create an inviting scene for late-nighters to enjoy one of the best 21-ounce porterhouses in town.

Best Special Occasion Restaurant
McCormick & Schmick's
2000 Main St., Irvine
(949) 756-0505 • www.McCormickandSchmicks.com

The area's finest seafood in a distinguished, tailored environment that is considered one of inland OC's premier dining choices.

Best Place To Buy a Gift
Fashion Island
401 Newport Center Dr., # A150, Newport Beach
(949) 720-3330 • www.shopfashionisland.com

One of the West Coast's most picturesque shopping centers, it combines big name luxury stores like Neiman Marcus and Bloomingdales with smaller independent shops.

Top Five Dates

#1. *I love the nightlife*
Shark Club
841 Baker St., Costa Mesa
(714) 751-6428 • www.sharkclub.com

Orange County has one of the hottest dance scenes in the area, especially for the 30 to 40 year old set. Make a late date around 10 p.m., and hit the Shark Bar or your favorite local nightclub. Depending on the chemistry, dance the night away or use it as a stepping board to an even later date.

#2. *Love is in the air*
Pacific Amphitheatre
100 Fair Dr., Costa Mesa
(714) 708-1870

Pacific Amphitheater offers outdoor concerts and performances by touring solo acts in addition to acclaimed local artists and musicians. The outdoor amphitheater allows patrons to bring in their own picnics, which is a great way to bring individuality to the date. Be sure to remember some candles and cloth napkins.

#3. *The allure of a civilized spirit*
Bowers Museum of Cultural Art
2002 N. Main St., Santa Ana
(714) 567-3600 • www.bowers.org

Living in Orange County gives people the ability to visit some of the best museums in the world. A great way to impress a date is to make a trip to a local museum. The Bower's Museum of Santa Ana offers one of the area's best and most extensive art and artifact collections in a stellar setting.

#4. *Make a formal date*
Orange County Performing Arts Center
600 Town Centre Dr., Costa Mesa
(714) 556-2787 • www.ocpac.org

With a local opera, ballet, and orchestra, Orange County is the perfect place to indulge in an evening performance. Rather than slinking in jeans and a button-down shirt to a third tier seat, why not splurge on the best seats you can get and go in a suit or even a tuxedo?

#5. *Sometimes it can get hot in the kitchen.*
St. Regis Monarch Beach Resort & Spa
1 Monarch Beach Resort, Dana Point
Call for other locations.
(949) 234-3200 • www.stregismonarchbay.com

Sometimes cooking is a talent that comes after a really positive cooking experience. With so many great restaurants and hotels in the area, why not go to a daytime cooking school to learn the tricks of the trade? Many of the classes are filled with hungry couples looking to nourish their relationships with good food and communication skills.

Orlando

Best Restaurant for Lunch or Brunch First Date
The Lake Eola Yacht Club
407 E. Central Blvd., Orlando
(407) 841-0033 • www.lakeeolayachtclub.com

This lakeside eatery borders Lake Eola with views of the downtown skyline. Feast on a tropical buffet or sandwiches and soups. Sit inside or outside on the breathtaking patio.

Best Restaurant for First Dinner Date
Houston's
215 S. Orlando Ave., Winter Park
(407) 740-4005 • www.houstons.com

This restaurant serves up juicy steaks and fresh seafood. Grab a drink at the beautiful bar. With comfortable seating and friendly staff, you won't be disappointed.

Best Cheap Date
Aloma Cinema Grill
2155 Aloma Ave., Winter Park
(407) 678-8214 • www.orlandomovietimes.com

For just two dollars you can watch blockbuster hits while you savor a cold beer, swallow a sandwich or pizza, or munch on a salad.

Best Restaurant for a Second Dinner Date
Carrino's Italian Restaurant Pizza and Deli
7572 W. Sand Lake Rd., Orlando
(407) 352-8407

This family style Italian restaurant is a hidden gem. Serving many delightful dishes such as pastas, veal, and homemade pizza — even submarine sandwiches.

Best Place for Coffee and Dessert
TooJay's Gourmet Deli
2400 E. Colonial Dr., Orlando
Other locations: Altamonte Springs, Dr. Phillips Marketplace
(407) 894-1718 • www.toojays.com

Your classic New York Jewish deli featuring mouthwatering favorites such as pastrami piled high on rye, blintzes and the most decadent and sinful desserts you can imagine. Be sure to try the black and white cookies or the "killer cake."

Best Place for a Laugh
Improv Comedy Club
129 W. Church St., Orlando
(321) 281-8000 • www.orlandoimprov.com

Enjoy dinner and a laugh-out-loud comedy show at America's premiere comedy showcase and restaurant. Featuring famous performers, like Michael Winslow — check out their website for upcoming shows.

Best Creative Date
GondEola at Lake Eola
2924 Mystic Cove Dr., Orlando
(407) 658-4226 • www.gondeola.com

Enjoy a romantic dinner while floating across beautiful Lake Eola. Lobster tail and happy hour cruises are available on this Venetian style tour. (Or, take an after dinner cruise, and order the chocolate and champagne!)

Best Club
Froggers Grill and Bar
6700 Conroy Rd. Suite 120, Orlando
Other locations: Apopka
(407) 293-4777 • www.froggers.com

This is a great place to mix and mingle with other single people — they even have their own online chat room. And their special events calendar is jam-packed. Check it out!

Best After Hours Place
Pat O'Brien's
Universal Studios Citywalk, Orlando
(407) 224-2106 • www.patobriens.com

This New Orleans style restaurant is located in the center of one of Orlando's busiest nightspots. Here you can feast on great food, drink specials, and listen to the music of tinkling keys from the nearby piano bar.

Best Special Occasion Restaurant
Le Coq Au Vin
4800 S. Orange Ave., Orlando
(407) 851-6980

Specializing in classic country French cuisine, everything on the menu is worth trying at this comfortable, upscale yet casual spot. Sample the namesake dish or the longtime favorite Bayou Tesche.

Best Place To Buy a Gift
The Mall at Millenia
4200 Conroy Rd., Orlando
(407) 363-3555 • www.mallatmillenia.com

An upscale mall where you're sure to find the perfect gift for his or her needs. Home to Neiman Marcus, Bloomingdales, and Macy's, as well as upscale boutiques like Louis Vuitton, Gucci, and Jimmy Choo.

Top Five Dates

#1. Pamper yourself and your date at the fabulous Canyon Ranch Spa Club
Gaylord Palms Resort and Convention Center,
6000 W. Osceola Parkway, Kissimmee
(407) 586-4772
www.canyonranch.com/spaclubs/gaylord/index.asp

Treat yourself and your date to the ultimate in relaxation with a combination of this top-notch spa's fabulous treatments. Choose from invigorating body wraps, rejuvenating facials and a massage or therapeutic body work session. Top it off with a healthy gourmet meal for a full-day of pampering that will leave you both positively glowing.

#2. Create something hot together
460 N. Orlando Ave. Ste. 106, Winter Park
(407) 644-8088 • www.glazeunderfire.com

Glaze Under Fire provides everything you need to create your own masterpiece. Bring a beverage and your favorite munchies and get creative. Watch your date unleash his or her creative juices. You can even work on a project together. And at the end of the date, you'll have a little treasure to take home as a keepsake.

#3. *DeLeon Springs*
DeLeon Springs State Park, 601 Ponce DeLeon Blvd., DeLeon Springs
(386) 985-4212
http://www.planetdeland.com/deleonsprings/
Take a trip to DeLeon Springs, a tropical frontier still rich in mystery and romance. Enjoy a unique dining experience at the Old Spanish Sugar Mill and Griddle House, where you'll be seated at a table with a built-in grill and given a pitcher of batter to create your own hotcakes.

#4. *Horseback Riding at the Hyatt Grand Cypress*
One Grand Cypress Blvd., Orlando
(407) 239-4700
http://grandcypress.hyatt.com/property/sportsrelax/activities/onsite_details.jhtml?id=10&ssnav=0
The Hyatt Grand Cypress Resort features a "world-class British Horse Society Approved" equestrian center with instruction for riders of all levels. It's a perfect place for an equestrian enthusiast to take a date with no riding experience; the caring and professional staff with make both of you feel equally at home.

#5. *Take your dream date to heavenly Discovery Cove*
6000 Discovery Cove Way, Orlando
(407) 370-1280 • www.discoverycove.com
Swim with the dolphins at this tropical hideaway. Languor in this paradise of grottoes, lagoons and reefs, then relax with your date on one of the beautiful white-sand beaches. Walk the nature trail and see some unique wildlife. And don't you worry about crowds — attendance at Discovery Cove is strictly monitored.

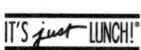

Philadelphia

Best Restaurant for Lunch or Brunch First Date
Reading Terminal Market
12th St. & Arch St., Philadelphia
(215) 922-2317 • www.readingterminalmarket.org

Here you will have hustle, bustle, chaos, and great food of every variety. The Reading Terminal Market is a great place to see if your date is as adventurous as you are. They have an incredible variety of places to eat, from sit-down cafés to dining at the counter.

Best Restaurant for First Dinner Date
Dolce
241 Chestnut St., Philadelphia
(215) 238-9983 • http://dolcerestaurant.com/

Dolce is about romance, romance, and more romance. It is a Southern Italian themed restaurant that is intimate and private. It is also conveniently located in a romantic walking area.

Best Cheap Date
Copabanana
344 South St., Philadelphia
(215) 923-6180

Copabanana is renowned for its margaritas, burgers, and fries. It is generally a Tex-Mex type of menu for a quick meal before you hit South Street. You pick your own toppings for your burger here.

Best Restaurant for a Second Dinner Date
Passion
211 S. 15th St., Philadelphia
(215) 875-9895 • www.passion.citysearch.com

Nuevo Latino is the theme of this restaurant that attracts a trendy crowd. It has an earthy, minimalist décor with draped ceilings and thumping salsa music playing. It has a creative and eclectic menu.

Best Place for Coffee and Dessert

Pink Rose Pastry Shop
630 S. Fourth St., Philadelphia
(800) ROSE-383 • http://pinkrosepastry.com

The Pink Rose pastry shop has a booming mail-order business that emerged from their renown as a great pastry and dessert bistro. Nonetheless, the shop remains a quaintly simple, English manor style bistro for coffees, teas, and desserts. It is light and airy with a homey feel to it. This is a superb little spot for desserts and teas.

Best Place for a Laugh

Tony and Tina's Wedding
18th and Snyder, Philadelphia
(800) 660-8462 • www.tonylovestina.com/city_philadelphia

Tony and Tina's Wedding is raucous, rowdy, and full of surprises. Sit down at a table with strangers and you never know if the person next to you is a cast member or a patron. Set amidst an authentically fashioned South Philly wedding, Tony and Tina's Wedding is a national hit and includes dinner and cake. It is hilarious and filled with unexpected twists and turns.

Best Creative Date

Shofuso, Japanese House and Garden
4700 States Dr., Philadelphia
(215) 878-5097 • www.shofuso.com

Shofuso is an authentically reproduced 'shoin-zukuri.' This is a 'desk-centered' house from the 16th century. It is located on the grounds of West Philadelphia's Horticultural Center in Fairmont Park. The house and garden are open for touring from April to October. Enjoy the complimentary machu green tea and seasonal sweets or participate in a Japanese Carpentry workshop with Japanese master carpenter Isao Okumura. This is an interactive date spot for anyone with an interest in architecture, botany, or Asian culture. It can be calming and deeply romantic.

Best Club

Alma de Cuba
1623 Walnut, Philadelphia
(215) 988-1799

Alma de Cuba has a Caribbean/South American menu with a happening bar downstairs. The atmosphere is sexy and they offer Mambo classes once a week. This place is fun and an excellent way to meet other singles.

Best After Hours Place
Buddakan
325 Chestnut St., Philadelphia
(215) 574-9440 • www.buddakan.com

Buddakan offers fun Asian cuisine. It has amazing décor, incredibly high ceilings, and each dining table has a massive statue of Buddha in the middle.

Best Special Occasion Restaurant
DiNardo's
312 Race St., Philadelphia
(215) 925-5115 • www.oldcity.org/memrestaurant/dinardos

If you love seafood, DiNardo's is the restaurant for you. The garlic crabs are transcendent. Bibs are supplied as diners plunge into seafood entrees renowned throughout the city. This is a great casual place to celebrate any occasion.

Best Place To Buy a Gift
Caviar Assoulline
505 Vine St., Philadelphia
(800) 521-4491 • www.icaviar.com

Caviar Assoulline is both a wholesaler and retailer of fine food gifts and gift baskets with an emphasis on caviar. This place can create according to budget or desire. They have excellent service and hard to find specialty foods and gifts that make this place a treasure.

Top Five Dates

#1. Ride the Ducks
The Philly Duck boats are WWII-era amphibious vehicles that have been extensively updated. Bring a date on an 80-minute tour through Philadelphia's land and water-based attractions. The water portion lasts 20 minutes and includes a splash into the river you will never forget with a complimentary "Wacky Quacker."

#2. Whale Watchers
Does anything melt hearts better than dolphins and whales? Head south to Cape May and jump aboard the Whale Watcher II for guaranteed sightings of marine mammals. There is something amazing

about seeing these huge creatures up close and in their natural habitat. This date is guaranteed to create a meaningful experience that will last a lifetime.

#3. Take in Some Culture and Some Treats

Rodin Museum has the most significant collection of 19th century sculpture in the city. Special events are planned throughout 2004, which marks the 75th anniversary of the opening of the museum. Have a fully prepared picnic delivered by Moose & Goose Picnic Catering on the grass near Schuylkill. If this doesn't melt hearts, nothing will.

#4. Make a Difference

Volunteer to make Philadelphia a better place through the many opportunities offered by Philadelphia Cares. They post schedules so you can pick an event to do together. They are extremely organized and are a great bunch of people too. It's a great way to get to know someone.

#5. Float through the Clouds

Take a beautiful drive out to Chester Spring to the launch site of Lollipop Balloons Inc. Soak in the scenery of Chester County's horse country. Then hop into the basket of one of Lollipop's hot air balloons and see it from the air. Take along provisions like caviar and champagne!

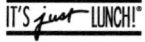

Phoenix

Best Restaurant for Lunch or Brunch First Date
Barrio Café
2814 N. 16th St., Phoenix
(602) 636-0240

Everyone loves Mexican food, but this neighborhood's gourmet version raises the bar. The cochinita pibil (chili-rubbed pork) is simply succulent.

Best Restaurant for First Dinner Date
Tarbell's
3213 E. Camelback Rd., Phoenix
(602) 955-8100 • www.tarbells.com

With a pleasing open layout and contemporary art, the low key atmosphere and moderate prices at Tarbell's are perfect for a relaxed and casual first date.

Best Cheap Date
Picnic at Arizona Falls
Northeast corner of Indian School Rd. and 56th St., Phoenix
Park at G.R. Herberger Park,
5802 E. Indian School Rd., Phoenix
www.srpnet.com/water/canals/azfalls.asp

This century old spot has been converted into an inviting design of industrial materials, sinuous curves, and cooling waterfalls. This is an unusual, romantic spot for a picnic.

Best Restaurant for a Second Dinner Date
Va Bene Ristorante
4025 E. Chandler Blvd., Phoenix (Ahwatukee)
(480) 706-4070

"I'll meet you anytime you want in our Italian Restaurant." This family owned restaurant could have inspired the Billy Joel song, with its generous portions and warm atmosphere.

Best Place for Coffee and Dessert
My Florist Café
530 W. McDowell Rd., Phoenix
(602) 254-0333

Open until midnight, this sophisticated spot is a lovely place to stop for homemade desserts, a cappuccino, dessert wine, and live jazz.

Best Place for a Laugh
The Improv
930 E. University Dr., Tempe
(480) 921-9877 • www.improvclubs.com/tempe/Tempe.htm

When top tier acts like Jerry Seinfeld and Kathy Griffin come to town, this is where they perform.

Best Creative Date
Drive-In Movie at Scottsdale 6 Drive-In
8101 E. McKellips Rd., Scottsdale
Other locations: Glendale 9 Drive-In, 5650 N. 55th Ave., Glendale
(602) 949-9451 • www.drive-ins.com/theater/aztscot

The only armrest you have to share is the one in your car. Pop some popcorn and snuggle up. Maybe you will even watch the movie.

Best Club
Marco Polo Supper Club
2621 E. Camelback Rd., Phoenix
(602) 468-0100 • www.azeats.com/marcopolo

A classy throwback to the Art Deco era, Marco Polo attracts a crowd old enough to appreciate it, yet young enough to get down and boogie.

Best After Hours Place
Five & Diner
5220 N. 16th St., Phoenix
(602) 264-5220

This '50s style diner with its mini jukeboxes on Formica tables, serves up comfort food like chicken fried steak and butterscotch milkshakes.

Best Special Occasion Restaurant

T. Cook's at the Royal Palms
5200 E. Camelback Rd., Phoenix
(602) 840-3610 • www.royalpalmshotel.com

Well reviewed and located in the beautifully refurbished Royal Palms resort, T. Cook's exudes a kind of graciousness that is rare in the Valley.

Best Place To Buy a Gift

Louis Vuitton
Scottsdale Fashion Square,
7014 E. Camelback Rd., Scottsdale
(480) 946-1700 • www.louisvuitton.com

Luxury monogrammed leather goods, including handbags and wallets, are always a stylish and sought after gift.

Top Five Dates

#1. It's like Being on Top of the World
Compass Room at the Hyatt Regency
122 N. 2nd St., Phoenix
(602) 252-1234 • www.phoenixhyatt.com

Spend and evening at the beautiful Compass Room at the Hyatt Regency Hotel. This revolving restaurant has an unparalleled view of the city lights and surrounding mountains. It creates an atmosphere like no other. Time your reservation for sunset, and it will be an evening neither of you will ever forget.

#2. Nothin' Says Lovin' Like Somethin' in the Oven.
Vincent's
3930 E. Camelback Rd., Phoenix
(602)-224-3727
Town & Country Mall
20th St. and Camelback Rd., Phoenix

Shop a local farmer's market and prepare a meal together. Vincent's on Camelback has a lovely Saturday morning market that includes cheeses, wine, and pastries. If you are inclined to cook from scratch, Town & Country Mall's Wednesday market features produce and other ingredients from local farms.

#3. Hold on to Each Other as you Brave the Local Haunts...
Haunted Phoenix
San Carlos Hotel
202 N. Central Ave., Phoenix
(602) 253-6668 • www.hotelsancarlos.com

Visit some of the city's reputed haunted locales. The Boutique Hotel and Hotel San Carlos, claim they have many ghosts. Leone Jensen, a heartbroken young woman, fell to her death from the hotel's high window in 1928. But not to worry, you will have each other to cling to if the ghosts make an appearance.

#4. Discover the Orient
Japanese Friendship Garden
Margaret T. Hance Park
1125 N. 3rd Ave., Phoenix
(602) 256-3204 • http://phoenix.gov/PARKS/jfg.html
Ichi Ban Japanese Sushi Express
2815 N. Central Ave., Phoenix
(602) 277-3559

On a Saturday afternoons, stroll the foot bridges, koi pond, and plants of the Japanese Friendship Garden. Then enjoy a tea ceremony in the tea house. Reservations are required. To continue the theme, go for sushi at a nearby restaurant, such as Ichi Ban.

#5. Paddle Boats
Tempe Town Lake
Mill Avenue and Rio Salado Pkwy., Tempe
(480) 984-8158
Encanto Park
15th Ave. and Encanto Blvd., Phoenix
(602) 262-6412

Go for low tech romance, rent a paddle boat at Tempe Town Lake or Encanto Park. Sitting side by side, paddle out to a quiet spot where you both can observe the shoreline at peaceful remove. Once you reach shore again, treat your date to ice cream or a sno-cone from a nearby vendor.

Pittsburgh

Best Restaurant for Lunch or Brunch First Date
Palomino
4 Gateway Center, Downtown
Other locations: 444 Liberty Ave.
(412) 281-7711 • www.palomino.com

Palomino's lively bar and sophisticated décor complements a Mediterranean menu rich in seafood. The atmosphere creates the ideal upscale hot spot for dinner, drinks, and conversation.

Best Restaurant for First Dinner Date
Mallorca
2228 E. Carson St., South Side
(412) 488-1818

Another Best of Pittsburgh winner and the best Spanish restaurant in the city. You can count on generous portions of delicious authentic dishes.

Best Cheap Date
Buca di Beppo
3 Station Square, Pittsburgh
(866) EAT-BUCA • www.bucadibeppo.com

Proof positive that cheap doesn't necessarily mean not as good as expensive when it comes to food, the "Immigrant Southern Italian" offerings at this family-run establishment is the best money can buy.

Best Restaurant for a Second Dinner Date
Kaya
2000 Smallman St., Strip District
(412) 261-6565 • www.bigburitto.com/kaya

Experience the tastes of the Caribbean right in your own backyard... well, in the Strip District anyway.

Best Place for Coffee and Dessert
Gullifty's
1022 Murray Ave., Squirrel Hill
(412) 521-8222 • www.gullifitysrestaurant.com

Gullifty's has been recognized as having "The Best Desserts in Pittsburgh" for almost 2 decades. With a legacy like that you can't go wrong.

Best Place for a Laugh
Improv
166 E. Bridge St., Waterfront
(412) 462-5233 • www.symfonee.com/Improve/Pittsburgh

Some of the freshest comedy, great drinks, and a lively crowd make this Pittsburgh's premier comedy stop.

Best Creative Date
National Aviary
Allegheny Commons West Ridge Ave
Pittsburgh, PA 15212
Cross Street: Arch Street and Ridge Avenue
(412) 323-7235

Look and learn about some of the most beautiful species of birds in the world as you are serenaded by winged wonders of the world at this delightful aviary.

Best Club
Matrix
7 E. Station Sq., Station Square
(412) 261-2220 • www.pghnightlife.com/matrix_home.php

Four distinctively themed rooms, providing house beats, hip-hop, Latin-dance, and Miami-style trance music. An ideal destination for any flavor of high-class dance club.

Best After Hours Place
Primanti Brothers
46 18th St., Strip District
(412) 263-2142

The city's signature sandwich shop since the 1920's, featuring the "sandwich that goes down like a meal", Primanti Brothers is one of the best spots for late night dining.

Best Special Occasion Restaurant
Le Mont
1114 Grandview Ave., Mt. Washington
(412) 431-3100

With it's great views of the Point, and a lavish menu, it has to be one of the city's most romantic restaurants.

Best Place To Buy a Gift
The Waterfront
285 E. Waterfront Dr., Homestead
(412) 476-8889 • www.waterfronttowncenter.com

You name the store — you'll find it here in this ever-expanding outdoor mall.

Top Five Dates

#1. Sittin' On Top of the World
Mount Washington
Grandview Ave., Pittsburgh

Just a little reminder — you live in (or near) one of the most beautiful city skylines in the world. Take your date and a camera up one of the inclines to the top of Mount Washington on a crystal clear spring or fall evening and play Austin Powers. "And, I'm spent...".

#2. Climb Every Mountain
Seven Springs Mountain Resort
777 Waterwheel Drive, Champion
(800) 452-2223

Western Pennsylvania is chock full of parks and outdoor activities. Everyone knows when winter rolls around that the ski-resort-packed Laurel Highlands just east of Pittsburgh make for a fun date. But, make an effort to check out this beautiful area of Pennsylvania for summertime activities like hiking and biking, too.

#3. Create Your Own Amusement
Kennywood
4800 Kennywood Blvd., West Mifflin
(412) 461-0500 • www.kennywood.com

C'mon, how long has it been since you were on a roller coaster? Kennywood is right around the corner in Homestead and you haven't had this much fun in a long time. Sneak a kiss at the top of the Ferris Wheel, scream out loud (always a good thing) on Phantom's Revenge, or become an instant hero and win her a teddy bear.

#4. Picnic By The Water
Moraine State Park
225 Pleasant Valley Rd., Portersville
(724) 368-8811

No matter where you are in Western PA, the water can't be far. If you work downtown, meet at the Point for a luncheon picnic by the fountain. If you are up north, my parent's favorite date is a sunset picnic on Lake Arthur at Moraine State Park. Add a romantic flare by bringing a portable CD player and that CD that will always makes her think of you.

#5. Massage This…
ESSpa Kozmetika SkinCare @ The Cross Keys Inn
599 Dorseyville Rd., Pittsburgh
(412) 963-0210 • www.esspa.net

Escaping your busy life and spending the day being pampered at a spa is pure luxury. It can be even more relaxing if you share it with someone you really like. For an evening of romantic indulgence, make a reservation for the Dinner Massage Special at ESSpa at The Cross Keys Inn in Fox Chapel. WARNING -this date is a sure fire success and will be difficult to top!

Portland

Best Restaurant for Lunch or Brunch First Date
Southpark Seafood Grill and Wine Bar
901 SW Salmon St., Portland
(503) 326-1300

Located in the heart of Portland's cultural district, the menu features the freshest Northwest seafood and produce in dishes inspired by the culinary traditions of the Mediterranean.

Best Restaurant for First Dinner Date
Dragonfish Asian Café at the Paramount Hotel
909 S.W. Park Ave., Portland
(503) 243-5991 • www.dragonfishcafe.com

Choose selections from their stunning Asian fusion menu and the staff will bring each out as a separate course, allowing you and your date to share food and friendly conversation.

Best Cheap Date
The Baghdad Theater
3702 SE Hawthorne Blvd., Portland
(503) 228-4651

This restored old movie theater shows second-run features for a buck. Every other row of seats was taken out and replaced with tables. Order pizza and a brew while you're there.

Best Restaurant for a Second Dinner Date
Portland City Grill
111 S.W. 5th Ave., 30th Fl., Portland
(503) 450-0030 • www.portlandcitygrill.com

Here's where it all happens in downtown Portland. Elegant dining, swanky clientele and a separate, yet hoppin' bar scene punctuates this romantic, panoramic view destination.

Best Place for Coffee and Dessert
Papa Haydn East
5829 S.E. Milwaukie Ave., Portland
Other location: N.W. 23rd Ave.
(503) 232-9440 • www.papahaydn1.citysearch.com

This Portland mainstay is an absolute dessert standout. Coat your fork with a mouthful of their Black Velvet cake and you'll think you've died and gone to heaven.

Best Place for a Laugh
The Greek Cusina
404 S.W. Washington, Portland
(503) 224-2288 • www.greekcusina.com

Wednesday through Sunday, the second floor fills up with raucous fun. Laugh the night away with Greek dancing, plate breaking, belly dancing and, of course, plenty of Ouzo.

Best Creative Date
Pasta Works
3735 S.E. Hawthorne Blvd., Portland
(503) 232-1010 • www.pastaworks.com

Browse the boutiques on S.E. Hawthorne Boulevard. Shop for candles and massage oil. Pick up pasta and wine from Pasta Works. End with dinner and a massage at home.

Best Club
Dante's
One S.W. 3rd Ave., Portland
(503) 226-6630 • www.danteslive.com

Complete with a glowing red bar, this club is as hot as its name. The big draws are the theme nights — like the DJs and exotic dancers that heat it up on "Sinferno Sundays."

Best After Hours Place
Le Bistro Montage
301 SE Morrison St., Portland
(503) 234-1324

Share banquet-like tables with your neighbors at this Cajun-style restaurant, known for macaroni dishes. Open until 4 A.M.. on Fridays and Saturdays and 2 A.M.. the rest of the week.

Best Special Occasion Restaurant
Hurley's
1987 N.W. Kearney St., Portland
(503) 295-6487 • www.hurleys-restaurant.com

This French restaurant was named by Citysearch as one of the top 10 newbies in the class of 2003. They have three dishes with Foie Gras. Reasonably priced for this category.

Best Place To Buy a Gift
Greg's
3707 S.W. Hawthorne Blvd., Portland
(503) 235-1257

Delightfully kooky cards, sensual candles, cleverly crafted housewares and handmade adornments alight in this fun Hawthorne District gift shop.

Five Great Dates

#1. Road Trip!
One of the biggest draws of Portland is its close proximity to so many different road trip destinations. Feel the surf flush your cheeks and sand beneath your feet while picnicking along the beach in Seaside, hike up to the Columbia River Gorge's Multnomah Falls or take the northeastern jaunt up to Hood River to windsurf or shop the local wares.

#2. Taste the Day Away
Various Oregon Wineries • www.oregonwine.org
Drive or take a chauffeured trip down scenic Hwy. 99 South from Tigard to McMinnville to taste your way in and out of the area's well-known wineries. During the summer months, many Oregon wineries also feature live music and tasting events. Check the Oregon Wine website for specific touring and event information.

#3. Walk on the Wild Side
Oregon Zoo
4001 SW Canyon Rd., Portland
(503) 226-1561 • www.oregonzoo.org
Meet and greet with Packy the elephant, hike through the snowcap-simulated Cascade Crest or stroll through Steller Cove, an underwater zoo odyssey. The Oregon Zoo also hosts several spe-

cial events, like their ultra-popular summer concert series. Don't want to drive? Take Portland's innovative MAX light rail system — it'll drop you off at the door.

#4. Asian Tour
Portland Classical Chinese Garden
N.W. 23rd and Everett, Portland
(503) 228-8131 • www.portlandchinesegarden.org
Explore the exotic at this authentic Suzhou-style Chinese garden. Tour the meandering paths through lush gardens and across flowing waterways, sit and chat on one of the welcoming benches among rare orchids and striking rock arrangements or take a class together — like seasonal flower arranging or Chinese script lettering.

#5. A Streetcar Named Desire
Portland Streetcar
Stops throughout Portland State University Campus, Pearl District and Nob Hill District
www.portlandstreetcar.org
Take the Euro-hip Portland Streetcar and hit all of downtown's hotspots in one fell swoop. Admire the upscale art galleries and chic eateries in the hot Pearl District, take in the local architecture near P.S.U. and window shop or grab a bite in the "trendy-third" area on N.W. 23rd St. Get to know one another while experiencing Portland in a day.

Providence

Best Restaurant for Lunch or Brunch First Date
CAV
14 Imperial Pl., Providence
(401) 751-9164

Both a restaurant and an antique store, CAV combines two favorite Sunday pursuits: brunch and browsing. The cuisine at CAV is as engaging as its carefully presented decor.

Best Restaurant for First Dinner Date
Capriccio
2 Pine St., Providence
(401) 421-1320

Carved from the cellars of a Providence landmark, Capriccio is the city's outpost for candlelight sophistication. You will be decidedly pampered and the food is divine.

Best Cheap Date
Twin Oaks Restaurant
100 Sabra St., Cranston
(401) 781-9693

Twin Oaks is a Cranston institution, serving traditional food in homey surroundings since 1933. The restaurant is still owned by the same family. The broiled chicken is like no other.

Best Restaurant for a Second Dinner Date
Neath's
262 S. Water St., Providence
(401) 751-3700

The restaurant's interior is just as impressive as the food. You'll find an open kitchen, gleaming bar and million-dollar view of the city and Providence River.

Best Place for Coffee and Dessert
Brewed Awakenings Coffee House
5 Memorial Blvd., Providence
(401) 421-2058

Try one of the 14 varieties of freshly brewed coffee or an

espresso, latte, fruit smoothie or chai. Or get your energy from cookies, biscotti, coffeecake, tortes, pies or muffins.

Best Place for a Laugh
Stitches Komedy Kafe
2 Dudley St., Providence
(401) 784-8243

Good comedy with gourmet eats like Brutus and Caesar salad and Groucho Sez Duck. Plus it does shows at Children's Hospital. That's something worth smiling about.

Best Creative Date
Harness Horse Association of New England
301 Washington St., Plainville

Only 15 miles from Providence awaits a very different experience. Trotters are beautiful and remind us of days past. An innovative way to show that you have depth!

Best Club
Metropolis
172 Pine St., Providence
(401) 454-5483

Metropolis is a Providence dance club that many say is its best. It pretends it's from NYC and looks like the offspring of a subway station and a TriBeCa loft. Open until 2 A.M..

Best After Hours Place
Atomic Grill
99 Chestnut St., Providence
(401) 621-8888

Eclectic entree specials, pasta, steaks and quesadillas are just a few of the choices at this hip, offbeat restaurant and bar. Lively late-night crowd!

Best Special Occasion Restaurant
Castle Hill Inn Restaurant
590 Ocean Dr., Newport
(401) 849-3800

New American cuisine perfectly served in a 19th-Century mansion with breathtaking views of Narragansett Bay. The elegance of yesteryear with the conveniences of today.

Best Place To Buy a Gift

Oop!
297 Thayer Street, Providence
Other Location: Providence Place Mall
(800) 281-4147 • www.oopstuff.com

Crafts, jewelry, furniture and toys by local and national artisans. Whether you need a 50-cent nose pencil sharpener or a hand-crafted $3,000 grandfather clock, it's here.

Top Five Dates

#1. The Spa at Norwich Inn
607 W Thames Street Route 32, Norwich CT
(860) 886-2401

Age-defying facials, 16 types of body treatments, astrology readings, hand and foot spa treatments and nine types of massages. Relax together in the country.

#2. Colt State Park
Route 114, Bristol
(401) 253-7482

Have a day by the bay. Picnic on the water. If it's chilly, call and reserve a fireplace so you can roast marshmallows and get to know each other. A beautiful, peaceful place.

#3. Spirito's
99 Hicks St., East Providence
(401) 434-4435

Under the Sons of Italy Hall is this town's best-kept secret. Everything is fresh, oversized, under priced, and made to order. The food is out of this world!

#4. Foxwoods Resort Casino
39 Norwich Westerly Rd., Mashantucket
(860) 312-3000

Dollar slots, video poker, blackjack, roulette. Great food of all kinds. A beautiful hotel and full-service spa. Go for an evening or go for a weekend and see the shows. What fun!

#5. Cliff Walk of Newport
Easton's Beach at Memorial Boulevard
175 Memorial Blvd., Newport
(401) 846-0813

The perfect walk in any season: On the right loom the Newport mansions in all their glory and on the left sits the ocean, majestically. Then feast at the Black Pearl!

Raleigh

Best Restaurant for Lunch or Brunch First Date
Brass Grill & Market
208 S. Wilmington St., Raleigh
(919) 833-9595
www.brassgrill.net

The Brass Grill is a warm and friendly family-owned place with the best cheesesteaks in town.

Best Restaurant for First Dinner Date
The Melting Pot
3100 Wake Forest Rd., Raleigh
(919) 878-0477

Each table serves a pot of fondue with an assortment of breads, veggies and fruits for dipping. Delicious and special, feeding your date never tasted so good.

Best Cheap Date
Raleighwood Cinema Grill
6609 Falls of Neuse Rd.,
Falls Village Shopping Center, Raleigh
(919) 847-0326
www.raleighwoodmovies.com

Dinner and a movie? Together? Now that's a classic date.

Best Restaurant for a Second Dinner Date
Est! Est! Est! Trattoria
19 W. Hargett St., Raleigh
(919) 833-2229
www.estest.com

This is Northern Italian cooking at its finest. Plus it's in a central location making it the perfect choice for a meal before strolling over to the BTI Center for a show.

Best Place for Coffee and Dessert
Maggie Moo's Ice Cream & Treatery
111 Weston Pkwy., Cary
Other location: Raleigh
(919) 678-9666
www.maggiemoos.com

With 40 different flavors, custom cake and shakes and great coffees to boot, Maggie's is a great place to come to.

Best Place for a Laugh
BattleZone
8311 Creedmoor Rd., Raleigh
(919) 847-4263
www.playlasertag.net

Say hello to your inner teenager and giggle with glee as you tag others — and each other — with a rousing game of laser tag.

Best Creative Date
Artspace
201 E. Davie St., Raleigh
(919) 821-2787
www.artspacenc.org

What is art? Is it beauty? Is it in the eye of the beholder? Is it a fun date? Wander through this huge place and find out.

Best Club
The Cantina
3011 Hillsborough St., Raleigh
(919) 832-4541

Laid back atmosphere in frat house style. At eleven A.M. the DJ starts spinning records and the dancing begins.

Best After Hours Place
Waffle House
3909 Hillsborough St., Raleigh
Call for other locations
(919) 833-1247

Not a lot of ambiance, but this classic American joint serves up a mean after-hours breakfast.

Best Special Occasion Restaurant
Waraji Japanese Restaurant
5910 Duraleigh Rd., Ste. 147, Raleigh
(919) 783-1883
www.waraji.citysearch.com

In an unpretentious setting comes one of life's little finds: Waraji, Raleigh's finest sushi restaurant.

Best Place To Buy a Gift
Uniquities
450 Daniels St., Raleigh
(919) 832-1234
www.uniquities.com

A unique selection of clothing and accessories whether it's a perfect fitting pair of jeans or a fabulous dress.

Top Five Dates

#1. *Up Up and Away*
Above and Beyond Hot Air Balloon Company
432 Crescent Ct., Raleigh
(919) 781-3433

See the world from a different perspective like, oh, from two-thousand feet above it. A hot air balloon ride is exciting and romantic. Make sure you pack a picnic lunch and some wine because when you finally do land, you'll still be up in the clouds.

#2. *Pony Up*
Dead Broke Farm
6921 Wildlife Tr., Raleigh
(919) 596-8975
www.horsebackridingstables.com/deadbrokefarm.html

Bring your date, saddle up on some friendly horses and check out the trails. It's relaxing, fun and something special to share.

#3. *Sailing, Sailing*
Apex Sailing & Windsurfing
6633 Apex Barbecue Rd., Apex
(919) 362-8729

Feel the spray hitting your faces, the pull of the tiller, the hum of the sail as your boat moves faster, faster...sailing.

#4. Hot and Spicy
Chef Rameaux's School of Cooking
704 N. Person St., Raleigh
(919) 834-2510
www.cheframeaux.com

Cooking together is a fun and rewarding thing to do, so why not take a Cajun cooking class? You just might stir up something extra special.

#5. Swing your Partner
Carolina Dancesport, Inc.
2409 Guess Rd., Durham
(919) 416-9213

The music plays, your date is in your arms . . . what could be more romantic? Learn to become the dancer you've always suspected you could be, then take your date to a club and show off your new moves.

Sacramento

Best Restaurant for Lunch or Brunch First Date
Pyramid Alehouse
1026 K St., Sacramento
(916) 498-9800 • www.pyramidbrew.com

Sit upstairs for a view overlooking the entire restaurant or try the covered patio to get away from the crowd and enjoy some conversation.

Best Restaurant for First Dinner Date
Joe's Crab Shack
1210 Front St., Sacramento
(916) 553-4249 • www.joescrabshack.com

This is a fun place for a first dinner date. It's casual and they serve up great seafood galore. Be forewarned though: the waiters may break out into dance every so often!

Best Cheap Date
Rivercats Game at Raley Field
400 Ballpark Dr., Sacramento
(916) 376-4700 • www.rivercats.com

Grab the grass seats and get a great view of the entire park. You can find ticket information online.

Best Restaurant for a Second Dinner Date
The Cliff House of Folsom
9900 Greenback Ln., Folsom
(916) 989-9243

The Cliff House is a wonderfully romantic date spot. It has incredible views of the American River and Rainbow Bridge; be sure to go prior to sunset and sit on the patio.

Best Place for Coffee and Dessert
Rick's Dessert Diner
2332 "K" St., Sacramento
(916) 444-0969

This place is absolute dessert heaven. They have exceptional cakes with very large slices, rich ingredients and it's all set in a 1950s diner atmosphere.

Best Place for a Laugh
Garbeau's Dinner Theatre
12401 Folsom Blvd., Rancho Cordova
(916) 985-6361 • www.garbeaus.com

A great dinner theatre where you will enjoy fun entertainment, good food and company. Catch a light-hearted performance and enjoy the laughs!

Best Creative Date
Jelly Belly Factory
One Jelly Belly Lane, Fairfield
(800) 9-JELLYBEAN • www.jellybelly.com

Learn the secrets as to how they create the legendary Jelly Belly and taste the world of flavors at the jelly bean sampling bar.

Best Club
Empire
1417 R St., Sacramento
(916) 448-3300 • www.empireeventscenter.com

The Empire is a huge dance venue with multiple bars. It's the new place to see and be seen; the destination for the trendy crowd.

Best After Hours Place
Infusions Lounge
1628 K St., Sacramento
(916) 442-8889

Unique sandwiches, great selection of coffee drinks and yummy dessert — all set in a modern and contemporary atmosphere.

Best Special Occasion Restaurant
Slocum House
7992 California Ave., Fair Oaks
(916) 961-7211 • www.slocum-house.com

This is truly a place of romantic and elegant dining, set atop hill of lush gardens and beautiful oak trees.

Best Place To Buy a Gift
William Glen
2651 El Paseo Ln., Sacramento
(916) 485-3000 • www.williamglen.com

A great place to find a gift for the chef in your life, William Glen stocks several lovely items for the kitchen and home.

Top Five Dates

#1. A Day on the Ranch
Apple Hill
Apple Hill, Camino
(530) 644-7692 • www.applehill.com
Enjoy a relaxing day in Apple Hill. Tour more than fifty ranches, wineries, orchards and more. Make a day of it by planning a picnic on the lush grounds. The options are endless. Apple Hill hosts several special events throughout the year, so plan ahead for a wonderful and relaxing outdoor experience.

#2. Picnic on the Lake
Adventure Sport Rentals
1609 Watt Ave., Sacramento
(916) 971-1800 • www.gearcloset.com
A great date doesn't have to break the bank. It can simply be a quiet get-together that stimulates conversation. Get innovative and spice up the date with a Spanish theme: bring a big bowl of paella and plenty of sangria and play festive music on your portable CD player. Or rent a boat for the afternoon and literally "picnic on the lake".

#3. Miniature Golf
Gold Mine Miniature Golf
4238 S. Hwy. 99, Yuba City
(530) 674-0475
There are few better ways to impress your date than by sinking an uphill 25-foot putt that goes through a lion and around an alligator by way of an abandoned ship. Just think of the possibilities!

#4. Just For Laughs
The Punchline
2100 Arden Way, #225, Sacramento
(916) 925-8500 • www.punchlinecomedyclub.com
Laughter is a natural aphrodisiac so why not warm up the mood and make a night of it? Visit The Punchline and laugh yourselves silly.

#5. *Get moving on the slopes*
   Lake Tahoe Ski Resorts
   www.sierratahoe.com

There's nothing like a day of fun in the cold to make a couple want to cozy up. So what are you waiting for? Don your skis and head for the hill. Or for those who aren't into hitting the slopes, nothing beats a fun snowball fight! Then head to lodge for a hot chocolate and schnapps before enjoying takeout and champagne served by the fireplace.

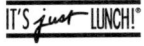

Salt Lake City

Best Restaurant for Lunch or Brunch First Date
The Garden Café
555 S. Main St., Salt Lake City
(801) 258-6708

The touched-with-elegance fare at this local garden-themed café makes for a refreshing Sunday brunch treat. It's served until 2 p.m.; be sure to arrive early to beat the crowds.

Best Restaurant for First Dinner Date
L'Avenue Bistro
1355 E. 2100 S., Salt Lake City
(801) 485-4494 • www.lavenuebistro.com

A quaint, yet elegant bistro is a perfect choice for a relaxed, conversational date. Try an order of their signature mussels with pomme fritesbut be sure to save room for dessert!

Best Cheap Date
Liberty Park
900 S. 700 E., Salt Lake City
(801) 972-7800

Bring your own lunch and then sample the many delights of this park. Walk around the pond, visit the aviary, check out the museums and on Sundays listen to the drum circle.

Best Restaurant for a Second Dinner Date
Stoneground
249 E. 400 S., Ste. 2, Salt Lake City
(801) 364-1368

This sleek second-story urban delight is the choice for a casual lunch or dinner date. Grab a seat overlooking the street and order one of the exceptional New York-style pizzas.

Best Place for Coffee and Dessert
Salt Lake Roasting Company and Café
320 E. 400 S., Salt Lake City
(801) 363-7572

The impressive coffee selection here is enough to keep up a conversation. Add to that the mouth-watering desserts and two-level seating and it's pretty close to perfect!

Best Place for a Laugh
Wiseguys Comedy Café
3500 S. 2200 W., Salt Lake City
www.wiseguyscomedy.com

Wiseguys consistently books some of the hottest national touring comics, so a laugh here is pretty much guaranteed. On Sundays, shows are only $5.

Best Creative Date
Family Search Center, Joseph Smith Memorial Building
15 E. S. Temple St., Salt Lake City
(801) 240-4085

Take a little time and look up each other's ancestors! They have millions of old documents, censuses and records of all types. It will keep you talking for years.

Best Club
Cabana Club
31 E. 400 S., Salt Lake City
(801) 355-9538

Cabana Club offers swanky seating, jazzy music and wonderful martinis to a mixed clientele — something that's tough to find in this area due to Utah State liquor laws.

Best After Hours Place
Port O' Call Social Club
78 W. 400 S., Salt Lake City
(801) 521-0589 • www.portocall.com

Whether you choose the main floor, the sports bar in the basement or the patio upstairs, you'll get delicious food, a good atmosphere, and live music. You can't miss here!

Best Special Occasion Restaurant
New Yorker
60 West Market St., Salt Lake City
(801) 363-0166 • www.gastronomyinc.com/ny

Highly rated by Zagat in many categories, this has been

the leading fine dining restaurant in Salt Lake City for more than 20 years. The menu is outstanding, and the service wonderful.

Best Place To Buy a Gift
Golden Braid Books
151 S. 500 E., Salt Lake City
(801) 322-1162 • www.goldenbraidbooks.com
So much more than just a killer independent bookstore, the Golden Braid also has music, candles, home accessories and even clothing.

Top Five Dates

#1. Setting the Stage
Salt Lake Acting Company
168 W. 500 N., Salt Lake City
(801) 363-7522 • www.saltlakeactingcompany.org
Enjoy a theatrical presentation at this popular venue, which was once a warehouse. From cabaret to contemporary drama, mainstream musicals to experimental local works, the Salt Lake Acting Company offers it all. They even allow theater-goers to bring their own food and drinks during their Saturday's Voyeur performances.

#2. Would You Like A Beer With Your Movie?
Brewvies Cinema Pub
677 S. 200 W., Salt Lake City
(801) 355-5500 • www.brewvies.com
Here's a great idea: Catch one of the hottest contemporary flicks (only a month or two out of the mainstream theater) while sipping on a Guinness and noshing on a slice of pepperoni pizza. Afterwards, challenge each other to a few rounds of pool in the lobby. Early seatings are only $2 and beers are extra cheap on Tuesday nights.

#3. Destination Downtown
The Gallivan Center
239 S. Main St., Salt Lake City
(801) 535-7780 • www.thegallivancenter.com
This outdoor amphitheater provides the perfect backdrop for a night of fun, no matter the season. Take in a free summer concert and dance the night away in

the grassed dance area. In the winter, bundle up and cozy together for a star-studded figure skating event. Once the leaves start to turn, party your way through fall's annual Blues & Brews Festival.

#4. *Travel the World*
International Peace Gardens
1000 S. 900 W., Salt Lake City
(801) 972-7860 • www.peacegarden.com

More than 26 countries are represented at this lush garden attraction. Originally designed to inspire world peace, each country is exquisitely represented and will not only stir conversation, but stagger the senses as well. Bring a picnic, then meander through the winding trails. You can have lunch in Rome, then go for a stroll through Paris.

#5. *Escape From It All*
Rocky Mountain Beauty Retreat
4751 Holladay Blvd., Salt Lake City
(801) 273-0266

This is not your average day spa by any means. Although they do serve up all the standards from massages to facials, the real draw here is the personalized and private service as well as the locale — tucked inside a historic Tudor mansion. Schedule intimate side-by-side treatments for the two of you and make a day of it!

San Antonio

Best Restaurant for Lunch or Brunch First Date
The Magnolia Pancake Haus
13444 W. Ave., San Antonio
(210) 496-0828 • www.magnoliapancakehaus.com

This is a local favorite, serving old-fashioned brunches and lunches. Their batter is mixed from scratch several times a day.

Best Restaurant for First Dinner Date
Paesano's
555 E. Basse Rd., Ste. 100, San Antonio
(210) 828-5191 • www.paesanaos.com

Paesano's serves great Italian and Mediterranean cuisine with a view of the Quarry Golf Course. Try the Shrimp Paesano.

Best Cheap Date
Rosario's
910 S. Alamo St., San Antonio
(210) 223-1806

This cheap Tex-Mex restaurant serves up tacos, enchiladas and other Mexican cuisine. The neon accented purple walls covered with decorative maracas evoke a playful scene.

Best Restaurant for a Second Dinner Date
Le Reve
152 E. Pecan St., San Antonio
(210) 212-2221

This French Riverwalk restaurant is both cozy and romantic, dishing up superb French cuisine with a leisurely, European pace.

Best Place for Coffee and Dessert
Nadler's Bakery & Deli
1621 Babcock Rd., San Antonio
(210) 340-1021 • www.nadlers.com

Originated in 1963, Nadler's is a family owned bakery

offering pastries, cakes, breads and anything else your sweet tooth desires.

Best Place for a Laugh
Howl at the Moon
111 W. Crockett St., San Antonio
(210) 212-4695 • www.howlatthemoon.com

This dueling piano bar will get you singing, dancing and laughing all night long, as the piano players get customers involved in the fun.

Best Creative Date
X-treme Bowling
13307 San Pedro Ave., San Antonio
(210) 496-3811

Visit the AMF Country Lanes and bowl like you've never bowled before. Be ready to stay up late, hear some music and bowl the night away.

Best Club
Tabu
315 E. Houston, San Antonio
(210) 224-4200

This club caters to ethnically diverse, young clientele. They play mostly techno, trance and salsa or meringue mixes.

Best After Hours Place
Rebar
8134 Broadway, San Antonio
(210) 320-4091

Patrons in their twenties and thirties keep this Alamo Heights bar jumping seven nights a week. You'll find a friendly crowd and free-flowing booze for laid-back fun.

Best Special Occasion Restaurant
Silo Restaurant
1133 Austin Hwy., San Antonio
(210) 824-8686

Too special to save just for Valentine's Day, the kitchen at Silo Restaurant makes a great Osso Buco — just be sure to save room for the stunning chocolate soufflé cake.

Best Place To Buy a Gift
Paper Garden
555 Bitters Rd., San Antonio
(210) 494-9602 • www.papergarden.com

Visit this paper store to find note cards, stationery and any other type of fine paper product you can imagine.

Top Five Dates

#1. Executive Surf Club
309 N. Water St., Corpus Christi
(361) 884-SURF • www.executivesurfclub.com

Rent a convertible, put the top down and soak up some sun on an enjoyable two-hour drive to Corpus Christi. Take a romantic stroll along the ocean and enjoy the waves while you relax. Afterwards, go for a plate of calamari and a few Mai Tais at the Executive Surf Club. You'll feel like you took a mini-vacation.

#2. Rivercenter Comedy Club
849 Commerce St., Ste. 893, San Antonio
(210) 229-1420 • www.hotcomedy.com

Laughter is a natural aphrodisiac, so warm up the mood and make a night of it at the Rivercenter Comedy Club. Sit back, laugh yourselves silly and get ready for a whole lot of fun.

#3. Dave and Buster's
440 Crossroads Blvd., San Antonio
(210) 515-1515 • www.daveandbusters.com

Why not score a different kind of game and invite her to play some pool at Dave and Buster's? It's a lot more fun than propping up a bar and guzzling beers. Raise the stakes by saying, "Whoever loses the game makes the other dinner." And just like that, you've got yourself a second round of love.

#4. Tower of the Americas
HemisFair Park, Bowie St., San Antonio
(210) 207-8615 • www.toweroftheamericas.com

Bringing your date to the highest point in San Antonio can be exhilarating for both of you. Enjoy a romantic gourmet dinner at the revolving Tower of the Americas. Make it a lasting memory by bringing a disposable camera and taking lots of pictures. Then, agree to meet up the following week to look at them.

#5. McAllister Park
13102 Jones-Maltsberger Rd., San Antonio
(210) 207-7275

A great date doesn't have to break the bank. It can simply be a quiet get-together, which allows for stimulating conversation. Get innovative and spice up the date with a Spanish theme, make a big bowl of paella, bring plenty of sangria and stick the Gypsy Kings on your portable CD player. Olé!

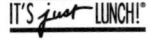

San Diego

Best Restaurant for Lunch or Brunch First Date
Meritage Restaurant & Bar
897 S. Coast Hwy. 101, Encinitas
(760) 634-3350 • www.meritage1.com

This intimate bistro is a charming setting for a lunch date. An extensive wine list is available, as well as an assortment of sandwiches, salads, steak, fish and pasta.

Best Restaurant for First Dinner Date
Baci Ristorante Italiano
1955 Morena Blvd., San Diego
(619) 275-2094 • www.bacicucina.com

This northern Italian restaurant has been a local favorite for over twenty-five years! They are very big on tradition and will treat you as a regular. Try their famous tiramisu.

Best Cheap Date
Sushi Deli 2
135 Broadway, San Diego
(619) 233-3072 • www.sushideli2.com

This is a fun, lively, and extremely inexpensive place to enjoy a lunch or possibly a snack before going out on the town. Take your sushi down to the harbor to enjoy, or eat in.

Best Restaurant for a Second Dinner Date
Old Venice Italian Restaurant
2910 Canon St., San Diego
(619) 222-5888

The quaint Old Venice restaurant is a fabulous place to go on any date, whether it's your second or your hundredth. Enjoy traditional pasta dishes, seafood, beef, chicken and veal.

Best Place for Coffee and Dessert
The Cheesecake Factory
7067 Friars Rd., San Diego
(619) 683-2800 • www.thecheesecakefactory.com

After coffee and dessert here, your date will surely be sweet on you. They offer forty different varieties of cheesecake, including the astonishing Chocolate Tuxedo Cream.

Best Place for a Laugh

Lips
2770 5th Ave., San Diego
(619) 295-7900 • www.lipsshow.biz

You never know which stars you'll see next during this bawdy female impersonator show. Don't miss Bitchy Bingo on Wednesdays and Gospel Brunch on Sundays.

Best Creative Date

Hot Air Balloon Ride over Del Mar
Panorama Balloon Tours
2730 Via De La Valle, Del Mar
(800) 455-3592 • www.gohotair.com

Take flight on a breathtakingly beautiful and romantic sunset ride over the Del Mar coastline. Complimentary hors d'oeuvres and champagne are included.

Best Club

Onyx
852 5th Ave., San Diego
(619) 235-6699 • www.onyxroom.com

This swanky, upscale club attracts the trendy set. Onyx features a hip piano bar in front and DJ-spun or live music in the back.

Best After Hours Place

La Posta de Acapulco's Taco Shop
3980 3rd Ave., San Diego
(619) 295-8982

What could be better than traditional Mexican fare at 3 A.M..? La Posta offers it all, from tacos to breakfast burritos, twenty-four hours a day.

Best Special Occasion Restaurant

Star of the Sea
1360 N. Harbor Dr., San Diego
(619) 232-7408 • www.starofthesea.com

The award-winning Star of the Sea is known for its legendary seafood as well as its spectacular view. You'll want to dress up for this elegant restaurant.

Best Place To Buy a Gift

Crutchfield Ranch
La Costa Ave. and Saxony, Carlsbad
(760) 942-2030

What started as a small produce stand has since expanded to a farmer's market, florist and gift shop. Grab a fresh flower bouquet or some chocolate-dipped strawberries.

Top Five Dates

#1. Wine and Dine
Thornton Winery
32575 Rancho California Rd., Temecula
(951) 699-0099 • www.thorntonwinery.com

Though it's not quite Napa Valley, the Temecula Valley is home to several wineries worth a visit. Inquire about wine-tasting packages when you rent a limousine for the sixty-mile drive from San Diego. Between winery stops, break at the Thornton Winery's Café Champagne for an elegant, delicious lunch.

#2. Corner Pocket
Tidewater Tavern
221 N. Hwy. 101, Solana Beach
(858) 755-4115

Invite your date to play pool. It's a lot more fun than propping up against a bar and guzzling beers. Raise the stakes by saying, "Whoever loses the game makes the other dinner." And just like that, you've got yourself a second round of love. The Tidewater Tavern in Solana Beach has plenty of pool tables and a full bar to support your game!

#3. Sea Worthy
San Diego Maritime Museum
1492 N. Harbor Dr., San Diego
(619) 234-9153

Tired of the standard movie date? On select Friday nights in July and August, the San Diego Maritime Museum presents *Movies Before the Mast*, in which nautical movies are projected upon the sails of the historical Star of India. This adults-only event is a great excuse to cuddle up under the stars beneath a warm blanket.

#4. *Nature-Lovers Morning Pick-Me-Up*
Hash House a Go Go
3628 5th Ave., San Diego
(619) 298-4646 • www.hashhouseagogo.com

Who says a great date must take place at night? Put together a morning date by starting with a refreshing early hike in Mission Trails Regional Park, eight miles northeast of Downtown San Diego. Conclude your date with a filling breakfast at the infamous Hash House a Go Go in Hillcrest.

#5. *Glow in the Dark*

A great date doesn't have to break the bank. It can simply be a quiet get-together that allows for stimulating conversation. Head to the beach at Mission Bay and light a small campfire within the designated fire pits. You can toast marshmallows and make s'mores, possibly providing the opportunity to kiss away a few crumbs on your date's face!

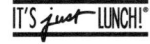

San Francisco

Best Restaurant for Lunch or Brunch First Date
Enrico's Sidewalk Cafe
504 Broadway, San Francisco
(415) 982-6223

A great place to sit back and get to know the person you're with while you sit outside and enjoy the people parade that is North Beach.

Best Restaurant for First Dinner Date
Grand Cafe
501 Geary St., San Francisco
(415) 292-0101

Opulent, romantic, located in the Hotel Monaco, close to the theater district — surely a place to impress your date.

Best Cheap Date
Crissy Field
Southeast Presidio, San Francisco
(415) 4-CRISSY • www.crissyfield.org

A former airbase now turned into a shoreline urban oasis for strolling or bike rides. Tidal marshes, meadows, sand beaches and dunes, and thousands of restored native plants.

Best Restaurant for a Second Dinner Date
Aziza
5800 Geary Blvd., San Francisco
(415) 752-2222 • www.aziza-sf.com

Modern twists on traditional Moroccan favorites, great prices and very romantic.

Best Place for Coffee and Dessert
Frog Hollow Farm
Ferry Plaza Farmers' Market, San Francisco
Other locations: Ferry Building, Embarcadero & Market
(888) 779-4511 • www.froghollow.com

Enjoy farm fresh produce turned into pastries as you gaze onto San Francisco Bay

Best Place for a Laugh
Cobb's Comedy Club
915 Columbus, San Francisco
(415) 928-4320 • www.cobbscomedy.com

San Fran's premium comedy club, with top national comedians in a 400-seat club in North Beach.

Best Creative Date
Cal Adventures
Various locations
(510) 642-4000 • www.oski.org

With classes in sailing, windsurfing and kayaking, their Full Moon Paddle was voted Most Romantic Date.

Best Club
Ruby Skye
420 Mason, San Francisco
(415) 693-0777 • www.rubyskye.com

San Fran's hottest dance club features multi levels, multi DJs and special events each month.

Best After Hours Place
Butterfly
Pier 33, San Francisco
(415) 291-9054 • www.butterflysf.com

Another great hot spot overlooking the Bay, with California-Asian fusion food.

Best Special Occasion Restaurant
Cityscape Restaurant & Bar
333 O'Farrell St., San Francisco
(415) 923-5002

On the top floor of the Hilton Hotel, with amazing views to go with a gourmet menu.

Best Place To Buy a Gift
Luscious Wear
1410 Polk St., San Francisco
(415) 440-0172 • www.lusciouswear.com

Silky intimate clothing for him or her, with friendly helpful staff to help you find that perfect gift.

Top Five Dates

#1. *Hornblower Cruises and Events*
Pier 41, San Francisco
Call for other locations
(888) 467-6256 • www.hornblower.com
What could be better than to enjoy a dinner on a ship sailing around San Francisco Bay with someone you care about?

#2. *Dolores Park Cafe*
501 Dolores St., San Francisco
(415) 621-2936 • www.doloresparkcafe.org
More than just a sidewalk café, it's across from beautiful Dolores Park, with its sculpted pathways and view of the city. A great place for a stroll on a sunny day.

#3. *Japantown*
Buchanan and Post St., San Francisco
Home to concerts, horticulture, martial arts presentations, tea ceremonies and the Spring Cherry Blossom Festival.

#4. *Alcatraz Island*
Golden Gate National Recreation Area,
Pier 41, San Francisco
(415) 705-5555
Not as strange as it sounds, Alcatraz has amazing views of the city, wonderful places to wander and the fun of seeing if you can fit in a cell together.

#5. *Coit Tower*
1 Telegraph Hill Blvd., San Francisco
(415) 362-0808
A perfect spot in North Beach. Go have a coffee at the Café Trieste, grab a sandwich at Molinari's Deli (on Columbus) and then enjoy some of the best views and people watching in all of San Francisco.

Seattle

Best Restaurant for Lunch or Brunch First Date
Place Pigalle
81 Pike St., Seattle
(206) 624-1756

This pretty, quaint bistro offers amazing views of the Sound and romantic French fare.

Best Restaurant for First Dinner Date
El Gaucho
2505 First Ave., Seattle
(206) 728-1337

Feel like you've stepped back in time. Service is properly formal and the seating is mink-lined. Well known for their steaks.

Best Cheap Date
Buca di Beppo
701 9th Ave. N, Seattle
(206) 244-2288 • www.bucadibeppo.com

Everything is served family style, so go ahead and order a feast to share! Listen to the soothing tunes of Frank Sinatra.

Best Restaurant for a Second Dinner Date
Blue C Sushi
3411 Fremont Ave. N, Seattle
(206) 633-3411

This is Fremont's first Kaiten (or conveyor-belt) sushi restaurant. There's a lot to see here from the projection wall murals to the ultra-cool scene and hipster diners.

Best Place for Coffee and Dessert
The Panama Hotel Tea and Coffee Shop
607 S. Main St., Seattle
(206) 515-4000

This place is rich in tradition and history. They boast beautifully done Italian and Pan-Asian desserts.

Best Place for a Laugh
Jet City Improv
5510 University Way NE, Seattle
(206) 781-3879

A comedy show that insists on participation; the audience must provide suggestions to the troop.

Best Creative Date
Wasabi Bistro and Cinerama Theatre
2311 2nd Ave., Seattle
(206) 441-6044 • www.cinerama.com

Enjoy sushi at the Wasabi Bistro, then head to the movies at the Cinerama Theatre. You're in for a luxurious treat with its velvet curtains and sparkling ceiling.

Best Club
Contour
807 First Ave., Seattle
(206) 447-7704

Contour caters to a diverse crowd of clubbers, all determined to dance the night away. If you are a chronic club hopper or simply refuse to go home, this party will last 'til 5 A.M..

Best After Hours Place
13 Coins Restaurant
125 Boren Ave. N, Seattle
(206) 682-2513

It's been open 24 hours a day since 1967. Where else can you order chicken piccata at 4 A.M..?

Best Special Occasion Restaurant
Canlis Restaurant
2576 Aurora Ave. N, Seattle
(206) 283-3313

Canlis is legendary in Seattle! The décoræ a textured and organic mix of stone, branches and natural light-æ is gorgeous. The martinis are fantastic.

Best Place To Buy a Gift
Burnt Sugar
601 N. 35th St., Seattle
(206) 545-0699

If you like flea markets, this is the store for you. From

shabby chic to funky, you can easily spend $20-$500 on must-haves. You won't come home empty handed.

Top Five Dates

#1. Sittin' On Top of the World
Space Needle
400 Broad St., Seattle
(206) 905-2100

Bring your date to the top of the Space Needle and get an exhilarating view for both of youæespecially at night. Make it a lasting memory by bringing a disposable camera and taking lots of pictures, then agree to meet up the following week to look at them.

#2. Bay Watch
Salty's on Alki
1936 Harbor Ave. SW
(206) 937-1600

If you're lucky enough to be within driving distance of Alki beach, then it's a perfect date location. Everyone feels relaxed walking by the Ocean and it's so romantic. If you're lucky maybe, you'll get a sneak peak of her in a bikini, but don't get your hopes upæmost women prefer not to get wet on a date. Afterward, you can go for a plate of Calamari and a few bloody marys at Salty's on Alki. You'll feel like you took a mini-vacation.

#3. Gameworks
1511 7th Ave., Seattle
(206) 521-0952

There are few better ways to impress your date than by sinking a tough, uphill, 25-foot putt that goes through a windmill, around a castle, by way of an abandoned gold mine or racing speedboats. Just think of the possibilities. It also affords great opportunities for some physical contact when you have to give your main squeeze a crash course on how to hold the iron. Just humor him, ladies.

#4. Unleash Your Inner Tiger (Woods)
Golf is for lovers. Well, okay, we made that up. But golf is a great couples activity, and if you're already a fan, this might be a good opportunity to get your date

hooked (on you *and* the game). Just look at Tiger Woods. He's a babe magnet. Sure, he has more money than Canada, but what the ladies are really attracted to are his putting skills. Right, ladies? The Interbay Golf Center offers this challenge in nine holes.

#5. *Dining In*
Seduction & Spice
(206) 406-1676

They say a way to a man's heart is through his stomach. Well, we've got news for you: It holds true for women, too. Making your date a home-cooked meal with all the trimmings (candles, flowers and champagne) says you really care. Kick it up a notch with a gourmet dinner prepared by Chef Alexi Faucherm with "Seduction & Spice" right in your own kitchen. It might cost a bit extra, but at least you won't have to clean up alone!

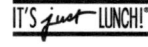

Silicon Valley

Best Restaurant for Lunch or Brunch First Date
Fuki Sushi
4119 El Camino Real at Page Mills Road, Palo Alto
(650) 494-9383 • www.fukisushi.com

This is Palo Alto's oldest sushi bar, with an authentic Japanese feel and specialties you won't find anywhere else.

Best Restaurant for First Dinner Date
Eight Forty North First
840 N. 1st St., San Jose
(408) 282-0840 • www.840.com

First dates are something to be remembered, and the white linens covering mahogany tables, the Cubist mural and awe-inspiring service, create a memorable atmosphere.

Best Cheap Date
San Pedro Square Farmer's Market
San Pedro Square, San Jose
Other locations: Willow Glen and Campbell

Farmer's Markets are a great way for health-conscious consumers to buy locally grown (mostly organic) produce at better than super-market prices. Open Saturday mornings.

Best Restaurant for a Second Dinner Date
Habana Cuba
238 Race St., San Jose
(408) 998-CUBA • www.998cuba.com

The hidden gem of San Jose, Habana Cuba has become the place where locals and tourists return again and again for generous portions of fresh, authentic Cuban cuisine.

Best Place for Coffee and Dessert
Cheesecake Factory
3041 Stevens Creek Rd., San Jose
Other location: Palo Alto
(408) 246-0092 • www.thecheesecakefactory.com

What can you say about a place that serves the best cheesecake around and is constantly coming up with new and better combinations to take your breath away

Best Place for a Laugh
Improv
62 S. Second St., San Jose
(408) 280-7475 • www.improv.com

Open-mic nights mixed with some of the nation's best comics combine to make this a must for a laugh.

Best Creative Date
Kayaking in Lexington Reservoir
Lexington Reservoir
www.parkhere.org

Surrounded by the Santa Cruz Mountains, this quiet and isolated spot is perfect for a romantic cruise in a kayak for two through beautifully clear blue-green water.

Best Club
Club Miami
177 W. Santa Clara St., San Jose
(408) 279-3670

This is the place to go if you are in the mood for a little salsa, meringue, or samba. Enjoy live music every Thursday through Saturday, and dance lessons are available.

Best After Hours Place
GLO
396 S. First St., San Jose
(408) 995-6414 • www.clubglo.com

This mega-lounge setting attracts an upscale mix of cool San Joseans and hotel guests seeking a fashionable and stylish setting for dancing the night away.

Best Special Occasion Restaurant
La Fondue
14510 Big Basin Way, Saratoga
(408) 867-3332 • www.lafondue.com

Treat yourself by dipping an array of breads, fruits, and

vegetables into creamy melted cheeses. Try a dessert of chocolate fondue with strawberries, bananas, and more.

Best Place To Buy a Gift
Only the Best
15954 Los Gatos Blvd., Los Gatos
(408) 356-7362

Looking for that certain something? Try a unique stationery store with an extensive selection of cards, gifts and specialty items.

Top Five Dates

#1. *Music in the Mountains*
The Mountain Winery
14831 Pierce Rd., Saratoga
(408) 998-8497

The Mountain Winery, set in lush hills with a backdrop of the sky, offers inexhaustibly breathtaking views from dawn to dusk to night. The before-concert buffet is excellent. Come for dinner then get out your blanket and cuddle with your dearest while the music serenades you at this spectacular mountain retreat.

#2. *Horse around at the Beach*
Sea Horse Ranch
Hwy. 92 West, Half Moon Bay
(650) 726-9903 • www.horserentals.com/seahorse.html

There's nothing more romantic than horseback riding along the beach in Half Moon Bay. A local favorite for Bay Area riders, enjoy the view and tranquility of the ocean while galloping down the sandy shores of the beach with your special date. You'll never forget or regret it.

#3. *Bon Appetit*
Draeger's Culinary Center
222 E. 4th St., San Mateo
(650) 685-3704

Food and wine are the heart and soul of romance, so why not enjoy them both with someone special? Participate in one of over 300 demonstrations and tastings. You're sure to find something you can look forward to preparing together.

#4. *Happy Trails*
Rancho San Antonio
Cristo Ray Dr., Los Altos

Pack a lunch, put on your sneakers or boots, and hike one of the many trails in Los Altos. Find that perfect spot with a view of the bay off in the distance. It's good for your heart, and your soul, too.

#5. *Treat Yourself*
Watercourse Way
165 Channing Ave., Palo Alto
(650) 462-2000 • www.watercourseway.com

Nothing says "I care" like a full day of pampering. Try private hot-tubbing with steam or a sauna, or a long massage to relax and refresh you. Melt away that tension. Treat yourself and someone special. You know you both deserve it and your body will thank you for it.

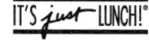

South Florida

Best Restaurant for Lunch or Brunch First Date
Houston's
17355 Biscayne Blvd., North Miami Beach
Call for other locations
(305) 947-2000 • www.houstons.com

Request a romantic table by the windows overlooking the bay. Have lunch and then walk outside, sit on a bench and watch the water and boats pass by.

Best Restaurant for First Dinner Date
Capriccio's
2424 N. University Dr., Pembroke Pines
(954) 432-7001 • www.capriccios.net

Known for "the best tossed salad in town," dining at Capriccio's is a true Italian experience. It's one of the area's great original restaurants.

Best Cheap Date
Da Leo Trattoria
819 Lincoln Rd., Miami
(305) 674-0350 • www.daleotrattoria.com

It sounds upscale but is actually quite affordable. Try the fisherman soup, veal with bruschetta or the rack of lamb.

Best Restaurant for a Second Dinner Date
Bed
929 Washington Ave., Miami Beach
(305) 532-9070 • www.bedmiami.com

No, they don't offer chairs or tables at Bed; enjoy French cuisine and premium drinks atop a white mattress! It's a very chic feeling and a good way to cozy up on a date.

Best Place for Coffee and Dessert
Segafredo Espresso
1040 Lincoln Rd., Miami Beach
(305) 673-0047

This awesome coffee venue has outdoor seating with fantastic drinks, large couches and chairs, and a very cool ambience with lounge music. It's great for people-watching.

Best Place for a Laugh
Palm Beach Skate & Ice Zone
8125 Lake Worth Rd., Lake Worth
(561) 963-5900

Bundle up and skate hand-in-hand at this full-sized ice skating rink. Or, take a blast to the past and partake in a bit of roller skating.

Best Creative Date
X-TREME Rock Climbing
13972 S.W. 139th Ct., Miami
(305) 233-6623 • www.x-tremerock.com

It's a challenge for the mind and the body. Enjoy premiere rock climbing in a safe, regulated environment. All levels are welcome.

Best Club
Mansion
1235 Washington Ave., Miami Beach
(305) 532-1525 • www.mansionmiami.com

This is a new happening spot on South Beach. Great DJs from all over the world spin here and celebrities consistently host the hottest functions.

Best After Hours Place
Jerry's Famous Deli
1450 Collins Ave., Miami Beach
(305) 532-8030 • www.jerrysfamousdeli.com

This restaurant and deli never closes. And with more than 700 items on the menu, there's sure to be something for everyone.

Best Special Occasion Restaurant
Solo Trattoria
208 S.W. 2nd St., Fort Lauderdale
(954) 525-7656

A great special occasion destination, Solo serves some of

the best classic Italian food around. Sample the Italian Lobster Ravioli in an authentic pink cream sauce — divine!

Best Place To Buy a Gift

Base
939 Lincoln Rd., Miami Beach
(305) 531-4982 • www.baseworld.com

From jewelry to footwear, perfume to rare books, Base is where to find something that's especially unique.

Top Five Dates

#1. Floating on Air
Captain Doug's Everglades Tours
200 S.R. 29, Everglades City
(239) 695-4400 • www.captaindougs.com

Home of the original jet boat tours, a day with Doug's is the perfect way to escape the hustle and bustle of the city. Remember to take a camera for snapping shots of the exotic birds, alligators, manatees and all the other wildlife indigenous to the area — plus a few of your date!

#2. Revolving Windows in the Sky
Pier Top Lounge Pier 66
2301 S.E. 17th St. Cswy., Fort Lauderdale
(954) 525-6666 • www.pier66.hyatt.com

Stop by the revolving bar that sits atop the Hyatt Pier 66 right over the causeway. It's one of the best views of the Fort Lauderdale beaches and city skyline. Watch the sun set, share a drink and listen to live jazz vocalists for a romantic evening date.

#3. Hot Rocks
Radiance Day Spa
1219 E. Las Olas Blvd., Fort Lauderdale
(954) 524-5533 • www.daysparadiance.com

Indulge in a relaxing hot stone massage from Radiance Day Spa and enjoy feeling the heat — as it flows from your feet to your legs and then swirls up into your back. Tranquil music and a cool room temperature top off the experience.

#4. Elegant Interludes
Miami City Ballet
2200 Liberty Ave., Miami Beach
(305) 929-7010 • www.miamicityballet.org
Enjoy an evening at the ballet. Miami City Ballet is one of the largest and most prolific dance companies in the country. Go to their website for ticket and performer information.

#5. Diving for Treasures
H20 Scuba
160 Sunny Isles Blvd., Sunny Isles
(305) 956-3483 • www.h2oscuba.com
Scuba is not only a great form of exercise, but it's a creative date idea as well. Instruction is offered for all levels at H20 Scuba; give it a try!

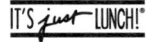

St. Louis

Best Restaurant for Lunch or Brunch First Date
Yia Yia's Eurocafe
15601 Olive Blvd., Chesterfield
(636) 537-9991 • www.yiayias.com

Relax in the Mediterranean feel of this West County upscale but casual eatery. They have a great brunch; the beef tenderloin for lunch will melt in your mouth!

Best Restaurant for First Dinner Date
Top of the Riverfront — Millennium Hotel
200 South 4th St., St. Louis
(314) 241-3191

For a romantic evening, sit atop St. Louis at this chic eatery at the trendy Millennium Hotel. The service is impeccable and you'll relax and dine right alongside the stars!

Best Cheap Date
Olympia Kebob House & Tavern
1543 McCausland Ave., St. Louis
(314) 781-1299

No matter how you say it, (gee-roh or ji-roh) their gyros are the best in town! You'll feel full and fine and without emptying your wallet. Try the fried cheese..."Opa"!

Best Restaurant for a Second Dinner Date
The Crossing
7823 Forsyth Blvd., Clayton
(314) 721-7375
www.saucemagazine.com/liluma_crossing/theCrossing

With cuisine that "crosses" French and Italian traditions, you'll love the sophisticated surroundings, incredible meat and seafood as well as the warm, inviting ambiance.

Best Place for Coffee and Dessert
Cyrano's
603 East Lockwood, Webster Groves
(314) 963-3232 • www.cyranoscafe.com

Grab two spoons and save some room, The Cleopatra will

knock your socks off! It's a decadent, vanilla ice cream treat with strawberries, bananas and light whipped crème.

Best Place for a Laugh

Johnny Gitto's
6997 Chippewa St., St. Louis
(314) 781-8111

For the diehard Karaoke fanatic, this is where Billy Idol meets American Idol. Not for the timid, check your pride at the door and bring your best vocals and sense of humor.

Best Creative Date

Murders, Games & More
7355 Idamor Lane, St. Louis
(314) 849-1346 • www.murgames.com

"Whodunit?" is what you'll ask while participating in a hilarious murder mystery and laughing with new friends. Laughter is the best aphrodisiac.

Best Club

M.P. O'Reilly's
14 Maryland Plaza, St. Louis
(314) 367-8111

Two dollar drinks, a game of pool or dirty-dancing — take your pick. This fun bristling hot spot is centrally-located at the heart of the Central West End.

Best After Hours Place

O'Connel's Pub
4652 Shaw St., St. Louis
(314) 773-6600 • www.saucemagazine.com/oconnells

The bar is open until three on weekends and you can't beat the burgers. A true St. Louis tradition since 1962, the bartenders and waitresses are nice too.

Best Special Occasion Restaurant

Top of the Riverfront, Millennium Hotel
200 South 4th St., St. Louis
(314) 241-3191 • www2.millenniumhotels.com

If the innovative American cuisine doesn't get your attention, the restaurant's 360 degree panoramic view of the city will. On Sunday, enjoy their plentiful brunch.

Best Place To Buy a Gift

*Louisiana Purchase at the
Missouri Historical Society Museum*
Intersection of Lindell Blvd. & Debaliviere
(314) 454-3172 • www.mohistory.org

For all things relative to St. Louis, stop by and choose from books on history, culture, architecture and more. There is something for everyone looking to connect with the city.

Top Five Dates

#1. *Sittin' on Top of the World*
Jefferson National Expansion Memorial Park,
Gateway Arch
Other locations: Top of the Riverfront, Millennium Hotel, St. Louis
(314) 982-1410
www.stlouisarch.com • www.gatewayarch.com

For a relationship that is reaching new heights, St. Louis boasts two of the most unique locations to savor that special time in your life. Start the evening with a sunset viewing of the city from atop the Gateway Arch. At a height of 666 feet, on a clear night you can see over 30 miles in all directions. When the sun goes down, head across the street to the top of the Millennium Hotel for dinner and drinks at Top of the Riverfront for the area's.

#2. *Tom Sawyer and Becky Thatcher Cruise Up the Riverfront*
St. Louis Riverfront, St. Louis
(877) 982-1410 • www.gatewayarch.com

Offering evening and daylight cruises, the Tom Sawyer and Becky Thatcher riverboats are an amazing way to see the St. Louis riverfront. Indoor and outdoor seating is available as well as concessions on these oldest excursion riverboats on the Mississippi.

#3. *Milo's Bocci Garden*
5201 Wilson Ave., St. Louis
(314) 776-0468

What better way to pass the time than learning to play Bocci Ball (pronounced bow chee)? Milo's Bocci Garden has become somewhat of a cult gathering and offers open court times as well as several leagues. Milo's is the place to be for a unique and incredibly entertaining date.

#4. *Jazz at the Botanical Gardens*
4344 Shaw Blvd., St. Louis
(314) 577-9400 • www.mobot.org

There's nothing like an evening at the Botanical Gardens listening to St. Louis' best live jazz performers such as the Quartet Tres Bien or The River City Ramblers. Attracting audiences of all ages, Jazz at the Gardens is romantic evening for two or even a group.

#5. *Tour of the Anheuser-Busch Brewery*
One Busch Pl., St. Louis
(800) DIAL-BUD • www.anheuser-busch.com

A true St. Louis landmark, the brewery of Anheuser-Busch is a remarkable venue of size and spirit. From the all red-brick buildings to the stables of the famed Budweiser Clydesdales, the brewery's hour-long tour takes you from the gathering of ingredients to the finished product. As a bonus, at the end of the tour you're free to do some sampling.

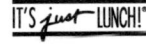

Tampa

Best Restaurant for Lunch or Brunch First Date
Noodle Lounge
3324 W. Gandy Blvd., Tampa
(813) 835-1434 • www.btrestaurants.com

This fusion of Vietnamese, Japanese, and Thai cuisine draws a high-class lunch crowd. All the homemade noodles and the dark chocolate mousse are sure bets.

Best Restaurant for First Dinner Date
Bonefish Grill
3665 Henderson Blvd., Tampa
(813) 876-3535 • www.bonefishgrill.com

The city's freshest fish, an extensive wine list, and the lively chatter that permeates this upscale but casual hotspot will ease your nerves and encourage conversation.

Best Cheap Date
Jimmy Mac's
5000 W. Gandy Blvd., Tampa
(813) 839-3449

The expansive patio overlooks a harbor, and the sandwiches couldn't be better in this supremely casual restaurant. Sunsets and live music are complimentary.

Best Restaurant for a Second Dinner Date
Catch 23
10103 Montague St., Tampa
(813) 920-0045

Enjoy the mouth-watering Caribbean Jerk chicken on the patio of this northwest Tampa seafood house.

Best Place for Coffee and Dessert
Blackhawk Coffee Cafe
1628 W. Snow Cir., Tampa
(813) 258-1600 • www.blackhawkcoffeecafe.com

Always open late, the Blackhawk in Hyde Park will satisfy

your sweet tooth with everything from gourmet pies to Krispy Kremes.

Best Place for a Laugh
Key West Comedy Club
2015 E. 7th Ave., Ybor City
(813) 248-2214

Tampa natives love this small and superb comedy club; no cover charge on Wednesdays & Thursdays.

Best Creative Date
Yacht StarShip Dinner Cruise
603 Channleside Dr., Tampa
(813) 223-7999 • www.starshipdining.com

Float across Tampa Bay while dining on scrumptiously prepared Asian Salmon, Veal Marsala and more. Live music and breathtaking views enhance your evening.

Best Club
The Empire
1902 E. 7th Ave., Ybor City
(813) 247-2582

An of-the-moment techno and hip-hop club for the hardcore dancers, The Empire caters to a young, energetic crowd.

Best After Hours Place
Sangria's
315 S. Howard Ave., Tampa
(813) 258-0393

Urbanites pack themselves into Sangria's until 2 A.M.. on weekends. Great tapas; try the Fromage en Croute.

Best Special Occasion Restaurant
The Palm
205 Westshore Plaza Dr., Tampa
(813)-849-7256 • www.thepalm.com

Begin with valet service, sample wines from their cellar and then dine on tender steaks and oversized lobsters, or the highly recommended crab cakes.

Best Place To Buy a Gift
La France
1612 E. 7th Ave., Ybor City
(813) 248-1381

Packed with vintage finds from every era, La France also

sells a selection of creative new jewelry certain to suit your lady's taste.

Top Five Dates

#1. CSI: Tampa
Adult Forensic Science Program: CSI: Tampa
Museum of Science and Industry, 4801 E. Fowler Ave., Tampa
(813) 987-6100 • www.mosi.org/adultprograms.html
This hands-on exploration of actual and fictional case studies from your favorite TV shows lets you analyze clues from a crime scene CSI style. Analyze fingerprints, DNA patterns and more with your sweetheart. You'll certainly have lots to talk about afterwards.

#2. St. Pete Beach
Gulf Blvd, St. Pete Beach
http://beaches.tbo.com/beaches/guide/spbeach.htm
Bask together in the sun or frolic in the surf at St. Pete's white sand beach. Then, walk over to The Undertow tiki bar for some fruity spirits before catching an art flick at the Beach Theatre.

#3. Splitsville
615 Channelside Dr., Tampa
(813) 514-2695 • www.channelside.com
This fancy bowling alley and retro lounge combination is sure to get you both laughing. Dress for a sock hop and munch the scrumptious white truffle pizza while you're there.

#4. Avoid Moderation
Channelside
615 Channelside Dr., Tampa
(813) 223-4250 • www.channelside.com
An evening made special by options and excess: watch a Hollywood film on Muvico's massive IMAX flat screen, stop for dinner at Jackson's Bistro or Grille 29 and then head over to Stump's Supper Club for a retro dance party.

#5. Big Cat Rescue
12802 Easy St., Tampa
(813) 920-4130 • www.bigcatrescue.org

Impress your date with your willingness to hand-feed a tiger. Better yet, embark on a night tour, or an up-close photo safari.

Twin Cities

Best Restaurant for Lunch or Brunch First Date
Kincaid's Fish, Chop, and Steakhouse
380 St. Peter St., St. Paul
(651) 602-9000 • www.kincaids.com
Other locations: Bloomington

This is a warm and upscale, yet reasonably priced fish, chop, and steakhouse.

Best Restaurant for First Dinner Date
Café Twenty Eight
2724 West 43rd St., Minneapolis
(612) 926-2800 • www.cafetwentyeight.com

Located in the historic Linden Hills neighborhood, this restaurant is in a converted firehouse with a cozy, intimate dining room.

Best Cheap Date
Bryant Lake Bowl
810 West Lake St., Minneapolis
(612) 825-3737 • www.bryantlakebowl.com

Besides bowling, check out the Cabaret Theater for hilarious comedies.

Best Restaurant for a Second Dinner Date
Three Fish
3070 Excelsior Blvd., Minneapolis (Calhoun Commons)
(612) 920-2800

The hotspot for local celebrities, Three Fish offers up fresh fish that is flown in seven days a week.

Best Place for Coffee and Dessert
Zeno Café, Dessert & Wine Bar
2919 Hennepin Ave., Minneapolis
(612) 746-4170 • www.zenocoffee.com

The desserts here are larger than life. Choose from an extensive wine list.

Best Place for a Laugh
Brave New Workshop
2605 Hennepin Ave. S., Minneapolis
(612) 332-6620 • www.bravenewworkshop.com

This is the longest-running original sketch comedy, music and comedy improvisation theater in the United States.

Best Creative Date
Aamodt's Balloon Rides
Aamodt's Apple Orchard, Stillwater
(651) 351-0101 • www.aamodtsballoons.com

Treat your sweetheart to an hourlong baloon ride. Upon your return, you will be greeted with champagne!

Best Club
Fahrenheit
322 1st Ave. N., Minneapolis
(612) 673-9694 • www.fahrenheitnightclub.com

The front bar has low conversational music; the back bar has Top-40 dance music. They cater to the upscale crowd and have a strict dress code.

Best After Hours Place
Figlio
3001 Hennepin Ave., Minneapolis (in Calhoun Square)
(612) 822-1688 • www.figlio.com

There are TVs to watch sporting events, the food and drink are always good and it's a very hip place, especially in the summer when you can people-watch on Lake and Hennepin.

Best Special Occasion Restaurant
Sophia
65 Main St. S. E., Minneapolis
(612) 379-1111 • www.sophia.twincitiesfun.com

Beautiful surroundings, located on the Mississippi riverfront with piano players nightly.

Best Place To Buy a Gift
Ampersand
5034 France Ave. S., Edina
(952) 920-2118
Other locations: Wayzata

This establishment is filled with pricey housewares, candles and scented bath products from New York apothecary Kiehl's.

Top Five Dates

#1. Bay Watch
Everyone feels relaxed walking by the water. It's such a romantic setting! Walk, bike or Rollerblade on one of the many paths around Lake Calhoun or Lake Harriet.

#2. Just For Laughs
Laughter is a natural aphrodisiac, so why not warm up the mood and make a night of it: Hey City Theater, ACME, Music Box Theater or stop by Nye's Polonaise Room.

#3. Paddle your own canoe
Enjoy the great outdoors and see some beautiful scenery up in Taylor's Falls while paddling your canoe on the St. Croix River.

#4. Outdoor Movie
What could be better than to be sitting under the stars enjoying an outdoor movie? Pack a picnic and blanket for Loring Park, Stevens Square Park and many others.

#5. Winery
The Alexis Bailey Vineyard in Hastings is the only vineyard around. Make it extra special by packing a picnic, picking up a bottle of wine and enjoying the sculpture park.

Washington, D.C.

Best Restaurant for Lunch or Brunch First Date
Eastern Market
7th St. & North Carolina Ave. S.E., Washington, D.C.
(202) 544-0083 • www.easternmarket.net

Wander among South Hall's food vendors until you get to Market Lunch, a small grill with great barbecue sandwiches and crab cakes.

Best Restaurant for First Dinner Date
Rice
1608 14th St. N.W., Washington, D.C.
(202) 234-2400 • www.ricerestaurant.com

This narrow, low-lit modern dining room serves up a fun twist on Asian cuisine and is a good place for people-watching. Try the unusual breadstick-shaped "spring rolls."

Best Cheap Date
The United States Botanic Garden
245 1st St. S.W., Washington, D.C.
(202) 225-8333 • www.usbg.gov

Admission is free and the indoor conservatory is open daily, so you can stroll among flora all year round.

Best Restaurant for a Second Dinner Date
Komi
1509 17th St. N.W., Washington, D.C.
(202) 332-9200

For starters, diners are treated to menu samples before they have to decide from brick-oven pizza, salads and other entrees.

Best Place for Coffee and Dessert
Love Café
1501 U St. N.W., Washington, D.C.
(202) 265-9800 • www.cakelove.com

Open until about 11 A.M. most nights, this outpost of the

CakeLove bakery has delicious custard-filled treats and comfy seating.

Best Place for a Laugh
Chaos
1603 17th St. N.W., Washington, D.C.
(202) 232-4141 • www.chaosdc.com

If you appreciate a good time intertwined with adventure, join the crowd and dance with well-dressed drag queens.

Best Creative Date
International Spy Museum
800 F St. N.W., Washington, D.C.
(202) 393-7798 • www.spymuseum.org

Tour the relics of espionage and get a look at the real world of spying, both past and present.

Best Club
Dream
1350 Okie St. N.E., Washington, D.C.
(202) 347-5255 • www.welcometodream.com

Hip-hop and R&B luminaries come here to play, so Dream pulls double-duty as both a nightclub and music venue with four floors, a deck and pool tables.

Best After Hours Place
Bob and Edith's Diner
2310 Columbia Pike, Arlington
Other locations: Arlington
(703) 920-6103

A local stalwart that has been around since 1969, Bob and Edith's still serves classic breakfast selections around the clock.

Best Special Occasion Restaurant
Asia Nora
2213 M St. N.W., Washington, DC
(202) 462-5143 • www.noras.com

The gold-leafed walls, silken draperies and Asian artifacts fashion an atmosphere that's intimate and exotic, which is enhanced by the very accommodating staff.

Best Place To Buy a Gift

The Shops at Georgetown Park
3222 M St. N.W., Washington, D.C.
(202) 298-5577 • www.shopsatgeorgetownpark.com
This upscale mall blends familiar stores such as H&M and Ann Taylor with smaller boutiques providing a wide selection of gifts to choose from.

Top Five Dates

#1. *Steeeee-rike!*
Strike Bethesda
5353 Westbard Ave., Bethesda
www.strikebethesda.com
A VIP Room in a bowling alley? Strike is one of the "new" bowling alleys, where martinis compete with beer and the pins glow fluorescent. Have dinner in the heart of Bethesda at Mon Ami Gabi, Red Tomato or South Beach Café.

#2. *A Landmark Occasion*
National Cathedral
Wisconsin and Massachusetts Avenues N.W., Washington, D.C.
(202) 537-6200 • www.cathedral.org/cathedral
Take one of the many tours offered at this landmark, or explore on your own. Be sure to climb the central tower and take in Bishop's Garden.

#3. *Fresh and Healthy*
Dupont Circle Farmer's Market
1500 block of 20th St. between Massachusetts Ave. and Q St., Washington, D.C.
(202) 362-8889
www.freshfarmmarket.org/markets.html
This Sunday morning market is year-round, but it only goes from 9 A.M.. until 1 A.M. (10 A.M.. in winter), so don't oversleep. There are several places to pick up fresh and healthy edibles, or even non-edible gifts. After shopping, take your goodies to eat in Dupont Circle, or stop at Teaism or Kramer's for brunch.

#4. *A Day in Georgetown*
Mie N Yu
3125 M St., N.W., Washington, D.C.
(202) 333-6122 • www.mienyu.com

Mie N Yu's is a great place for drinks. Differently themed rooms offer lots of sensory input, comfortable cushioned banquettes, and great people watching. Consider a walk in Georgetown beforehand or stop by the Govinda Gallery, which often features great rock photography. Another good daytime destination is the Dumbarton Oaks garden.

#5. *Cozy Up*
Chi-Cha Lounge
1624 U St. N.W., Washington, D.C.
(202) 234-8400

Chi-Cha has lots of cozy, closely placed couches plus a smaller den off the main room. It's a great place to get a drink and snacks, especially when they have live Latin music. Of course, it's not a bad place to snuggle, either; neither is Soussi Lounge on 18th Street (upstairs) or the back room of Spy Lounge, also on 18th next to Felix.

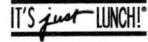

Western New York

Best Restaurant for Lunch or Brunch First Date
Brodo
765 Elmwood Ave., Buffalo
(716) 881-1117

Brodo is colorful and flavorful. They're best known for their soups, but everything on the menu is delicious.

Best Restaurant for First Dinner Date
Sonoma Grill
5050 Main St., Buffalo
(716) 204-2743 • www.sonomagrille.com

Choosing a meal from Sonoma's expansive menu helps gives you an idea of your date's preferences. Ask to be seated in the fireplace room; it's more quiet and cozy.

Best Cheap Date
Ice Skating at the Pepsi Center
1615 Amherst Manor Dr., Williamsville
(716) 631-7555 • www.amherstpepsicenter.com

You don't have to be Dorothy Hamil or Wayne Gretzky to enjoy a few laps around the rink. It's a good excuse to hold hands! The rink is open all year long.

Best Restaurant for a Second Dinner Date
Calvaneso's Cosmopolitan Grille
5185 Transit Rd., Williamsville
(716) 633-6683

The "to-die-for" house dressing turns a simple steak and salad meal into an incredible dining experience.

Best Place for Coffee and Dessert
Dessert Café
Snyder Square, Main St., Snyder

This is a quaint little café for dessert and coffee. Don't miss the Oreo cake, it's fabulous. They also serve a great lunch.

Best Place for a Laugh

Clifton Hill
4960 Clifton Hill, Niagara Falls, Ontario, Canada
(905) 358-3676 • www.cliftonhill.com

Check out fun places like the FX Thrill Ride (a motion simulator/movie) or the Ghost Blasters. All guaranteed to make you laugh and leave you begging for more.

Best Creative Date

Niagara Clipper Cruises
Erie Basin Marina, Buffalo
(716) 856-6696 • www.niagaraclipper.com

Try a romantic dinner cruise aboard one of the Niagara Clipper cruise ships. Along with the wonderful menu, the sunset ride along the lake is breathtaking.

Best Club

Sphere Entertainment Complex
681 Main St., Buffalo
(716) 852-3900 • www.spherebuffalo.com

This self-proclaimed "5,000 watt-pounding nightclub" features Top 40 dance, hip-hop, and house music to get you out of your seat and moving.

Best After Hours Place

Alton's
2250 Walden, Buffalo
(716) 681-7055 • www.altonsrestaurant.com

The servers are always smiling, even at 4:00 A.M..! Alton's has the best late-night breakfast food. Be sure to try the ham and cheese omelet with rye toast and coffee.

Best Special Occasion Restaurant

Riverside Inn
On the Waterfront, Lewiston
(716) 754-8206 • www.riversideinn.net

Candlelit tables and a scenic view of the Lower Niagara River make for a romantic evening. You'll quickly see why it's such a popular location for wedding receptions.

Best Place To Buy a Gift
Graser's Florist
399 Amherst St., Buffalo
Other location: East Amherst
(716) 947-5901 • www.graserflorist.com

Show her how special she is by sending a beautiful bouquet of her favorite flowers from Graser's. They deliver to most of Western New York.

Top Five Dates

#1. The Bright Lights of Vegas, Close To Home
Niagara Fallsview Casino Resort
6380 Fallsview Blvd., Niagara Falls, Ontario
(888) 888-1089
www.discoverniagara.com/fallsviewcasino

Feel like a celebrity at the world-class Niagara Fallsview Casino Resort. Try your hand at the slot machines or gaming tables, have a great meal, visit the spa, or watch live entertainment in the intimate setting of the Avalon Ballroom. No matter how you spend your visit, you and your date are sure to feel glamorous in this special setting.

#2. Instant Culture
The Albright-Knox Art Gallery
1285 Elmwood Ave., Buffalo
(716) 882-8700 • www.albrightknox.org

Surround yourself and your date with works of art at the Albright-Knox Art Gallery. This gallery houses some amazing works of art, including works by Picasso and Rembrandt. After you've worked up an appetite soaking up all that culture, have brunch or lunch at The Garden Restaurant inside the gallery.

#3. Get a Little Wet
The Maid of the Mist
Base of the Observation Tower, Prospect Point
(716) 284-8897 • www.maidofthemist.com

Chances are you and your date haven't been on the Maid of the Mist since you were kids, or maybe you've never been on it at all! This boat ride is the best way to experience the beauty and glory of Niagara Falls. You also can visit Terrapin Point, Three Sisters Island, Goat Island, and the Cave of the Winds.

#4. Get Spirited Away
Bully Hill Vineyards
8843 Greyton H. Taylor Memorial Dr., Hammondsport
(607) 868-3610 • www.bullyhill.com

If you enjoy fine wine but find most wine tastings too stuffy and formal, Bully Hill Vineyards is the perfect place for you. You and your date will experience a fun day tasting fabulous wine at great prices! Your tour guide tastes the wine along with you, so prepare for a day that gets progressively more fun!

#5. Sail through the Clouds
Aurora Balloon Company
132 Grant St., Depew
(716) 685-7908 • www.auroraballooncompany.com

What better way to experience the sights of Western New York than by air? Aurora Balloon Company offers champagne sunrise and sunset flights over most of Western New York. Just select your site and view it from 2,000 feet above as you sail in a majestic hot air-balloon.

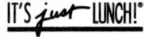

Wilmington

Best Restaurant for Lunch or Brunch First Date
Washington Street Ale House
1208 N. Washington St.
(302) 658-2537

A small place in the heart of it all. The great location, laid back atmosphere and extensive menu makes this an awesome spot for the first date.

Best Restaurant for First Dinner Date
Eclipse Restaurant
1020 N. Union St.
(302) 658-1588

A trendy, 4-star restaurant in the heart of Little Italy. The wine menu is out of this world. Winner of the Wine spectator Award of Excellence for 1999-2003.

Best Cheap Date
Blue Rocks at Frawley Stadium
801 S. Madison St.
(302) 888-2583 • www.bluerocks.com

Spend the evening watching our very own baseball team: the Blue Rocks. Cheap seats, two hotdogs, and two Cokes will run you less than $20!

Best Restaurant for a Second Dinner Date
Buckley's Tavern
Rt. 52, 5812 Kenneth Pike, Centerville
(302) 656-9776

A casual atmosphere in the heart of Centerville. Wonderful bar for after work drinks, plus a tavern-type menu. The sweet potato shoestring fries are the best!

Best Place for Coffee and Dessert
Rossi's
1835 W. 4th St.
(302) 656-8584 • www.joerossisays.com

Their Bananas Foster is simply melt-in-your-mouth wonderful. At the edge of little Italy, and providing a warm, romantic atmosphere.

Best Place for a Laugh
Comedy Cabaret
1010 N. Union St.
(302) 652-6873

The only comedy club in Wilmington is now housed in the bar at the Air Transport Command. Come by and see some top-level comedians every Saturday night.

Best Creative Date
Habitat for Humanity
1603 N. Jessup St.
(302) 652-0334

Nonprofit organizations everywhere are in constant need of volunteers. Grab a hammer and paintbrush and go to work. You've never had a date like this!

Best Club
Epoch Night Club
1206 N. Union St.
(302) 429-6633

One of the best dance spots in Wilmington. Epoch has been a staple of the party scene for years. Crowd is mostly young professionals in their 20s and 30s.

Best After Hours Place
Golden Castle
2722 Concord Pike
(302) 478-7701

Open 24 hours, this is the hot spot after the bars close in Wilmington. Stop on by for some coffee and breakfast and meet the night owls!

Best Special Occasion Restaurant
Christiana Hilton
100 Continental Dr., Newark
(302) 454-1500

The only 5-diamond restaurant in Delaware. Try the Caesar salad made table side! Lots of fun, with a great atmosphere.

Best Place To Buy a Gift

Everything but the Kitchen Sink
Hockessin Corner
(302) 239-7066 • www.thekitchensink.com

Yes, they really do have everything! Robes, ties, picture frames, kitchen accessories and more. If you can't find something here, then you can't find it anywhere!

Top Five Dates

#1. *Tall Ships at Riverfront Park in Wilmington*
www.riverfrontwilmington.com

Head on down to the park and check out the ships. Often you can even board them and take a look around. You can also take a ride on the water taxi up to the Ship Yard Shops and outlets for the afternoon. Wind up the evening with dinner at one of the many nearby restaurants.

#2. *Blue Rocks at Frawley Stadium*
801 S. Madison St., Wilmington
(302) 888-2583 • www.bluerocks.com

Spend the evening watching our very own baseball team the Blue Rocks. Cheap seats, two hotdogs, and two Cokes will run you less than $20!

#3. *Snow and Sun!*
UD Sporting Center
Rt. 896, Newark
(302) 831-2868 • www.udel.edu/icearena

Start out ice skating, an especially refreshing way to spend a summer day. Then go across the parking lot to the UD outdoor pool. Drop in rates are $5.

#4. *Let's go Bowling!!!!*
Pike Creek Bowling
5100 Pike Creek Blvd., Wilmington
(302) 994-7474

The home of Rock 'N Bowl! Grab your blue suede shoes and knock down some pins with the 30-40 something professional and trendy crowds!

#5. *Cultured Discussion*
Theatre N, 1007 N. Orange, Wilmington
(302) 658-6070 • www.theatren.org
Toscana's, 1412 N. Dupont St., Wilmington
(302) 654-8001

Head on over to Theatre N on a Friday or Saturday night. Afterwards, have a discussion about the film over dessert and drinks at Toscana's.

Vermont

Best Restaurant for Lunch or Brunch First Date
Toscano Café Bistro
27 Bridge St., Huntington
(802) 434-3148

The Toscano sets the stage with a rustic and comfortable Mediterranean menu. During the warmer months, enjoy your lunch or Sunday brunch out on the inviting patio.

Best Restaurant for First Dinner Date
Kitchen Table Bistro
1840 W. Main St., Richmond
(802) 434-8686

With an impressive wine list and American nouveau fare that's served amid a late 18th Century farmhouse, an evening at the Kitchen Table is an exercise in leisurely fine dining.

Best Cheap Date
The Country Bear Bookshop
Rt. 5, Lyndonville
(802) 626-3469 • www.countrybearbookshop.com

Enjoy a cup of coffee (or hot chocolate) and a baked goody while you browse their thousands of new and used books, tapes, CDs, toys, puzzles and more!

Best Restaurant for a Second Dinner Date
The Lakeview Inn
295 Breezy Avenue
Greensboro, VT 05841
(802) 533-2291 • www.lakeviewinn.biz

The Lakeview Inn creates its menus based on what's in season. You get only the freshest ingredients here and the American and Mediterranean cuisine is quite sophisticated.

Best Place for Coffee and Dessert
Mist Grill Café
92 Stowe St., Waterbury
(802) 244-8522 • www.mistgrill.com

Enjoy a cup of steaming coffee or something more specialized like the Vermonter, a latte with a shot of Vermont maple syrup. Don't forget dessert; Mist is a bakery as well!

Best Place for a Laugh
Laugh Out Loud Series
North Lounge at The University of Vermont, Burlington
(802) 656-3131 • www.uvm.edu/~cmpacttm

This ongoing comedy series brings the best national comedians out of the woodwork. Also be sure to check out the University's other giggle-inspiring events, like poker nights.

Best Creative Date
Vermont State Parks
Statewide
(802) 241-3655 • www.vtstateparks.com

You're within minutes of many beautiful Vermont state parks wherever you are! It's a great chance to talk, walk and hold hands while you enjoy beautiful scenery!

Best Club
Club Metronome
188 Main St., Burlington
(802) 865-4563

Wear your hippest outfit and hit the dance floor at this eclectic club, where mod décor meets with stylish patrons and cutting-edge acts.

Best After Hours Place
135 Pearl
135 Pearl St., Burlington
(802) 863-2343 • www.135pearl.com

You'll find local DJs, live music, theater and internationally known talent here most anytime. Whether you want to dance, listen or sing karaoke, this is the place!

Best Special Occasion Restaurant
The Blue Seal
Bridge St., Richmond
(802) 434-5949

This local institution serves up heaps of American- and

Southwestern-inspired cuisine and was Yankee Magazine's Editor's Choice in 2004. Be sure to save room for ice cream!

Best Place To Buy a Gift
Stowe Craft Gallery & Design Center
55 Mountain Rd., Stowe
(877) 456-8388 • www.stowecraft.com

The place to find gorgeous one-of-a-kind local artistry, pick up some gorgeous handmade jewelry, eclectic fine art, a whimsical kaleidoscope or handcrafted home furnishings.

Top Five Dates

#1. Setting the Stage
Weston Playhouse Theatre Company
703 Main St., Weston
(802) 824-5288 • www.westonplayhouse.org

Kick up the romance with a high-energy cabaret act or off-Broadway production at this dazzling theater locale, which has been entertaining audiences since the 1800s. Make an evening of it by dining before the show and then, after the final curtain, walking through the lovely Weston village.

#2. Play with Your Hands
Shelburne Craft School
54 Falls Rd., Shelburne
Other location: Shelburne
(802) 985-3648 • www.shelburnecraftschool.org

Try some hands-on fun and take a class together. Shelburne offers courses in fine arts, woodworking, stained glass and more, with convenient weekend workshops and clinics. After class, grab a bite to eat at one of the charming area lunch stops, then explore historic Shelburne Village attractions like Mt. Philo State Park and Shelburne Museum.

#3. A Romantic Performance
Middle Earth Music School
Barton St., Bradford
(802) 222-4748 • www.middle-earth-music.com

This intimate venue seats only 150 people, but books the largest live rock and folk music acts to come through the state. At a locale this cozy, you and your date will feel as though the performance is solely for you!

#4. *Be a Tourist*
Downtown Montpelier • www.montpelier-vt.org
Spend the day in Vermont's historic capital. Start off with a tour through the gilded Capitol Building and the State House. Then go for a romantic stroll and picnic in gorgeous Hubbard Park, home to a stone observation tower with stunning views of the city. Before heading home, enjoy a dessert of ice cream samples at Ben & Jerry's factory.

#5. *The Ultimate Date*
Stoweflake Mountain Resort & Spa
1746 Mountain Rd., Stowe
(802) 253-2232
There's nothing like escaping from the daily hustle and bustle. Reserve Stoweflake's Spa Renewal Package and enjoy a couple's tandem massage, chilled champagne and resort accommodations, which include an intimate breakfast and dinner. Or upgrade to a package with activities like golf, hiking and skiing. It doesn't get any better than this!

West Texas

Best Lunch Or Brunch Date
Stella's
4646 50th St., Lubbock
(806) 785-9299

A delightful, yet romantic setting for lunch, which offers a wide range of cuisine to tempt the most delicate of palates.

Best First Dinner Date.
Sedona Grill
2101 W. Wadley, Midland
(432) 570-9600

The food is amazing, the service is wonderful and if you want proof that little things add up, check out their wonderful side dishes like mashed sweet potatoes and sauteed spinach.

Best Cheap Date
Picnic in Mackenzie Park
4th St. & I H 27, Lubbock
(806) 763-2719

Relax on a blanket in a cozy setting among the beautiful trees and lake. Feeding the ducks and geese is a great way to break the ice on a first date.

Best Restaurant For a Second Date and Beyond
Chez Suzette
4423 50th St., Lubbock
(806) 795-6796 • www.lubbocktv.com/chez

Enjoy your choice of French or Italian cuisine at a sidewalk café. This restaurant is known as one of Lubbock's finest choices for a romantic dinner.

Best Place for Coffee and Dessert
Daybreak Coffee Roasters
19th Street and Quaker, Lubbuck
(806) 799-1994 • www.dbcr.com

Daybreak serves the finest roasted coffee from around the world — and you can't go wrong with their famous recipe cinnamon or pecan rolls.

Best Place For a Laugh
Texas Tech Football Tail Gate Parties
Jones Stadium
Texas Tech University, Lubbock
(806) 742-2770

Enjoy ice cold beer, good old fashioned Texas barbeque and live music with friends. Sit in beach chairs and watch the crazy antics around you. You will definitely enjoy plenty of laughs.

Best Creative Date
Mountain bike and picnic in Palo Duro Canyon
11450 Park Rd. 5, Canyon
(806) 488-2227 • www.palodurocanyon.com

Just a short drive from Lubbock, enjoy rustic bike trails and beautiful deep canyon views. A must see for outdoor romantics.

Best Club
Graham Central Station
2201 S. Western #111, Amarillo
Other location: Lubbock
(806) 457- 0444 • www.grahamcentralstationamarillo.com

With six nightclubs in one, you get to choose from country-western, rock, Latin, sounds of the seventies and more. GCS is extremely crowded on weekends.

Best After-Hours Place
Wall Street Bar & Grill
115 E. Wall St., Midland
(432) 684-8686

Great food, great service and you'll fall in love with the salad and the bread. If you like trout, it's outstanding here.

Best Special-Occasion Restaurant.
Frenchman Inn
4409 19th St., Lubbock
(806) 799-7596

Delight yourself with country French cuisine set in a quaint atmosphere. Call for reservations.

Best Place To Buy A Gift

Jay Keith Jewelry
8001 Quaker Ave., Lubbock
(806) 791-0092

Jay is known as one of the finest craftsmen in west Texas. This is a fabulous spot to find the perfect gift for the special person in your life.

Five Great Dates

#1. Cuddle While They Huddle
Texas Tech Football Game
Jones Stadium
Texas Tech University, Lubbock
(806) 742-2770

Football and Texas go together like beer and hot dogs at a stadium. Why not spend an afternoon cheering for the Red Raiders? In a crazy way, there's something romantic about going on a date with thousands of other people who are rooting for the same thing — a Red Raiders victory.

#2. Drive Down Memory Lane
Stars and Stripes Drive-In.
5013 Clovis Hwy., Lubbock
(806) 749-SHOW (7469) • www.driveinusa.com

Take a drive down memory lane, or make some new memories at the Stars and Stripes Drive-In. There's something special about sitting together in a car in the dark and watching the big screen. Get there early and eat at the Concession Café. Try a famous Chihuahua sandwich and wash it down with a frozen lemonade. Or just order some home-made hot chocolate.

#3. Some Mighty Fine Wine
Wine Tasting at Cap*Rock Winery
Route 6, Lubbock
Other location: Grapevine
(806) 863-2704 • www.caprockwinery.com

Take a tour of the Cap*Rock Winery. Afterwards, you and your date can taste a variety of award-winning wines ranging from Cabernet Sauvignons to Orange Muscats and Merlots. Make it a night to remember by buying your date an engraved wine bottle at the gift store.

#4. *Horsin' Around*
Horseback riding at the Kerschner Four Bar K Ranch
Kershner's Inside Four Bar K & Four Bar K Ranch
2811 98th Street, Lubbock
(806) 789-8682

Take a break from your computer, your cell phone, and all the stresses of modern life. Pick out a pair of beautiful horses and go for a ride together. You'll feel like you've entered a whole other world. When your ride is over and you finally dismount, see which one of you can do the best John Wayne imitation.

#5. *The Sound of Music*
Depot District
1-27 and 19th St., Lubbock
(806) 747-2648 • www.depotdistrict.com

The historic area has many clubs with live music of all types, from country western to the blues. There can literally be ten live bands playing here at one time. Stroll around and sample whatever suits your mood with the all-inclusive Depot pass.

Appendix

What's Your Dating IQ?

Take our dating quiz and see how your answers compare to those of other singles nationwide.

1. At what point would you introduce someone to your best friends?
    a. After 3 dates
    b. More than 5
    c. After 5 dates
    d. After 1 date

2. Women Only! Have you ever asked a man out on a date?
    a. Yes
    b. No

3. If not, why?
    a. Fear of rejection; I'd be crushed if he said no.
    b. I'm old fashioned — the man should do the asking.
    c. I'm worried I would appear desperate.
    d. I'm too shy; I'd be tongue-tied.
    e. No need, I always get asked.

4. Which date option do you think would most entice a man?
    a. Dinner
    b. A movie
    c. A drink after work
    d. A sporting event
    e. Lunch
    f. A concert

5. If you do the inviting, would you expect to pay for the date?
    a. I'd be prepared to pay, unless he offered.
    b. Of course, I'd pay.
    c. No, the man should pay, no matter what.

6. After how many dates would you utter the six magic words, "Would you like to come in?"
    a. After we're officially a couple.
    b. After a third date.
    c. Never. I'd wait until the man asks to come in.
    d. After the first date.

7. Men Only! Has a woman ever asked you out on a date?
    a. Yes
    b. No

8. How do you feel about a woman asking you out for a date?
    a. I'm flattered; it's a real turn-on.
    b. Depends on the woman.
    c. Too aggressive; not my type.
    d. Regret that I didn't take the lead.

9. What do you think it means when a woman invites you in after a first date?
    a. Yippee, I've scored a home run!
    b. Does she want coffee... or something else?
    c. I'm afraid to say no, it might hurt her feelings.
    d. Makes me nervous.

Both sexes from this point...

10. At what point in a relationship would you feel comfortable bringing your significant other home for the holidays?
    a. Dating at least two months.
    b. Dating for at least a month.
    c. Dating at least six months.
    d. With my family? Never!
    e. After dating for at least two weeks.

11. Of all the following, I would be LEAST interested in dating:
    a. My friend's ex
    b. A co-worker
    c. A client
    d. Someone my mother wants to set me up with

12. After how many dates would you use the term "boyfriend" or "girlfriend?"
    a. 7 - 9 dates
    b. 5 - 6 dates
    c. more than 10 dates
    d. 3 - 4 dates

13. You are meeting your significant other's parents for the first time during the holidays. Which would you do?
    a. Bring a card, candy, flowers, bottle of wine or other similar gift.
    b. Pick out a modest gift for the two of them.
    c. Come empty handed, after all, we're just meeting for the first time.
    d. Do some research and purchase something exceptional.
    e. Sign your name to your boyfriend's/girlfriend's gift.

14. On a first date, I'd prefer:
    a. A casual lunch date
    b. Drinks after work
    c. A dressy dinner or other formal affair
    d. A concert, play or movie

15. You've been dating for a couple of weeks. How many times a day should you be calling your new boyfriend/girlfriend before 6 P.M.?
    a. You'd never think to call during work hours.
    b. Once. You want to check in and see how their day is going.
    c. 2 – 3 times. You just want to let them know you're thinking about them.

    d. More than 4 times. You're thinking about them every minute.

16. The shoes a person is wearing on a date tell the other:
    a. About their personality.
    b. How in tune that person is with fashion.
    c. About their personal hygiene.
    d. How much money they have.

17. Of all the dating conversation killers, the worst would have to be:
    a. Marriage
    b. Politics
    c. Past relationships
    d. Dieting/body image

18. What's the biggest turnoff on a first date?
    a. Talking only about oneself.
    b. Bad manners.
    c. Poor eye contact.

19. Which dating mistake do you think is the most common?
    a. Talking too much.
    b. Having too high expectations for the date.
    c. Judging your date like a "book by its cover."
    d. Spilling your "history" and being too honest.

20. If you'd like to go on a second date, how do you pursue him/her?
    a. Wait to be pursued.
    b. Call the next day.
    c. Email them the same night as the date.
    d. Wait 3 – 4 days, then call.

See How You Compare!

Below are our national averages based on various surveys of singles.

1. a. 46%, b. 17%, c. 30%, d. 7%
2. a. 58%, b. 42%
3. a. 25%, b. 39%, c. 18%, d. 9% e. 9%
4. a. 12%, b. 3%, c. 44%, d. 32%, e. 7%, f. 2%

5. a. 70%, b. 24%, c. 6%
6. a. 24%, b. 59%, c. 7%, d. 11%
7. a. 67%, b. 33%
8. a. 63%, b. 34%, c. 1%, d. 1%
9. a. 18%, b. 62%, c. 7%, d. 14%
10. a. 37%, b. 19%, c. 34%, d. 3%, e. 7%
11. a. 60%, b. 14%, c. 8%, d. 17%
12. a. 25%, b. 22%, c. 47%, d. 6%
13. a. 60%, b. 18%, c. 9%, d. 12%, e. 1%
14. a. 44%, b. 43%, c. 4%, d. 8%
15. a. 44%, b. 52%, c. 4%, d. 0%
16. a. 45%, b. 39%, c. 12%, d. 4%
17. a. 15%, b. 15%, c. 49%, d. 21%
18. a. 35%, b. 51%, c. 10%
19. a. 13%, b. 27%, c. 35%, d. 25%
20. a. 28%, b. 38%, c. 7%, d. 27%

To participate in one of our dating surveys, which change each month, go to www.itsjustlunch.com.

About the Authors

Andrea McGinty founded *It's Just Lunch* almost 14 years ago after her engagement was suddenly called off. She attended her first *It's Just Lunch* wedding after the company had been in business for just 5 months. Since then, she has been responsible for many *It's Just Lunch* weddings and she still gets goosebumps when she hears about another engagement! With over 65 offices worldwide now, she has been featured on Oprah, CNN, People and The New York Times.

Nancy Kirsch joined forces with Andrea McGinty 12 years ago to pursue her dream job...being a Yenta!! Nancy has been featured and quoted in The Washington Post, The Today Show, and The Wall Street Journal. And 12 years later, she feels as though she still has the most interesting job on the planet.

Alana Beyer has always believed that there truly is someone for everyone. That's why she loves *It's Just Lunch*. She comes to work every day doing something that she loves—working with people and helping others find that special someone. She loves hearing about that "great" first date because she knows it *just* takes one.

Here's how to reach the It's Just Lunch office nearest you

Office	Phone
Headquarters	619.234.7200
Albany	518.482.8400
Albuquerque	505.244.1050
Ann Arbor	734.327.2700
Atlanta	404.588.2700
Atlanta Perimeter	770.590.4910
Austin	512.476.5566
Baltimore	410.659.6699
Birmingham	205.986.6050
Buffalo	716.839.2787
Central PA	570.522.9922
Charlotte	704.332.6081
Chicago	312.644.9999
Chicago Suburbs	630.775.6633
Cincinnati	513.929.4499
Cleveland	216.830.9999
Columbus	614.233.9999
Dallas	972.991.4161
Denver	303.292.2600
Detroit Suburbs	248.273.1000
Ft.Lauderdale/Boca Raton	954.725.8500
Ft.Lee, NJ	201.363.9594
Ft. Myers	239.939.3900
Ft. Worth	817.870.9999
Grand Rapids	616.235.6700
Harrisburg	717.234.3400
Honolulu	808.532.7300
Houston	713.572.0900
Huntsville	256.519.3600
Jacksonville	904.281.0277
Kansas City	816.421.5600
Las Vegas	702.436.4600
LA Century City	310.229.9393
LA South Bay	310.937.8200
LA The Valley	818.548.9988
Miami	305.381.8888
Milwaukee	414.224.9600
Minneapolis	612.376.7373
Naples	239.597.4100
Nashville	615.312.9700

New York City	212.750.8899
No. Virginia	703.506.6767
Omaha	402.991.9388
Orange County	949.251.9494
Orlando	407.835.8888
Palm Beach County	561.799.9955
Philadelphia	215.772.9999
Phoenix	602.279.3366
Phoenix—East Valley	480.785.4949
Pittsburgh	412.263.2499
Portland	503.248.9995
Raleigh-Durham	919.836.9199
Sacramento	916.564.1400
San Antonio	210.525.9988
San Diego Downtown	619.232.8999
San Diego North County	760.268.0004
San Francisco	415.989.9500
Sarasota	941.362.7702
Scottsdale	480.730.6023
Silicon Valley	650.969.1100
St. Louis	314.863.7300
St. Paul	651.228.0070
Seattle	206.340.0100
Tampa	813.204.9688
Tucson	520.299.6338
Walnut Creek	925.287.8700
Washington, D.C.	202.466.6699
West Texas	806.687.4440
Wilmington, DE	302.651.9999

International

Singapore	65.6536.0100
Toronto	416.703.3900

Call Today, Date Tomorrow

www.itsjustlunch.com

dating for busy professionals®